The Crisis of the
Early Italian Renaissance

The Crisis of the Early Italian Renaissance

Civic Humanism and Republican Liberty in an Age of Classicism and Tyranny

By HANS BARON

RESEARCH FELLOW AND BIBLIOGRAPHER
THE NEWBERRY LIBRARY, CHICAGO

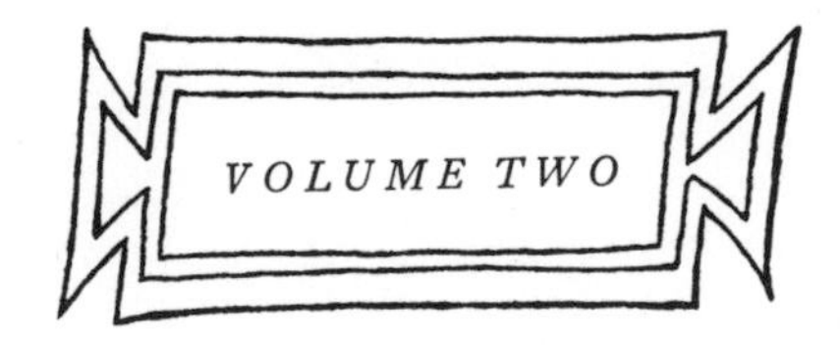

PRINCETON, NEW JERSEY
PRINCETON UNIVERSITY PRESS
1955

London: Geoffrey Cumberlege, Oxford University Press

L. C. Card No. 54-6073

Printed in the United States of America
by Princeton University Press at Princeton, New Jersey

CONTENTS

VOLUME TWO

APPENDICES

NOTES: DOCUMENTARY, CHRONOLOGICAL, CRITICAL

WITH CONTENTS OF MAJOR NOTES

Appendices

APPENDIX 1

INTERPRETATIONS OF THE POLITICAL BACKGROUND OF THE EARLY RENAISSANCE

(Annex to Vol. I, pp. 36 and 317)

IN THE year 1402—thus we concluded our analysis of the political events around 1400[1]—the real issue of the Florentine-Milanese contest stood revealed; out of the struggle had come the decision that the road was to remain open to the civic freedom, and to the system of independent states, which became a part of the culture of the Italian Renaissance. Throughout the present book, the knowledge that many a contemporary in the first decades of the Quattrocento must have been aware of this decision and of the new role of Florence, serves as a key to not a few otherwise confusing aspects of the genesis of Quattrocento thought.

Since so much depends upon the correct historical perspective of the political struggle on the threshold of the new century, it is desirable to define the relationship in which the picture that has so naturally emerged from the testimony of our sources stands to earlier interpretations of the political background of the Renaissance. For the opinion that Florence's war for independence played a crucial role in the beginnings of Renaissance thought cannot be said to be generally accepted; and even where this role is recognized, very different interpretations have been placed on it. On the other hand, even a brief glance at the history of the earlier interpretations will prove that the estimate of the political changes at which we have arrived is a logical and necessary advance from the positions held in earlier phases of the historiography on the Renaissance.

1 In the section "A Struggle for Civic Liberty, 1390-1402. Giangaleazzo Visconti and the Challenge of the Year 1402," esp. p. 36.

The first dominant view of the Florentine-Milanese struggle, as was natural in the light of political experience in the nineteenth century, was based on the long-range effects of the Renaissance upon the modern history of the Italian nation. If Giangaleazzo had succeeded, the argument ran, in building a permanent large state, Italy would have grown into a unified and centralized monarchy as did the West-European nations. The Viscontean propaganda with its calls for unity and peace on the Peninsula was piece by piece recovered from the sources by a group of north-Italian historians that reached its greatest influence with G. Romano in about 1900.[2] The aims of the Visconti were thought by these historians to have heralded the modern ideal of national unity. The Florentine resistance to Giangaleazzo, on the other hand, seemed to have initiated the petty egoism of local states which since the Renaissance kept the Peninsula in a state of disunity, and which had to be swept away around the middle of the nineteenth century by a new movement of unification coming from the north—this time under the House of Piedmont-Savoy. Among Italian scholars, this interpretation has not

2 On Romano see note 29 to Chap. 2, and Valeri's appraisal quoted in note 14 below. Another cause of Romano's sympathies for the expansionist Italian politics of the Visconti lay in Giangaleazzo's endeavours (above Vol. One, p. 23) to replace most of the Papal State by a secular "regnum" in central Italy that would be closely allied with, and dependent upon, the north-Italian State of the Visconti; see the fine portrait of the historian Romano in G. Volpe's *Storici e Maestri* (Florence, 1924), pp. 65-84. As Volpe notes, this interest of Romano's reflected the bent of mind of the generation which had grown up under the impact of the struggle of the Italian "Risorgimento" with the secular power of the Papacy until the overthrow of Papal rule over Rome in 1870. In the eyes of the scholars of Romano's generation, the historical significance of the process of secularization characteristic of the late Middle Ages was to be sought in the growing "criticism of the temporal power of the Church," and the fight against it, rather than in the cultural and intellectual transformation achieved by the humanistic Renaissance. (Volpe, *loc. cit.*, pp. 74-76). It is obvious that such an approach made it still more difficult for Italian historians in the latter part of the nineteenth century to do justice to the tendencies embodied in the culture and politics of anti-Viscontean, Guelph Florence.

lost its persuasiveness to this day.[3] It did not lose it even after research in the archival documents had brought to light much of the deeper motives of the Florentine resistance, and of the heroism of the Florentine defense.

We must examine in some detail the unavoidable inconsistencies of the resulting interpretation. For instance, F. Landogna, who in 1928 in a basic monograph furnished our knowledge of Florence's reaction to Giangaleazzo's central-Italian policies with a firm documentary foundation,[4] was encouraged by his sources to give the following objective and vigorous description of the Florentine resistance: "It is of unusual and arresting interest to observe the untiring work, now open and now secret, of the Florentine Republic. Immersed in danger, she tightens her bonds with Bologna, turns her eyes toward France, and extends her hand to Siena and Perugia, all of whom in the end accept the Viscontean protectorate. . . . But her tenacity will receive its reward. Already close to ruin and completely surrounded by enemies ready to divide the spoils; after resisting for years with a fierce passion that seems to be folly; on the verge of definite collapse—she is saved unexpectedly by the death of the man who had nearly brought her to destruction."[5] Yet when it comes to the historical evaluation of the political convictions that

3 For instance, the excellent article by G. Falco on "Signorie e Principati" in the *Enciclopedia Italiana* (vol. XXXI, 1936) sees the significance of the era of the *principati* in the fact that the establishment of an Italian Monarchy by the most powerful dynasty, that of the Visconti, became a genuine historical possibility ("più che un vuoto motivo cortigiano e letterario, una possibilità"), and that Giangaleazzo's diplomacy, although it was as ruthlessly practical and crafty as lies in the nature of most political action, represented a conscious effort to realize an ideal held by many of his contemporaries. See esp. p. 758. An American example of the same school of thought, using Mussolini's dictatorship as a guide to an understanding of Italy's need, around 1400, for unification by a tyrant-dictator, is E. Emerton, *Humanism and Tyranny. Studies in the Italian Trecento* (Cambridge, Mass., 1925); see note 38 to Chap. 7.

4 *La politica dei Visconti in Toscana* (Milan, 1929); also published in *Bollettino della Società Pavese di Storia Patria*, XXVIII, 1928.

5 *Bollettino*, p. 157.

had rendered the long and heroic struggle possible, all this resistance appears to the same author to have no meaning, to be a waste of precious energies—a tragic error. "Throughout the later Middle Ages, the Florentine Republic represents the source of that resistance to Viscontean expansion which definitively put an end to the ideal of an Italian kingdom—a kingdom which, even if its origin was lust for power, would certainly have prevented the great historical tragedy which the dawn of the modern epoch brought about for Italy."[6]

Another able monograph which reconstructed the conditions in Tuscany during the expansion of the Visconti—S. Favale's "Siena nel quadro della politica Viscontea," 1936[7]—reveals still more of the a priori bias that characterizes this school of thought. Florence, we hear, "saved that city-state liberty which was already about to give way before the rising power of the Medici, and the glamour of culture which has issued from that rule causes us to consider the outcome fortunate. But if death had not struck down the cruel Duke of Milan when he was still young and in his vigor, who knows but there might have risen at that time, at least over a large part of Italy, that national state which would have spared our nation the disgrace and injury of foreign domination which sprang from, and were strengthened by, the fragmentation into, and enmities among, powerless tiny states."[8] Is it not obvious

6 "La repubblica fiorentina rappresenta, durante tutto il Basso Medioevo, il principio di quella resistenza all'espansione viscontea, che segnerà il definitivo tramonto dell' ideale di un regno italico, il quale, se anche ispirato da cupidigia di potere, avrebbe certamente impedito che gli albori dell'età moderna segnassero per l'Italia l'inizio di una grande tragedia storica." *Bollettino*, p. 79.

7 *Bullettino Senese di Storia Patria*, n. s., vol. VII.

8 "Firenze . . . salvò quella libertà comunale che già si preparava a piegare dinanzi alla sorgente potenza dei Medici, e il fulgore di civiltà che da essa è sortito ci porta a considerare fortunato l'epilogo. Ma se la morte non colpiva, ancor giovane e vigoroso, il crudele Duca di Milano, chi sa che non fosse sorto allora, su gran parte almeno dell'Italia, quello Stato nazionale che avrebbe risparmiato alla nostra nazione l'onta e il danno delle dominazioni straniere, nate e rafforzate dalla divisione e dalle inimicizie dei minuscoli e impotenti statarelli italiani." P. 345.

how far the historical estimate must have swerved from an objective appraisal if the only alternative to standards taken from the after-effects of the struggle of the Florentine Republic on the modern national state is found in the benefits which indirectly accrued to the flowering of Florentine culture in the "Medicean age" one or two generations after the great contest? In the most complete survey of Renaissance politics attempted in the 1920's and 1930's, the widely read *Problemi Politici del Rinascimento* by F. Cognasso,[9] we have a balance-sheet of the contest which notes to the credit of Visconti Milan that Milan had been given an historic "mission in Italy," whereas "the Florentines claimed they were acting as the avengers of the so-called Italian liberty, but instead they defended only the old egotisms of city-states and social class."[10]

What all these judgments are lacking to a truly astonishing degree is evident: while the indirect effects of the decision of around 1400 on the Italy of the 16th, 17th, and 18th centuries are weighed with thoroughness, none of these authors ever brings out, let alone evaluates, the fact that the failure of the Visconti to achieve an Italian Monarchy was the necessary condition for Italy's becoming intellectually, artistically, and culturally the birthplace of the Renaissance and, in Burckhardt's sense, the "first-born son" of the modern European family of nations. Until deep into the second half of the 15th century, all of the new elements in Humanism and in art that constitute the essence of the Renaissance not merely appeared first of all in Florence, to be accepted in Milan only later, but in Milan they met with the greatest resistance and never succeeded in being accepted unadulterated. No one familiar with this fact can have any illusions that the growth

9 Turin, 1930.

10 ". . . a Firenze si pretendeva farsi vindici della così detta libertà italiana, mentre invece si defendevano solo i vecchi egoismi di comuni e di classe." ". . . Gian Galeazzo ebbe della sua missione in Italia una più chiara coscienza, sentì tutti i doveri e tutti i diritti che dalla sua potenza gli venivano." Pp. 32, 29.

of the Renaissance would have been nipped in the bud if Florence had become a provincial town within an Italian kingdom under despotic Viscontean rule. By the same token, the decisive traits of the later Renaissance are unthinkable without the existence of a Venetian republic, and without independence of life in Rome and Naples. Since the statements cited earlier lack all awareness of these basic facts of Renaissance history, they are not only guilty of a certain one-sidedness such as is unavoidable; they represent an essentially unhistorical approach to the past which, in raising the question of the effects of events on later times, forgets their significance in their own time. In the last analysis, the controversy over the political "tragedy" of the Italian Renaissance is the Italian counterpart to the long controversy among German scholars over the "imperial policy" of the German kings in Italy during the Middle Ages—a controversy which, looking on history from the perspective of the German national state of the nineteenth century, saw in every conquest and act of Germanization in Slavic territories east of the Elbe by a medieval prince a preparation for the distant future, while the policies of the Salian and Hohenstaufen emperors appeared as the fateful "error" and the "tragedy" of German history. But just as the transference of the standards of the nineteenth-century national state to the German history of the Middle Ages came eventually to be recognized as inadequate, just so the application of nineteenth-century national standards to the world of the republics and signories of Renaissance Italy was bound in due time to become obsolete.

The actual development of political historiography on the Renaissance did not, however, take this simple course; it was deflected by the rise of another trend in historical research. The authors who took sides with the Visconti State on the grounds that it could have become the forerunner of an Italian national state were almost of necessity inclined to infuse into their descriptions of Giangaleazzo's aims something of their own national passion. With the growth, toward the end of the nineteenth century, of realistic tendencies in historiography there arose a growing distrust of the possibility that the maxims and emotions guiding modern nationalism had played a substantial part in the power-politics of Renaissance tyrants and Renaissance states. The more the study of the archival records of diplomatic actions moved into the center of historical research, the more frequently the assertion that Giangaleazzo had harbored far-flung plans of national unification came to be considered as a misinterpretation of the evidence. Non-Italian scholars, as is natural, were the first to recommend a program of matter-of-fact diplomatic research free of national-Italian prejudices. French students especially, in their investigations of the constantly shifting alliances of both Milan and Florence with France, were inclined to conclude that the continuous changes in the attitude of the Italian powers were motivated by sheer Machiavellianism, and that the diplomatic game was not ennobled by any higher goals or political traditions. Two generations ago, in 1896, this was the opinion expressed by E. Jarry in a commentary accompanying the first collection of the documents of the French-Italian relations. (*Les origines de la domination française à Gênes, 1392-1402; documents diplomatiques et politiques*); and it was still the conclusion reached by M. de Boüard in 1936 in an exhaustive analysis of the interrelations between France and the Italian states (*Les origines des guerres d'Italie. La France et l'Italie au temps du grand schism d'Occident*).[11] The cool scepticism of this French school, and

11 Cf. De Boüard, p. 14f. Some well-substantiated objections against de Boüard's inclination to find in Italian politics around 1400 "Machiavellianism" in the bad sense were raised at once by E. Dupré Theseider in *Rivista Storica Italiana* (ser. v, vol. 1 [1936], fasc. 3, p. 101ff.). Dupré Theseider stressed that the Florentines needed the French alliance to survive the threat of Giangaleazzo Visconti, even though "in their hearts they considered [the alliance] an 'inevitable evil'," and a danger to Italy, "and endeavoured to free themselves of it as soon as an opportunity offered."

its full reliance on the testimony of archival-diplomatic documents, had their influence also on the only large work about the politics of the Giangaleazzo period written in the English language: D. M. Bueno De Mesquita's *Giangaleazzo Visconti, Duke of Milan, 1351-1402*,[12] the best handbook in existence for the study of the diplomatic and military occurrences on the North and Middle Italian scene. Throughout Mesquita's learned book, we are given the impression that of the alleged far-reaching designs of Giangaleazzo no more existed in reality than can be found in the official diplomatic documents; we are told that Giangaleazzo often merely reacted to Florentine moves, while both sides were motivated by parochial interests and narrow-minded local egoisms. It has already been noted[13] that, to the detriment of De Mesquita's work, what results is a narrative in which the history of the Giangaleazzo period appears an endless sequence of diplomatic moves and countermoves, devoid of any higher aspirations or political passions.

The extent of this swing of the pendulum toward "realism" is shown by the fact that Italian scholars did not remain unaffected. If we compare the Italian literature on the Visconti that was produced around 1900, when G. Romano occupied the leading position, with F. Cognasso's *Problemi politici del Rinascimento* of 1930, we are struck by the shift of accent from the description of a Milanese struggle for a national program to the disillusioned presentation of a world dominated by mere power-politics.[14] What distinguishes the Italian authors of this group from a scholar like De Mesquita is their more emphatic adherence to the notion that even though modern national feelings were still alien to the Visconti, yet the destruction of so many smaller dominions and their incorporation in the Milanese State did in fact create a possi-

12 Cambridge, 1941. 13 See note 13 to Chap. 2.

14 See the informative sketch of this development by N. Valeri in *Archivio Storico Italiano*, anno XCIII (1935), vol. II, pp. 110-116.

bility to establish a unified Italian kingdom, and that consequently the resistance of Florence and the collapse of Milan after Giangaleazzo's death were a "tragedy" for Italy. In this form—combining a conviction of the national mission of the Visconti State with an extreme scepticism toward the supposition that the Visconti themselves were conscious of this mission—the "realistic" school of thought has still quite recently made its way even into the old handbook *Storia Politica d'Italia* with L. Simeoni's revision of the volume *Le Signorie* (published in 1950). The slogan of a unified Italy, Simeoni tells us, served in the fourteenth and fifteenth centuries merely as a "means of propaganda," or at best expressed the "isolated feeling of a few superior personalities like Petrarch, without any effect on the general sentiment of the nation or the conduct of the statesmen."[15]

Anyone who with an open mind examines the contemporaneous literary documents collected and discussed in the present book must judge that the result of the diplomatic-realistic phase in the study of early Renaissance politics constitutes a loss as much as a gain. Self-restriction to the study of diplomatic actions, and of the official documents about them, has had the effect of focussing attention on a mere fraction of historical reality. In spite of the constant kaleidoscopic changes in the diplomatic situations, *literati* and large groups of the populations throughout Italy looked with hope or fear on Giangaleazzo's sweeping conquests as the revolutionary upheaval which would lay the lasting foundations for a unified monarchy. There is sufficient appropriate evidence: pamphlets of publicists, political poems, public speeches, and the political reasonings of chroniclers influenced by Humanism. From all this evidence there emerges the picture of both partisans and opponents of Giangaleazzo living in the awareness that the

15 ". . . artificio polemico o sentimento isolato di pochi individui superiori come il Petrarca, senza efficacia sul sentire generale della nazione come sulla condotta degli uomini politici." Simeoni, *op. cit.*, p. 3.

Milanese-Florentine struggle was destined to bring about a crucial and historic decision.

The error of the Italian-"nationalist" evaluation of the Visconti enterprise was not, as the historians of the realistic school supposed, an unjustified attribution to Renaissance statesmen and citizens of motives foreign to their period; for most of the elements of the modern national idea did indeed appear for the first time in the struggles of the Trecento and Quattrocento. The error lay in the tacit assumption that national political unification would have had the same effect on life and culture of Renaissance Italy as it had (or, at least, was supposed to have had) on Italy in the nineteenth century. An unhistorical identification of modern and Renaissance conditions was at the bottom of the rash neglect of the counterforces that struggled against peninsular centralization under one head. Unification by the Visconti was not the sole antidote to medieval localism around 1400; and the defeat of national unity during the early Quattrocento consequently did not mean the triumph of the remnants of an out-dated kind of localism. The wars of the Giangaleazzo period were a struggle of ideas as well as material resources that was to decide between two possible courses of history. If a final victory of the Visconti would have meant national unification of Italy at an earlier date, the survival of the Florentine Republic did not mean parochialism or "Kleinstaaterei" in the nineteenth-century sense. Rather it meant the emergence of the world of the Italian Renaissance: a competition among regions and city-states recalling the situation of ancient Greece, and a civilization which offered a place in the sun to civic liberty in an age in which, under Italian conditions, universal despotic absolutism would have been the price of nation-wide integration.

In a political picture of the early Renaissance due weight must be given, then, to two essential elements: first, both dimensions of the political scene, republicanism as well as the belief in tyrant rule, must be recognized; there must be an end to the black-and-white treatment characteristic of the "nationalist" school. And second, our basis in the sources must be broadened sufficiently to admit the voices that can be heard through the writings of the humanists and other contemporaneous literature; there must be an end to the limiting of inquiries to archival documents which is the hall-mark of the diplomatic-"realistic" school. With these necessities taken into account, a new, third phase in the study of the Renaissance background opens—a phase in which it is possible to recognize the interdependence of Quattrocento politics and thought, and to make live again the fears, sorrows, and exultations of a generation that was experiencing the clash of irreconcilable forces and convictions in an historic crisis.

Since the late 1930's and quickened by the political experiences of our own generation, this third approach has gradually emerged, and in it we find the setting and the justification for our own analysis. Some of the observations made in the present book about the political frame of Quattrocento Florence were first outlined by the writer in 1938 in an essay "The Historical Background of the Florentine Renaissance";[16] others were sketched in 1942, in a paper "Articulation and Unity in the Italian Renaissance and in the Modern West."[17] At about the same time similar viewpoints were being suggested in Italy, in a programmatic essay, *La libertà e la pace. Orientamenti politici del Rinascimento Italiano*, by N. Valeri, published in 1942. In 1950, Valeri carried out his program in a comprehensive narrative of the development of Italy from the mid-Trecento to about 1500—a work of fundamental significance, which will give the new approach a permanent place

16 In *History*, n. s., XXII (1938), 315-327, and in an Italian version, "Lo sfondo storico del rinascimento fiorentino," in *Rinascita*, I (1938), 50-72.

17 Published in the symposium volume, *The Quest for Political Unity in World History*, ed. S. Pargellis; volume III of the *Annual Report of the American Historical Association for 1942* (Washington, D.C., 1944), 123-138.

especially in the interpretation of the second half of the Trecento.[18] A study by the present writer, also finished by the end of 1950—"A Struggle for Liberty in the Renaissance: Florence, Venice, and Milan in the Early Quattrocento"[19]—has used the new approach in reviewing Florence's part in the turn-of-the-century upheaval and in the subsequent political developments down to the middle of the Quattrocento.

Now it is true that even if war, and post-war, conditions had not kept Valeri and this author in mutual ignorance of each others' results after 1938, certain differences in method as well as in the historical evaluation of Florentine liberty would be discernible between studies made in an American atmosphere and studies more closely joined to the earlier course of Italian scholarship. But these are differences that concern shades of opinion; they must not make us overlook the essential fact that during the last ten or fifteen years a basically new approach to the background of the early Renaissance has emerged—a fresh view of the political situation on the threshold of the Quattrocento which, if found correct, is bound to modify substantially the picture familiar from the work of the two older historiographical schools.[20]

18 N. Valeri, *l'Italia nell'Età dei Principati dal 1343 al 1516* ("Storia d'Italia," ed. A. Mandadori, vol. v). Verona, 1950.

19 Published in the *American Historical Review*, LVIII (1953), 265-289 and 544-570, with a companion essay, "The Anti-Florentine Discourses of the Doge Tommaso Mocenigo (1414-23): Their Date and Partial Forgery," published in *Speculum*, XXVII (1952), 323-342, and again in *Humanistic and Political Literature*, Chapter IX.

20 For a closer comparison of Valeri's *L'Italia nell'Età dei Principati dal 1343 al 1516* with the preceding phase of scepticism toward the humanistic sources, as well as with the picture given in the present book, see the writer's review-essay "Die politische Entwicklung der italienischen Renaissance," *Historische Zeitschrift*, CLXXIV (1952), 31-56.

It is of great interest to note that the appraisal of the inter-state relations among the city-states of ancient Greece has recently resulted in a kindred opposition to the use of "national unification" as an absolute historical standard, and in a similar emphasis on analogies with the modern states-system. See H. E. Stier's *Grundlagen und Sinn der Griechischen Geschichte* (Stuttgart, 1945), pp. 144 ff., 167 ff., and A. Wucher, "Das Bild der griechischen Geschichte: Forschungsbericht," *Saeculum*, II (1951), 619 f.

APPENDIX 2

A VENETIAN CONTRIBUTION TO THE QUATTROCENTO CONTROVERSY ON CAESAR

(Annex to Vol. I, p. 55)

AN INTERESTING epilogue to Poggio's 1435 controversy with Guarino on Caesar is still imperfectly known. In 1440, a Venetian humanist and jurist in Papal services, Pietro del Monte, then nuncio of the Curia in England and later Bishop of Venetian Brescia,[1] composed a letter of pamphlet length, addressed to Poggio, in order to strengthen Poggio's position against Guarino.[2] This letter, which Poggio took pains to make known in Italy,[3] represents an effort further to discredit Guarino's glowing appraisal of Caesar by bringing together all the statements from antiquity that were unfavorable to Caesar, and by the demonstration in minute detail that Caesar had been a bad citizen and a tyrant.

We have here a document that is of unusual interest for several reasons. In the first place, it furnishes rare evidence of the part played by the new Florentine historical outlook in

1 On Pietro del Monte see two papers by A. Zanelli in *Archivio Storico Lombardo*, 1907, and J. Haller's introduction to his *Piero da Monte. Ein Gelehrter und päpstlicher Beamter des 15. Jahrhunderts. Seine Briefsammlung* ("Bibliothek des Preussischen Historischen Instituts in Rom," vol. XIX, Rome, 1941).

2 Attention was first drawn to Pietro del Monte's letter to Poggio by E. Walser in his *Poggius Florentinus, Leben und Werke* (Leipzig, 1914), p. 172f. Only a few sentences from the letter have been published in J. Haller's cited edition of Pietro del Monte's *Briefwechsel*, p. 142f. The passages quoted on the following pages are reproduced from extracts made by this writer many years ago from the then Ms. Lat. Fol. 366 of the Preussische Staatsbibliothek Berlin, fol. 63v-64r, 66v-67r, and 69v. The version in the Berlin manuscript is the original form of the text which, according to Walser, *loc. cit.*, is also preserved in the Ms. Bibliothèque de la Sorbonne, no. 229. For other manuscripts containing Pietro's letter see Haller, *op. cit.*, p. 142, and R. Weiss, *Humanism in England during the Fifteenth Century* (Oxford, 1941), p. 24, n. 7.

3 Poggio presented the letter to the Pope; Walser, *op. cit.*, p. 173.

loosening the tongues of republican citizens elsewhere in Italy. Pietro del Monte had received his humanistic education from Guarino during the period when Guarino was teaching in Venice.[4] As Pietro reports at the opening of his letter, Guarino had even then used his lectures to sing the praises of Caesar at the expense of the *Respublica Romana*. Previously, in the 1390's, Guarino had pursued his studies under the guidance of Giovanni Conversino in Padua, and, as is shown elsewhere in this book, Conversino in his Paduan days had been a literary champion of the spirit of north-Italian Tyranny; his defense of the *Imperium Romanum* against the *Respublica Romana* had heralded the debates of the 1430's.[5] Thus, Guarino's classroom had introduced a slice of the intellectual life at the north-Italian princely courts of Giangaleazzo Visconti's days into the education of young citizens of Venice. Pietro del Monte, as he tells us in his letter, had been revolted even as Guarino's student by the teacher's advocacy of "the enemy of his *patria* and destroyer of sweet liberty." But it was Poggio who finally introduced him to the arguments refuting Guarino, and in the letter Pietro congratulates himself "that I have found in you [Poggio] so good, so strong, and so eloquent an advocate and defender of my long-held views and opinions."[6]

Thus enlightened and confirmed in his original reaction, Pietro ventures upon a frank discussion of the roots of his attitude. The verdict that Caesar's "conspiracy and plot against the *patria*" has effaced the merit of his military achievements for Rome sounds natural and convincing, says Pietro, in the ears of a person born in a commonwealth which to the present

4 Haller, *op. cit.*, p. 11. Guarino was teaching in Venice during the years 1414-1419, with interruptions.

5 See Vol. One, p. 118f.

6 Already in his youth he had learned to regard Caesar a "turbulentus civis" and "patrie hostis eversorque libertatis dulcissime." In later years he had rejoiced ". . . quod te talem tantumque ac tam disertum veteris sententie et opinionis mee patronum ac defensorem . . . nactus sum."

day has remained an "inviolate temple of liberty." Venice, he says, knows only too well that kind of "passionate desire to extinguish liberty" found in Caesar; for the same desire has incited many emperors and princes to conspire against the liberty of the Republic of Venice. But the Venetians, after overcoming these aggressors, formed for themselves the maxim "that if liberty ends, let life end also";[7] and they have learned to follow the political program "that, if possible, all Italy, which has been crushed under so many disasters caused by tyrants, may at some time achieve peace, tranquillity, quiet, repose, and the sweetest and most coveted of all human things, liberty. How, then, should it seem strange to anybody if I, who was born, raised, and bred in the strongest fortress of liberty, and who have never felt the heavy and harsh yoke of tyranny (for all of which I am in the debt of the immortal gods)—if I emphatically and frankly express detestation for Caesar the infamous patricide, destroyer of Roman liberty, and bitter enemy of his *patria*? For even if there were no other reasons, Nature, mother of all things, drives and compels me to say what I have said."[8] This statement of a Venetian humanist presents a remarkable demonstration of the relationship connecting the Quattrocento controversy on Caesar with the deep-rooted differences between the convictions of civic humanists and the outlook of humanists at the princely courts.

It also testifies to the spirit of a period in which the republics of Florence and Venice had at last become political allies

7 ". . . ut qui libertatis finis fuerit, idem sit et vite."

8 ". . . ut, si fieri posset, universa Ytalia, que tantis cladibus tyrannorum oppressa est, aliquando pace, tranquillitate, quiete, ocio ac rerum omnium mortalium dulcissima et optatissima libertate potiretur. Quid igitur cuiquam mirum videri debet, si in libertatis arce munitissima natus, nutritus, educatus, gravissimumque ac durissimum tyrannidis iugum nusquam expertus, quamobrem diis immortalibus omnia debeo, Cesarem scelestissimum patricidam, eversorem romane libertatis, hostem patrie acerbissimum, pleno ore ac libera voce detestor? Ad id enim, ut dixi, etiam si cetera deessent, me cogit compellitque natura, rerum omnium parens."

against the Visconti, and in which the conceptions of Roman history and of *libertas Italiae* that in Florence had emerged on the threshold of the century, spread also to Venice. Pietro was in close relation with two of the spiritual and political leaders of the Venetian alliance with Florence, Francesco Barbaro and Andrea Giuliano. These two Venetian patrician citizens, together with Guarino, are the partners of the conversation in a dialogue from Pietro's pen.[9] In Pietro's youth, Giuliano had been a paternal friend to him,[10] and Barbaro, to whom Poggio's criticism of Caesar had been addressed, is referred to as the arbiter of the Caesar controversy at the end of Pietro's letter. In view of these personal relations we may, then, say that Pietro's proud claim—that Venice was striving to see all Italy escape from long suppression by tyrants, and enjoy "the most coveted thing, liberty"—reflected the political climate characteristic of Venice during the decades of the Florentine-Venetian league against the Visconti. It is this community of sentiment between humanists born and bred in the two republics which makes Pietro in his letter uphold and advocate the Florentine republican interpretation of Roman history. In the concluding section of this book we shall have an opportunity to confirm from many other sources the dissemination of the common belief in the *libertas Italiae* during the 1420's, 1430's, and 1440's.[11]

9 Haller, *op. cit.*, p. 18, n. 34, and p. 22.

10 Haller, *ibid.*, and S. Troilo, *Andrea Giuliano, Politico e letterato veneziano del quattrocento* (Florence, 1932), p. 173.

11 See in particular for Barbaro and Giuliano, Vol. One, p. 345f.

APPENDIX 3

INTERPRETATIONS OF LEONARDO BRUNI'S *DIALOGI AD PETRUM PAULUM HISTRUM*

(Annex to Vol. I, p. 205)

IN WEIGHING a problem of interpretation which in the course of time has been probed from as many different directions as that of the *Dialogi*, we should know which of the possible forms of approach have been tried by earlier scholars. For it is with a view to the history of the problem that we must chart the course of our study and avoid avenues already explored to the limits of their usefulness.

The precursor of all those who sought the nerve of Bruni's discussions in the first dialogue was Wesselofsky who, in 1867, was the first among modern scholars to read both dialogues *in extenso* (in a manuscript of the Biblioteca Laurenziana in Florence). True, in this inspection he convinced himself that the attacks of the Niccoli of the first dialogue are eventually refuted; and consequently he judged that they play only the role of a rhetorical feat in the structure of the dialogues. Nonetheless they seemed to him to represent the essential part of the work when it is considered as an historical source. For they do echo, he argued, the most important intellectual movement of the time, as is shown by the fact that Niccoli's challenges "are taken seriously, and discussed seriously" in the conversations.[1] Wesselofsky, therefore, looked upon the dialogues as a veiled testimony for the rise of the classicistic trend. This trend he tried to reconstruct by proving that the ideas of the Niccoli of the first dialogue are identical with what we can learn about the classicistic movement from the contentions of its adversaries, the adher-

1 ". . . la sua opinione . . . presa sul serio e seriamente discussa." Wesselofsky, vol. II, pp. 24-40, esp. p. 40.

ents of Trecento culture, whose works—the *Paradiso degli Alberti*, the two invectives of Cino Rinuccini and Domenico da Prato, and other minor writings—Wesselofsky was the first to recover from the manuscripts, and the first to appraise historically.[2]

This interpretation of the *Dialogi* fell on well prepared ground, for only a few years earlier the first comprehensive survey of Italian Humanism, G. Voigt's *Die Wiederbelebung des Klassischen Altertums* (first edition 1859), had also—though from a somewhat different starting-point—arrived at the conclusion that the meat of Bruni's work was in the challenge of *Dialogus I*. When Voigt prepared the first edition of his work he had known the *Dialogi* merely through the few extracts contained in L. Mehus' *Vita Ambrosii Traversarii* (Florence, 1759). In that standard work of the eighteenth century on Florentine Humanism in Bruni's time, some important passages of both Niccoli's attack and his recantation could be found.[3] From these selections Voigt gathered that the theses of the first-dialogue Niccoli were a true reflection of the mind of the historical Niccoli, and of the historically important intellectual tendencies in Florence about 1400, while the second dialogue did no more than somewhat to "temper and soften" (*mässigen und mildern*) the sweep of these new ideas.[4] By 1880, when the second edition of his work appeared, Voigt had read the complete first dialogue in the Basel print of 1536, and for the second he had available the more copious extracts contained in Wesselofsky's *Paradiso* introduction. But even with this fuller knowledge of the sources he insisted[5] that the attack of the first dialogue "did not seem" to be refuted in any essential points by Niccoli's recantation, nor did the second dialogue seem to him to show the color of real life characteristic of the first-day conversations. "The accusations [made by Niccoli] are not really re-

2 See Vol. One, p. 251ff.
3 Esp. pp. CLXXVI and CCXXVIf.
4 Ed. 1859, pp. 195-197.
5 Ed. 1880, vol. I, p. 385ff.

tracted, or refuted. The praise for the Triumvirs [Dante, Petrarch, and Boccaccio] moves on other planes than the attack and seems to lack basic motivation. The second dialogue does not have the titillating charm of the first. . . ."[6] Before long, these ideas were echoed in an important monograph on *Il Petrarca e i Carraresi* by A. Zardo.[7]

When both dialogues became available in print in 1889, emphasis on the ideas of the first continued among the vast majority of scholars, supported either with Wesselofsky's or with Voigt's arguments—a striking example that a broadening of the source basis alone is impotent to modify established tradition, as long as new sources are not viewed from a changed historical perspective. The three editors of 1889 (Klette, Wotke, and largely even Kirner, the most independent and critical mind in this younger group of scholars) merely adopted and elaborated Wesselofsky's and Voigt's views. So did M. Lehnerdt who prepared the third revised edition of Voigt's *Wiederbelebung* in 1893. Basically the same opinions were repeated by G. Zippel, the Italian reviser of Voigt's work, in his *Niccolò Niccoli* (in 1890); by R. Sabbadini in a review of the works of Kirner, Klette and Wotke;[8] by O. Zenatti in his *Dante e Firenze*;[9] and by the authors of more general historical works, such as C. Trabalza in *Storia della grammatica Italiana*,[10] and Th. Zielinsky in *Cicero im Wandel der Jahrhunderte*;[11] and still quite recently by A. Buck in a paper on *Dante im Urteil . . . des italienischen Humanismus*.[12]

6 "Die Vorwürfe werden doch nicht zurückgenommen oder widerlegt. Das Lob der Triumvirn [Dante, Petrarch, and Boccaccio] bewegt sich auf anderen Gebieten als der Angriff und scheint der tieferen Begründung zu entbehren. Dem zweiten Dialog fehlt der prickelnde Reiz des ersten. . . ."

7 Milan, 1887.

8 *Giornale Storico della Letteratura Italiana*, XIV (1889), 288ff., and also, though with certain modifications, *ibid.*, XCVI (1930), 132f. For the three editions, see note 29 to Chap. 11.

9 Florence, 1899, p. 179f.

10 1908, p. 43.

11 4th edn.: Leipzig, 1929, pp. 177, 340.

12 *Deutsches Dante-Jahrbuch*, XXVIII (1949), 8.

Apparently the first to reverse the perspective and seek the message of Bruni's work in the concessions of the second Niccoli, was A. Gaspary, in the second volume of his *Geschichte der italienischen Literatur* published in 1888.[13] Since then the *Dialogi* have made the same impression on other readers.[14] The most forceful statement of this view has come from G. Gentile, who in his *La Filosofia*[15] called Niccoli's recantation a "magnificent eulogy of Dante" which "demonstrates the childishness, lack of substance, and injustice of the judgments passed on the day before."[16] "Compared with the feebleness and artificiality of the accusations of the previous day, [Niccoli's recantation] reveals perfect sincerity."[17] The gross incompatibility of this opinion with Voigt's earlier verdict makes it strikingly clear how little personal impressions and value-judgments, derived from a single source, can do to produce a convincing new historical perspective, as long as they do not refute apparent "facts" or put their views to the test by applying them to other sources.

The first to compare the viewpoint of the Niccoli of the second dialogue with kindred ideas found in contemporary documents, and thus to produce a match to Wesselofsky's appraisal of the first-dialogue Niccoli, seems to have been M. Korelin in his work on early Italian Humanism, published in Moscow in 1892.[18] From the coincidences between the key-ideas of the second Niccoli and Bruni's appraisal of Dante and Petrarch in 1436, Korelin concluded that Bruni's own

13 Pp. 179, 661.

14 See, still quite recently, C. Vasoli, *Rinascimento*, III (1952), 131-133.

15 For the important reinterpretations of the ideas of about 1400 given in Gentile's work, see notes 32 to Chap. 13 and 8 to Chap. 14.

16 ". . . dimostra la puerilità, l'insussistenza, l'ingiustizia dei giudizii del giorno prima."

17 ". . . paragonata alla debolezza e artificiosità delle accuse del giorno precedente, ne dimostra la perfetta sincerità." p. 217.

18 *The Early Italian Humanism and its Appraisal in Historiography.* In the series: Memoirs of the University of Moscow, 1892. See the analysis of the Russian work by F. Dukmeyer in *Deutsche Literaturzeitung*, XXVI (1905), 69-75.

convictions must have been identical with the concessions made by the second Niccoli. On the other hand, Korelin failed to do justice to the important fact, already noted by earlier students, of the concordance between the ideas of the first-dialogue Niccoli, and those of the historical Niccoli as we know him from other sources. In consequence he did not touch upon the essential point that Bruni in the second dialogue obviously took issue with, and modified, the ideas of the historical Niccoli reproduced in the first dialogue.

Thus, even if the appraisal of the Russian scholar were not difficult of access to western students because of the language in which it is written, it would be surpassed in importance by E. Santini's treatise "*La produzione volgare di Leonardo Bruni Aretino e il suo culto per 'le tre corone fiorentine,'*" which enlarges on a systematic comparison of the first-dialogue Niccoli with the historical Niccoli, and of the second-dialogue Niccoli with the historical Bruni.[19] So long as one persists in seeing Bruni's own position exclusively either in one or the other of the diverging views of the two dialogues, Santini's interpretation of the *Dialogi* is the most mature and comprehensive that can be achieved.[20]

The only attempt to go beyond this alternative, and to

19 *Giornale Storico della Letteratura Italiana*, LX (1912), esp. pp. 290-295.

20 See Santini, pp. 292ff. Santini's reference to the affinity between Niccoli's recantation and Bruni's own later opinion known from his *Vita di Dante* ought to have prevented R. Sabbadini from reaffirming, as late as 1930, the old error of Voigt that the crucial part of the challenge of the first-dialogue Niccoli is not retracted in the second dialogue, and that the heart of the new criticism, to Bruni as well as Niccoli, is the attack "sulle opere volgari dei tre fiorentini e in particular modo sulla *Commedia* di Dante." (*Giornale Stor. della Lett. Ital.*, XCVI, 133). For a characterization of Bruni's attitude to the *Commedia* it is sufficient to quote his verdict from his *Vita di Dante* that "Dante in his principal work is superior to every work of Petrarch," i.e., obviously, even including Petrarch's Latin works (*Bruni, Schriften*, p. 69). Furthermore, it will be pointed out (Vol. One, pp. 302, 305f.) that Bruni took a positive and appreciative stand precisely on the question of the value of the Volgare, and that, even in those early days when he composed the *Laudatio*, he was far from being a classicist extremist.

interpret the difference of attitude between the two dialogues as revealing two frames of mind both characteristic of the author, was made by V. Rossi as late as 1921.[21] In our chapter on the *Dialogi*, we have discussed at length the progress brought about by this latest approach, and also the remaining vital problems which even Rossi's theory is powerless to solve.[22] There we examine in detail whether, along the trail made by this third approach, it may not be possible to reach an interpretation other than that proposed by Rossi, who deemed that Bruni in each of his two dialogues illuminated the central problems of early Quattrocento Humanism from a different angle, but that he was unable to bring into harmony, or reconcile, these partial views.

21 See note 31 to Chap. 11.

22 See notes 31 and 47 to Chap. 11.

APPENDIX 4

FRANCESCO DA FIANO, ROMAN HUMANIST, AND THE DATE OF HIS INVECTIVE "AGAINST THE DETRACTORS OF THE POETS"

(Annex to Vol. I, p. 273)

IN VIEW of the lack of any monographic study on Francesco da Fiano, and his omission from nearly all general accounts of early Humanism, a few words are needed to introduce his personality, and to determine the date of his unpublished major work, *Contra Ridiculos Oblocutores et Fellitos Detractores Poetarum.* The brief extracts from it, reproduced in our chapter on Francesco's role in the vindication of ancient religion, will have shown the need for a brief delineation of the life of this friend and correspondent of Florentine humanists in the time of the intellectual transition about 1400.[1]

Two of the ablest students of early Humanism, F. Novati and V. Zabughin, quite aware of this lacuna in our knowledge, planned years ago monographs and editions of Francesco da Fiano, but they failed to publish more than a few bits of information in the context of related studies.[2] Some of the pre-

1 Cf. Vol. One, p. 282f.

2 See the few pages on Francesco's life and letters in Novati's *La giovinezza di Coluccio Salutati* (Torino, 1888), esp. pp. 91 ff.; Novati's statement in *Archivio Storico Lombardo*, ser. III, vol. XIX (1903), 374f.; and Zabughin's by no means exhausting notes on the contents of Francesco's *Contra Detractores* in his *Vergilio nel Rinascimento Italiano*, vol. I (Bologna, 1921), pp. 110ff. Between the time (about 1930) when the writer collected the material on Francesco da Fiano used in this book, and the composition (in 1947) of the critical notes below and the chapter on Francesco da Fiano in Vol. One, Part Four, no scholar seems to have given attention to this Roman humanist; but, more recently, interest in him has been revived. After a brief discussion by R. Weiss and E. Panofsky of a poetical invective of Francesco against an unnamed Englishman, in the *Journal of the Warburg and Courtauld Institutes*, 1947 and 1949, R. Weiss in his *Il Primo Secolo dell' Umanesimo* (Rome, 1949) has published the letters exchanged between Francesco da Fiano and Petrarch, and has collected the data referring to Francesco's humanistic education under Pietro

paratory work already done by Novati, including in particular a collection of references to manuscripts that contain writings of Francesco, has been preserved in the archives of the *Società Storica Lombarda* in Milan, where this writer has had an opportunity to consult it.

The period when Francesco's role in the history of Humanism was relatively most conspicuous, was the short pontificate of Innocent VII (November 1404 to November 1406) during which the Roman University was reorganized and eminent humanists—indeed the best talents of the younger generation—were for the first time called to the Curia as Papal *scriptores* and *secretarii.* Before that time, or more precisely before the later years of the pontificate of Innocent's predecessor Boniface IX, Francesco had experienced much of the misery that was the lot of so many chancery-humanists of the late Trecento. For a while, fortune had driven him restlessly about the Peninsula, from the northern reaches of central Italy down to Naples. Nonetheless the Curia, which employed him intermittently in various positions, always remained the spiritual home of this Roman-born scholar[3]—a fact sufficiently shown by the following evidence (it could, undoubtedly, be greatly enlarged through specialized research): 1379, papal *scriptor*;[4] 1381, papal *scriptor*;[5] 1387, papal *computator*;[6] 1389, signing documents in Registrum Vaticanum 347, fol. 49r and 57r;[7] some time between January 1399 and September 1404, appointed by Pope Boniface IX "*Cancellarius litterarum dilectorum filiorum populi Ro-*

da Muglio in Bologna around 1370 and at the court of Pandolfo Malatesta at Pesaro. A comprehensive biographical study on Francesco da Fiano has just been promised by don Igino Taù. For Zabughin, see note 22 below.

3 Fiano is a little township in the Roman territory.

4 Cf. F. Th. Ripoll, *Bullarium ordinis fratr. Praedicatorum*, vol. II (Rome, 1730), p. 297, and Graf's reference to Francesco, next note.

5 Cf. T. Graf, *Urban VI*, Berlin doc. diss., 1916, p. 20a (1379 and 1381).

6 Cf. Graf, *op. cit.*, p. 11a.

7 Originals seen by this writer.

mani penes . . . Conservatores camerae urbis";[8] 1404, February, signing a document as a papal *scriptor*.[9]

In 1406, therefore, when, after the return of the Curia from Viterbo to Rome, such men as Bruni, Poggio, Vergerio, and Loschi were employed in the papal chancery simultaneously, Francesco could by comparison with these newcomers consider himself a Roman of long standing, and play the part of Nestor among the younger humanists. The exchanges which he then had with members of the younger generation—he vied with Loschi in a kind of contest in writing Latin verses—are the only episodes of Francesco's life that are not wholly forgotten. Besides the record which has remained of them in Loschi's works,[10] a Latin poem by Vergerio has quite recently come to light in which the contest between Francesco and Loschi is echoed.[11] In addition, we have a description of those Roman years in Latin verses, written in retrospect in 1425, by a humanist of Brescia, Bartolomeo Bayguera, who in the time of Innocent VII's pontificate was forced to leave his native city on account of party strife, and took refuge at the Curia from about 1405 to 1410. In this poem,[12] the figure of Francesco da Fiano stands out as that of a cicerone who showed the younger humanists around the ruins of ancient Rome, and

8 This fact results from the reappointment diploma by Pope John XXIII of 1412, Sept. 1 (see note 14 below), which says that Francesco had already been appointed "cancellarius . . . camerae urbis" by Pope Boniface IX (1389-1404). Since in December 1398, according to Registrum Vat. 316, fol. 83 (seen by this writer), Tebaldo di Cencio de' Cancellieri was appointed chancellor of Rome, Francesco's appointment by Boniface must have been made some time between January 1399 and September 1404.

9 See Kochendörffer's list of Papal curial officials during the Schism, *Neues Archiv der Gesellschaft für Ältere Deutsche Geschichtskunde*, XXX (1904-5), 578 nr. 38, and the documents quoted in *Festgabe für K. Th. Heigel* (Munich, 1903) p. 154f.

10 Cf. G. Da Schio, *Sulla vita e sugli scritti di Antonio Loschi* (Padua, 1858), pp. 47, 67, 92, 149.

11 Vergerio's poem was published by L. Smith in *Archivio Veneto*, ser. V, vol. IV (1928), 134-137.

12 *Itinerarium*, according to the text in Cod. Ambros. A 6 inf., fol. 1ff.; or *Libellus Itinerarii*, according to the text in Cod. A. V. 6, manuscript of the Biblioteca Qeriniana at Brescia.

inspired them with enthusiasm for the ancient poets and the remains of classical art.[13] After Innocent's brief pontificate, Francesco's positions in Rome must have continued for some time, for under John XXIII, in 1411 and 1412, we still find him a papal *scriptor* and *abbreviator*, and, in September 1412, see him confirmed as "*Romani populi principalis et maior cancellarius penes Conservatores. . . .*"[14] Francesco was still alive in 1416, and active enough so that he could be asked to compose an invective against the "destroyers" (*perversores*) of the ruins of ancient Rome.[15] By 1425, however, he had died, after living his last days in Rome.[16]

There can be no doubt that in Francesco da Fiano we have before us a member of an age group somewhere between that of Salutati and that of Bruni, who exerted considerable influence on his coevals and many younger humanists. Of the nature of this influence we may some day be able to form an adequate idea with the help of Francesco's numerous letters and poems, still scattered unpublished through Italian libraries. From what this writer knows of this material, and from Francesco's *Contra Detractores* and his letter to Bruni,[17] it would appear that Francesco's literary production shows marked intellectual quality, in spite of a style which fell short

13 See the article by S. Locatelli, "Bartolomeo Bayguera e il suo 'Itinerarium,'" in *Commentari dell' Ateneo di Brescia per l'anno 1931* [1932], 83-90, which is, however, extremely meager in information and does not even mention Francesco da Fiano. The section of Bayguera's *Itinerarium* which deals with his Roman sojourn and his exchanges there with Francesco is found in Cod. Ambros. A 6 inf., fol. 33r ff., according to a photostat in the author's possession.

14 For 1411 see entries in Registrum Vat. 341, fol. 26r, 88v, and 104v. (Seen by this writer.) Pope John XXIII's diploma, dated Sept. 1, 1412 (see note 8 above) calls Francesco "scriptor et abbreviator litterarum apostolicarum" and reappoints him "dictarum litterarum Romani populi principalem et maiorem Cancellarium penes Conservatores prefatos ad vitam tuam . . ."; Registrum Vat. 344, fol. 201v-202r. (According to a photostat.)

15 So we are told in a letter of one of his former pupils, Cencio de' Rustici; see Vol. One, p. 282f.

16 As we read in Bayguera's *Itinerarium*.

17 For Francesco's letter see notes 44 and 45 to Chap. 14.

of the standards that were being rapidly accepted in the beginning of the Quattrocento. The mediocrity of form goes a long way toward explaining why Francesco, despite the esteem in which he was held by a number of more famous humanists, was little successful in his literary and professional career; but it must not cause us to overlook his place in the history of the classicist ideas around 1400. Almost every letter and poem from his pen is in some way a document of the aggressive attitude of classicism characteristic of those years. But the strongest expression of this sentiment is found in his one surviving major work: the invective *Contra Detractores Poetarum.*[18]

Ascription of Francesco's invective to the years around 1400 implies, however, a change from the date so far attributed to it. For even this work has not escaped the fate of virtually the entire literary production of that transition period: to have been obscured in its historical value through a mistaken chronology assumed by modern readers. At some future time it may be possible to determine the date of Francesco's work so accurately that no place will be left for error or for doubt. For the invective originated with a local Roman event, a sermon preached by a certain *magister* Stephanus Aretinus assaulting the ancient poets. As long as this figure has not been identified,[19] we must base our inferences on the observation that Francesco's invective, according to its preface, was dedicated to a certain "Cardinalis Bononiensis." Whereas Sabbadini, without taking cognizance of this essential key, as late as 1914 chanced upon the wholly subjective guess that the

18 Preserved in the autograph in Cod. Vat. Ottob. Lat. 1438, a manuscript with marginal corrections and insertions evidently made by the author.

19 Zabughin, in his *Vergilio nel Rinascimento Italiano*, vol. I, p. 129, was on a wrong track with his reference to a certain Stephanus Aretinus named in Bruni's letters *Ep. VI 2* and *Ep. X 17* of 1430, for this "Stephanus" from Arezzo was evidently a young man in 1430, and, in the letters, is not called "magister," as he would have been.

invective originated "in the last decade of the Trecento,"[20] Novati, who was the first to pay attention to the manuscript of Francesco's work (in 1905), also made the first attempt to base the dating on the identification of the addressee. He identified him with Antonio Correr, nephew of Gregory XII, who was appointed "Cardinalis Bononiensis" in 1406;[21] and this hypothesis was accepted by Zabughin.[22] If the assumption were sound, 1407 would be the earliest (and, according to Novati, most probable) date. But Novati did not give any reasons for his preference for this particular "Cardinalis Bononiensis" over any other. Equally consistent with the data just produced for Francesco's life in Rome would be identification with Antonio Correr's predecessor, Cosimo de' Migliorati, who was "Cardinalis Bononiensis" from December 18, 1389, to October 17, 1404, on which date he became Pope Innocent VII.[23] When the austere, saintlike figure of Correr is compared with Innocent VII, patron and friend of humanists,[24] it would appear that the "Cardinalis Bononiensis" who was to be Innocent VII is the much more likely choice as patron of a work tinged, as is Francesco's *Invectiva*, with unbounded enthusiasm for the ancient poets.

Among Francesco's minor writings a document has been

20 "La difesa fu scritta, se non erriamo, nell' ultimo decennio del Trecento." Sabbadini, *Le Scoperte*, vol. II (1914), p. 267f.

21 Novati, in his edition of Salutati's *Epistolario*, vol. IV (1905), pp. 171 and 196.

22 Zabughin, *loc. cit.* Like Novati, Zabughin was engaged in special studies of Francesco's works, as follows from a note by Sabbadini sent to this writer in June 1929: "Il volume delle opere di Francesco da Fiano promesso da me non si pubblicherà, perché è morto tragicamente il prof. Zabughin, che ne aveva assunto l'incarico."

23 Compare the list of cardinals with their titular names in M. Souchon, *Die Papstwahlen in der Zeit des grossen Schismas, 1378-1417*, vol. II (Braunschweig, 1900), pp. 278-279. Correr's kinship with Gregory XII, emphasized by Novati, *op. cit.*, p. 196, was not the reason of Novati's preference; for Francesco says nowhere that the "Cardinalis Bononiensis" addressed by him was a relative of the reigning pope.

24 Cf. L. v. Pastor, *Geschichte der Päpste*, $I^{8/9}$ (1926), pp. 281f. and 175ff.

preserved which makes this probability a certainty. For some reason, Francesco was for a while in a position to donate live game to high-ranking personalities at the Curia, and on such occasions he liked to accompany the hunting-spoils with some appropriate Latin verses. Among several of such poems preserved in Cod. Marcian. Lat. XII, 139 is one entitled "Live pheasant presented and donated by Francesco da Fiano to the Cardinal of Bologna who later was Innocent VII. The Cardinal is addressed as follows."[25] Given this identification of Francesco's patron, there can be no question to whom the *Contra Detractores* was dedicated.

These findings, though leaving an unfortunately long range of time for the date of the pamphlet, refute the accepted chronology. The true *terminus ad quem* is September 1404; for not only must Francesco's work have been finished before Cosimo de' Migliorati was elected Pope and ceased to be "Cardinalis Bononiensis" (October 17, 1404), but the predecessor, Boniface IX (died October 1, 1404), in whose presence, according to the preface, *magister* Stephanus Aretinus preached his sermon, was evidently still alive at the time of the dedication. Accordingly, the period in which Francesco's invective must have been composed runs from January 1390 to September 1404.

While these are the chronological boundaries which we can establish with assurance, we may further infer that the exact date will most probably not have been many years earlier or later than 1400. In the first place, a work as rich in quotations from classical and patristic writings as Francesco's pamphlet, clearly required some length of time for preparation; accordingly, Stephanus Aretinus' sermon and the beginnings of Francesco's work can hardly be placed later than 1403. On

25 "Fasianus vivus presentatus et donatus a Francisco de Fiano Cardinali Bononiensi qui postea fuit Innocentius Septimus. Cardinalem ipsum ita alloquitur." Cod. Marcian. Lat. XII, 139, fol. 95v-96r; quoted from a photostat.

the other hand, we have good reasons to conclude that Francesco's contacts with his patron, Cosimo de' Migliorati, fell in the later part of Migliorati's cardinalate. For the position which enabled Francesco to donate game was still held by him when Migliorati had become Pope, as is proven by another poem of Francesco superscribed "Stag caught and donated by Francesco da Fiano to Innocent VII, addressing the Pope as follows."[26] Finally, the contemporary history of the debate on the ancient poets, which in the cases of Salutati, Vergerio, and others was occasioned by the rumor of the vilification of the Virgil statue in Mantua in 1398,[27] also makes it very unlikely that Stephanus Aretinus' attack and Francesco's answer were made before the widespread discussion which followed that event.

In any case, establishment of September 1404 (or the year 1403) as the *terminus ad quem* allows us to deal with Francesco's *Contra Detractores* as a further document from the period of transition on the threshold of the Quattrocento: not as an historical source pertaining to the year 1407 or even later, but as one roughly coeval with Cino Rinuccini's *Invettiva* against the Florentine classicists.

26 "Cervus captus et donatus a Francisco de Fiano Innocentio Septimo, ipsumque papam ita alloquitur." *Ibid.*, fol. 93v; from a photostat.

27 Cf. note 16 to Chap. 14.

APPENDIX 5

AN INFORMANT ON NICCOLÒ NICCOLI: LORENZO DI MARCO DE' BENVENUTI

(Annex to Vol. I, p. 292)

OUR portrait of Niccoli[1] includes features of his political conduct and social attitude which are not familiar from the figure of Niccoli the classicist and man of letters that is usually pictured in the histories of Humanism. These features are taken from a diatribe written about 1420 (and published by 1421) by the Florentine citizen Lorenzo di Marco de' Benvenuti under the title *Oratio in Niccolaum Nicholum*. Benvenuti's work has been accessible since 1894,[2] but as no biographical

1 See Vol. One, pp. 292ff. and 352f.

2 *Laurentii Marci de Benvenutis in Niccolaum Nicholum Oratio*, ed. G. Zippel in *Giornale Storico della Letteratura Italiana*, XXIV (1894), 168-179. Two manuscripts, unknown to Zippel, of Benvenuti's pamphlet include a short dedication preface, addressed to Ambrogio Traversari, that is lacking in the Florentine manuscript of the Biblioteca Riccardiana reproduced by Zippel. The writer owes his knowledge of this preface to the kindness of Prof. Paul O. Kristeller, who has in his possession microfilms of the two texts, which are preserved in cod. 13 of the Biblioteca Capitolare of Viterbo (described by L. Dorez in *Revue des Bibliothèques*, v [1895], 245f.), cited as *V*, and cod. 1/45 of the library of the Collegio di S. Isidoro in Rome, cart. misc. s. XV, cited as *R*. Benvenuti's dedication (*V* fol. 106v, *R* fol. 28v) runs: "Laurentius Benvenutus Ambrosio monaco S.D. [S.D.E. *R*]. Evomui tandem diu conceptum virus, et [et *om. R*] que [que *addidi*] maximis iniuriis provocatus in Nicolaum perscripseram (prescripseram *R*), e manibus nescio quomodo delapsa sunt atque in vulgus exiere. Ea igitur ad te mitto, non ut hominis tibi noti flagitia cognoscas, que tibi iam pridem fuere [fuere *om. R*] notissima, sed ut censor rerum mearum [mearum rerum *R*] existas et quid in illis perfecerim tu ipse idem intelligas. Vale. [*Contin.*: Indixeram ego michi . . .]." Unfortunately, these passages are of little help in the establishment of the precise date of the invective; they do not add anything to the data which may be derived from other sources, except the information that the work had been composed some time before it was given to the public. As for the inscription to Traversari, this fact is known from Traversari's *Ep. VI 21*, a letter which discusses Benvenuti's dedication angrily, protesting against the injury done by the invective to Niccoli. Regarding the date of this letter, two theories have been proposed, differing only slightly. According to R. Sabbadini's inferences made in 1887 (*Gior-*

study of Niccoli has appeared since 1890, and no manuscript of Benvenuti's pamphlet was known when Voigt's *Wiederbelebung des klassischen Altertums* was last revised in 1893,[3] the interesting portrait of Niccoli the citizen contained in Benvenuti's *Oratio* has not been seriously considered to this day, and has not even been used to complement the traditional portrait of Niccoli in any of its details.[4]

The fact that Niccoli's early biographers tell little about the sort of citizen he was need not arouse suspicion against Benvenuti's assertions. If Benvenuti's contention is true, that Niccoli had condemned the resistance of the Florentine Republic to the threats of Giangaleazzo and Ladislaus, and had seen nothing but evil in the building of a Florentine region-state, Niccoli's political demeanor was a subject which a benevolent biographer, writing mainly for Florentine readers, might best pass over in silence. Vespasiano da Bisticci, the main source of our ideas of Niccoli the humanist, was just such a benevolent reporter, and in addition he wrote two

---

nale Stor. della Lett. Ital., x, 367), the letter originated in the second half of 1420; this assumption was adopted by Zippel (p. 183). Subsequently, in 1898, F. P. Luiso, in his *Riordinamento dell' Epistolario di A. Traversari* (p. 38), adduced documentary evidence that the letter was written on an August 23; and, as Luiso argued, no August before that of 1421 appeared to be a likely date. When to these findings and interpretations we add that Poggio, then in London, knew in October 1420 that Benvenuti had composed an invective, and in July 1421 asked Niccoli in a letter from London to let him see a copy of Benvenuti's work as basis for a possible rejoinder (see Zippel, *loc. cit.*, p. 182; Zippel, *Niccolò Niccoli*, p. 31; E. Walser, *Poggius Florentinus*, p. 75), we may conclude that, although the time of the composition of the invective can only be given vaguely as "around 1420" (*verso 1420*), as Zippel (p. 182f.) inferred from circumstantial evidence, the date of publication can be exactly established as 1420 or 1421. For if Traversari's *Ep. VI 21* was written in August 1420, Benvenuti's invective must have been published in the first half or middle of 1420; if Traversari's letter originated in August 1421, the publication date of the invective may be assigned to the first half of 1421.

3 See the note by the editor, M. Lehnerdt, in the chapter on Niccoli, *Wiederbelebung*, vol. 1, 3rd edn. (Berlin, 1893), p. 304, n. 4.

4 Thus, for instance, not the slightest indication of Niccoli's political attitude and conduct is given in his appraisal in Rossi's *Il Quattrocento*, 3rd edn. (1934), pp. 30f., 105ff., and passim.

generations later, at a time when the memory of the opening decades of the century had shrunk to retain only the humanistic achievements, but no longer the political decisions, of those years. On the other hand, Manetti, Niccoli's younger contemporary, by stating repeatedly that Niccoli never strove for public office, and "abstained from public occupations,"[5] has given us a framework into which Benvenuti's remarks about Niccoli's lack of patriotism and civic sentiment can easily be fitted. Years ago, R. Sabbadini, in editing an invective by Guarino against Niccoli,[6] advised biographers of Niccoli not to by-pass the products of contemporaneous polemics—the invectives of Guarino and Benvenuti, and a later invective from the pen of Bruni—because these three documents, "in spite of natural exaggerations, help, when due allowance has been made, to reconstruct the traditional figure of Niccoli, and serve as a corrective to the biography of Vespasiano da Bisticci, which is prejudiced in Niccoli's favor."[7]

To be sure, because of the difficulty of determining the extent of that "due allowance" the use of diatribes as source material always involves a certain risk. But we shall hardly wander too far afield from the truth as long as we employ the following two main criteria: We may accept as true those statements of an assailant which are in uncommonly close harmony with the characteristics of the man under attack as we know him from other sources; and we may look with a degree of confidence upon assertions concerning conduct in public, because they would at once have been generally recognized as lies if they did not contain a considerable core of truth. The anecdote attributing to Niccoli the remark that the only thing he could have learned among the wool workers in his family's shop was "barking,"[8] is of the first kind; the

5 See Vol. One, p. 290.
6 In *Epistolario di Guarino*, vol. I, pp. 33-46, and in Sabbadini's commentary, vol. III, pp. 23-25.
7 *Op. cit.*, vol. III, p. 24.
8 See Vol. One, p. 293.

expression, in fact, is in such excellent accord with Niccoli's habitual sarcasm reported in our other sources, and the business of the wool merchant enjoys usually such high esteem in Florentine literature as the basis of Florence's industrial greatness, that the anecdote can hardly be thought mere invention. Again, the assertion that Niccoli protested publicly against the wars with Giangaleazzo, Pisa, and Ladislaus, and against the expansion of the Florentine territorial state, would have served only to cast a doubt on the general veracity of Benvenuti's invective if something of this sort had not been known to the Florentine public. Nor does it seem unlike Niccoli to have expressed his opposition publicly in such a vitriolic manner. Allusions, however, such as that Niccoli hoped for, or actually received, personal rewards from Ladislaus,[9] may have to be counted among those calumnious exaggerations for which the humanistic invectives are notorious. We have, therefore, ignored this spicy passage.

Other observations will confirm our assumption. Concerning Niccoli's attitude in 1413, when the danger threatening from Ladislaus' conquests was at its height, we have, in addition to Benvenuti's words written about seven years later, another testimony dating from the crucial year itself—Guarino's invective mentioned above.[10] In 1413, Guarino had been teaching at the Florentine university; and since he, a foreigner, was struck by precisely those aspects of Niccoli's political attitude for which Niccoli would later be censured by Benvenuti, we must conclude not only that Benvenuti's statements are based on truth, but that they point to actions of Niccoli which, in 1413, caught the attention of the Florentine public. Guarino says in his invective: "Whom does he spare, this man who incessantly insults and harbors ill will for Florence, most flourishing city on earth and his own birth-place

9 Benvenuti, *Oratio*, ed. Zippel, p. 178, and Zippel's comment p. 185.

10 P. 411. The date 1413 has been established by Sabbadini, *Epistolario di Guarino*, vol. III, p. 24f.

and *patria*? This worthless and ungrateful citizen condemns the republic and inveighs against the wisest counsels of the city."[11] These sentences state clearly that Niccoli gave public expression to his disapproval of the policies of the Florentine government, policies which in 1413 can only have been the resistance and military preparations against Ladislaus; and that Niccoli did so not just as a citizen who differed from the government on methods of foreign policy, but in a manner which impressed Guarino, a foreign observer, as that of a bad and irresponsible citizen.

Finally, great significance must be attributed to the fact that in matters of political opinion and conduct, Benvenuti does not echo mere rumors, but speaks from his own experience. From 1412 until 1423, the year when he, still a young man, died in a plague, he continuously held important offices, including some concerned with the foreign affairs and wars of the Republic.[12] Accordingly, he may be expected to have taken an immediate interest in Niccoli's political conduct in 1413. That Benvenuti himself intended his information to be looked upon as an eye (or, ear) witness account is clear from the way in which he establishes his reliability in the case of an earlier event. In referring to Niccoli's comments on the conquest of Pisa in 1405-06, a time when Benvenuti had not yet taken an active part in political life, he is careful to state that he himself had heard Niccoli make the utterance in question.[13]

In the last analysis, Benvenuti's *Oratio* is not simply one of those typical humanistic invectives in which an author, in the

11 "Cui parcet ille, qui florentissimam orbis terrarum Florentiam et natalem sibi patriam lacerare execrarique non cessat? Rem publicam improbat et contra prudentissima civitatis consilia nequissimus civis invehitur." *Epistolario*, ed. Sabbadini, vol. 1, p. 39. Attention was drawn to this passage already by Benvenuti's first editor and commentator, G. Zippel, *op. cit.*, p. 185, n. 1.

12 See the list of his offices in Zippel, *op. cit.*, p. 180.

13 ". . . audientibus nobis." *Oratio*, ed. Zippel, p. 178, line 18.

heat of a purely personal quarrel, piles up all sorts of insinuations not grounded in any serious matter of dispute; it is the outburst of an opponent who—even though he exaggerates in the fashion of the humanists and casts aspersion on his adversary—wages at bottom a more than personal fight, taking issue with Niccoli from the point of view of a different trend in Florentine Humanism.[14] Benvenuti, in fact, is the prototype of the kind of citizen-humanist that was later represented by Matteo Palmieri, the author of the *Della Vita Civile*; perhaps it was his premature death that prevented him from playing at least in part the role in the literature of Florentine civic Humanism which Palmieri was to perform soon afterward. In his invective, Benvenuti pays homage to Bruni by calling him the man "than whom Latin letters, through eight hundred years or so, have produced no one more eloquent, and who is so learned also in Greek letters that there never has been anyone among us who knew more profoundly the proper use of that language, nor translated it more gracefully into Latin."[15] This passage bears such striking resemblance to the well-known appraisal of Bruni in Palmieri's *Della Vita Civile*, written about a dozen years later,[16] that

14 Benvenuti states expressly that, in his eyes, Niccoli's failure to conduct himself as a citizen was the central fact among Niccoli's vices, and that the accusations on this score were a major objection of his diatribe: "Nunc ad ea dumtaxat veniamus que et erga rempublicam et erga cives truculenter fecisti; nam ad ea iampridem festinat animus, ut in arcem flagitiorum tuorum evasisse me sentias." *Ibid.*, p. 177.

15 ". . . Leonardum Aretinum, virum sane prestantissimum ac doctissimum, et quo per octingentos fere annos eloquentiorem neminem latine littere peperere, quique adeo grecis etiam eruditus est, ut nullus unquam fuerit e nostris, pace aliorum dixerim, qui illius lingue [usum *to be added?*] ac proprietatem doctius norit elegantiusque in latinum traduxerit." *Ibid.*, p. 175f.

16 "Delle lettere et liberali studii sarè meglio tacere che dire poco. Queste principalissime conducitrice et vere maestre d'ogni altra buona arte per più d'ottocento anni sono in modo state dimenticate nel mondo, che mai s'è trovato chi n'abbia avuto congnitione vera, . . . oggi veggiano per padre et hornamento delle lettere essere mandato nel mondo el nostro Leonardo Aretino come splendido lume della eleganzia latina, per rendere

Palmieri may easily have had the older work from Bruni's circle in mind when phrasing his statement on Bruni. Benvenuti is shown to belong to Bruni's school of civic Humanism also by the emphasis he places on the Florentine conquest of Pisa, an event which in his eyes is the climax of the perennial contest with the old rival and enemy, and "the most famous and most glorious victory" in Florence's history[17]—words reminiscent of Bruni's statement on the Pisa conquest in the preface to his *Historiae Florentini Populi*.[18]

When all these facts are considered, Benvenuti's *Oratio* reveals itself as a precious source that allows us to see a trace of those deeper tensions which had since long been developing between Niccoli, withdrawn and somewhat bohemian man-of-letters, and the more public-spirited citizen-humanists around Bruni, until, about 1420, these tensions issued in an open clash. The booklet from Benvenuti's pen gives us our only chance to observe the quarrel through the eyes of Niccoli's citizen-minded adversaries, for the text of Bruni's own invective against Niccoli, written in 1424, is only incompletely preserved in all the manuscripts which are known, breaking off before the point at which Bruni might have come to deal with Niccoli's political attitude.[19] To a degree, therefore, Benvenuti's invective can be accepted as a source which for the later period of Niccoli's life and relationship to Bruni may render services comparable to those rendered for Niccoli's and Bruni's youth by the invective of Cino Rinuccini.[20]

---

agl' huomini la dolcezza della latina lingua." *Della Vita Civile*, Ms. Florence Bibl. Naz. II, IV, 81, fol. 17r-17v; ed. Battaglia, p. 37.

17 "Cum expeditionem in Pisanos factam victoriamque vidisti, qui semper cubile ac receptaculum inimicorum nostrorum omnium extitere . . ." "Pisas vero cum adepti sumus atque victoriam, que sola inter reliquas famosissima ac gloriosissima numeratur, . . ." *Oratio*, ed. Zippel, p. 178.

18 See Vol. One, p. 324.

19 See Zippel, *loc. cit.*, p. 185, n. 1.

20 Already the contemporaries wondered whether Benvenuti's pamphlet might not express opinions which could be traced to Bruni. This is shown by a colophon of the scribe of the Viterbo manuscript expressing his sus-

picion that Bruni was the true author: "Explicit oratio rabida in rabiem ... effusa. Et est ornatissimi viri Leonardi Aretini in Nicolaum Florentinum, licet . . . dicatur Laurentii Benvenuti. Ego autem non sic opinor, attento contextu verborum. P. Lunensis." The copyist was chancellor of Norcia in Umbria. He had written a letter, reproduced in the manuscript, to Bruni in 1434; he may have copied his manuscript—and, consequently, composed the cited colophon—during a stay at Viterbo in 1441, as his last entry in the manuscript would seem to suggest. See Dorez, *loc. cit.* (in note 2 above), p. 246.

APPENDIX 6

THE *PARADISO DEGLI ALBERTI* AND THE FIRST BOOK OF BRUNI'S *HISTORIAE*: THE DISSOLUTION OF THE FLORENTINE LEGENDS OF TOTILA AND ATTILA

(Annex to Vol. I, p. 299)

ONE of the literary relationships that must be considered in determining the place of the *Paradiso degli Alberti* is Giovanni da Prato's possible dependence upon the first book of Bruni's *Historiae Florentini Populi*, written in 1415. Once the first group of books of Bruni's history had become known to the reading public, they completely dominated and shaped historical interest among Florentine citizens. It is of considerable importance for an appraisal of the relationship of the *Paradiso* to Bruni's humanistic school to know whether the numerous discussions on historical subjects which characterize the novel are mere adaptations from Bruni's masterpiece, or whether they reflect older, pre-humanistic interests among the Florentine citizenry.

The latest editor of Bruni's history, E. Santini, thought that he was able to detect the influence of the first book of the *Historiae* in several passages of Giovanni's novel.[1] His observations are worthy of careful scrutiny.

Apparently the strongest of the criteria brought forward by Santini is that, while Bruni in the first book of his Florentine History subjects the medieval legend of the destruction of Florence by either Totila or Attila to a searching criticism,

1 E. Santini, "La Fortuna della Storia Fiorentina di L. Bruni nel Rinascimento," *Studî Storici*, XX (1911), 185. Oddly enough, Santini in that connection did not pay any attention to the inevitable implication of his thesis: that if Giovanni was substantially dependent on Bruni, this fact would amount to a veto against the custom (see the survey of the appraisals of the *Paradiso*, in *Humanistic and Political Literature*, Chapter I, Section 1, notes 5-6) to consider the *Paradiso* a document for the year 1389 and a *forerunner* of Bruni's historiography.

Giovanni's novel at its conclusion proposes the same subject for discussion in a subsequent chapter (which was never written, or else lost) under the title "Whether the desolation of Florence was the work of Attila or of whom, and whether Attila is confused with Totila, or where the matter stands."[2] The fact is that, if this formulation is exactly compared with the discussion of the problem in the *Historiae Florentini Populi*, the result, contrary to Santini's inference, is that Giovanni not only did not use Bruni's account, but presumably did not even know it. For the phrasing of the theme given in the *Paradiso* indicates that Giovanni was going to discuss the question whether Totila or Attila was responsible for the destruction of Florence, or how else the contradictory reports could be reconciled. Bruni, on the other hand, by means of both literary sources and conclusions drawn from the political and geographic conditions of Italy between A.D. 450 and 800, proves that Florence was not destroyed at all, and therefore was not rebuilt later by Charlemagne, as medieval tradition had it.[3] An understanding reader of Bruni, consequently, would no longer ask Giovanni's question about the historical personage responsible for the "desolation of Florence."

As to the identity of the presumable destroyer, Giovanni did not have to know Bruni's *Historiae* to feel the need for some plausible reconciliation of the conflicting earlier accounts.[4] Long before Bruni had undermined the foundations

2 "Se la desolazione di Fiorenza fu fatta da Attila o da chi, e se Attila si piglia per Totila o come?"; *Paradiso*, II, p. 243.

3 Bruni, *Historiae*, ed. Santini, p. 24. What an attentive reader would learn from Bruni's account, can best be seen from Biondo's *Italia Illustrata* ("Secunda Regio: Etruria") where, after a reference to Bruni as the authority on Florentine history, we read: "Multis ea civitas (Florence) per Gothorum tempora incommodis agitata est. Nec tamen a Totila aut alio quopiam tunc aut alias unquam destructa fuit. Idque quod de reaedificatione a Carolo magno facta aliqui sentiunt non probamus . . ." (Edn. Verona, 1482, fol. A VIIIv). See also Vol. One, p. 82 and note 13 to Chap. 5.

4 A. D'Ancona's fundamental treatise "La Leggenda d'Attila Flagellum Dei in Italia," in his *Studj di critica e storia letteraria* (1880), pp. 361-500—a work which forms the basis of what we know today about the

of the medieval legend, Totila had been named as the destroyer of Florence in the medieval *Chronica de Origine Civitatis*, in Giovanni Villani's chronicle, and also by Dante, according to one group of the manuscripts of the *Divina Commedia*; and the same opinion continued to be expressed by some others until the end of the Trecento and later, for instance, by Marchionne di Coppo Stefani in his chronicle, by Lapo da Castiglionchio in his well known *Epistola* to his son, and still later by Gregorio Dati in his *Istoria di Firenze* of about 1407/08.[5] On the other hand, in many of the accounts of the legend in the Trecento Totila had been replaced by the towering historical figure of Attila—a change which appears already in the chronicle of Ricordano Malespini as well as in most of the manuscripts of the *Divina Commedia*; and later in Boccaccio's *Vita di Dante*, in Filippo Villani's *De Origine*

---

history of the Totila and Attila legends, and includes a chapter on the Florentine local version (pp. 379-389)—does not by itself establish this fact clearly. However, D'Ancona's collection of evidence is rather incomplete for the later part of the Trecento, because his chief concern is the nature of the legend during the Middle Ages, and only secondarily the history of its criticism and dissolution on the eve of the Quattrocento. If D'Ancona's account is supplemented in the manner suggested in the present appendix, the background of Bruni's and Giovanni's discussions of the legend appears different.

5 O. Hartwig, *Quellen und Forschungen zur aeltesten Geschichte der Stadt Florenz*, vol. I (1875), p. xvii f. (for Totila in the *Chronica de Origine Civitatis*); Giovanni Villani, II 1 and II 3 (see also the comments by N. Rubinstein, "The Beginnings of Political Thought in Florence. A Study in Mediaeval Historiography," *Jour. Warburg and Courtauld Institutes*, v [1942], esp. 200ff., 215f., 220, on Totila and Charlemagne from the *Chronica de Origine* to Giovanni Villani); Dante, *Inferno* XII 134 and XIII 149; Marchionne di Coppo Stefani, *Cronaca fiorentina*, lib. I, Rubr. 27, 28, 30 (ed. N. Rodolico, in "Rerum Italicarum Scriptores," tomo XXX, parte I [1903]), although it should be added that in at least one of the best manuscripts preserved of Marchionne's work, the alleged invader and destroyer is in most cases called "Attila" rather than "Totila," and that all manuscripts speak of "Totila" and "Attila" alternately, a confusion ascribed by Rodolico (*loc.cit.*, p. 15) to Marchionne himself; Lapo da Castiglionchio, *Epistola o sia Ragionamento*, ed. Mehus (Florentiae, 1754), p. 65; Gregorio Dati, *Istoria di Firenze*, ed. Pratesi, p. 113f.—A similar reference to "Totila, Dei Flagellum," as the destroyer of Florence is found in Salutati's *Invectiva*, ed. Moreni, p. 170. Cf. Vol. One, p. 83.

Civitatis Florentiae, and in a vernacular medley of Antonio Pucci. Confronted with this discord of opinion, critically-minded authors in the last third of the Trecento began to point out that a southward advance of Attila as far as Florence was irreconcilable with the account given by Paul the Deacon—an observation made both by Boccaccio in his later years, and by Benvenuto Rambaldi da Imola, in their commentaries on Dante. While these two writers did not yet realize the falsity of the entire legend about the destruction of Florence (Boccaccio in fact practiced a genuine cult of Charlemagne as the rebuilder of Florence), anyone after the late Trecento could take it from Benvenuto that the connection of Attila with Florence's history was a mere imagination of local chroniclers and that, whatever testimonies had been adduced, Benvenuto "did not believe it."[6] When this rise of scepticism before 1400 is remembered, we will not find it at all surprising that Giovanni da Prato should have brought up the dilemma, even while he had no knowledge as yet of Bruni's new approach to the old problem.

Turning to Santini's other criteria for the alleged dependence of Giovanni da Prato upon Bruni,[7] we may call insignificant his reference to the fact that the name of Florence ("Florentia" or "Fluentia") is discussed both in Bruni's

6 Ricordano Malespini, *Storia Fiorentina*, chap.XX-XXII, XXVI, XXXV-XXXVIII. Boccaccio, *Trattatello* and *Compendio della vita di Dante* (in Boccaccio, *Il Comento alla Divina Commedia E Gli Altri Scritti Intorno A Dante*, ed. D. Guerri [Bari, 1918, vol. I, pp. 6 and 68f.]). Filippo Villani, *Liber de origine civitatis Florentiae*, lib. I c. 18, ed. Galletti, p. 4. Antonio Pucci, in his *Zibaldone*. (Quoted, from the manuscripts, pp. 385-389, in D'Ancona's treatise referred to in note 4 above). Boccaccio, *Il Comento alla Divina Commedia*, ed. Guerri, *ed. cit.*, vol. III, pp. 113ff., 152f. (The so-called Paulus Diaconus, whom Boccaccio mentions as his source, is really the *Historia Miscella*). Benvenuto de Rambaldis da Imola, *Comentum super Dantis Comoediam*, ed. Lacaita, vol. I, pp. 463f. (Benvenuto's criticism, after referring to "Paulus Diaconus," ends: ". . . vel forte vidit aliquem autorem autenticum dicentem hoc, quem ego non vidi; sed quidquid sit de isto facto [i.e., that Attila had allegedly invaded Tuscany and destroyed Florence] ego nihil credo.")

7 Santini, "La Fortuna della Storia Fiorentina," *loc. cit.*, p. 185.

Historiae and in the *Paradiso*; for the same discussion is already found in Salutati's *Invectiva*.[8] As for the importance attached in the *Paradiso* conversations to the Etruscan past,[9] closer study shows that Giovanni puts the emphasis on a legendary glorification of the "piety" of the ancient Etruscans, and completely fails to mention the main point of Bruni's rediscovery of Etruscan history: the recognition of the Etruscan city-state system and its political significance for the freedom of Etruria. As far as an interest exclusively in the religious culture of Etruria is concerned, this was entirely possible in the Florence of the 1420's without any guidance from the first book of Bruni's *Historiae*. For in Gregorio Dati's *Istoria* (a work which in all certainty preceded the first book of Bruni's history) we find a very similar and even more emphatic picture of ancient Etruria, great through her rites and piety, and the cradle of medieval Guelph Tuscany, most loyal child of the Christian Church.[10] When we add that before 1429 the first book of Bruni's history was hardly known beyond the circle of his friends,[11] there remains no reason to believe that Giovanni da Prato who wrote his *Paradiso* in 1425/26,[12] had then been familiar with Bruni's work.

8 Bruni, *Historiae*, ed. Santini, p. 5. *Paradiso*, II, p. 240f. Salutati, *Invectiva*, ed. Moreni, pp. 31-35. A precise analysis of this paragraph of Salutati's *Invectiva* may be found in *Humanistic and Political Literature*, Chapter I, Section 1; see esp. note 10.

9 *Paradiso*, I, pp. 71-75; II, pp. 235-236. (Santini's reference to p. 231 is evidently a mistake.)

10 *Istoria di Firenze*, ed. Pratesi, pp. 108-112.

11 Cf. the chronology in *Bruni, Schriften*, p. 176, and the fact, discussed in Vol. One, p. 258, that Domenico da Prato did not yet know anything of Bruni's *History* by about 1420.

12 See *Humanistic and Political Literature*, Chapter I, Excursus "The Date of the *Paradiso*."

APPENDIX 7

BRUNI'S ALLEGED CLASSICISM IN THE CONTROVERSY ON THE ORIGIN OF THE VOLGARE

(Annex to Vol. I, p. 304)

Of fundamental importance for the appraisal of Bruni's attitude to the Volgare is the motive, or motives, that may have prompted his hypothesis that a sort of Italian vernacular, substantially identical with the Volgare, was already current at the time of Cicero and Terence, existing side by side with literary Latin. Recent students have been unanimous in the conclusion that Bruni's thesis that Latin could not have been spoken by Romans lacking a literary education betrays the mind of a classicist who thought his beloved Latin too noble for vulgar people, and who consequently disdained the vernacular, and the Volgare culture.

This common interpretation of Bruni's position in the humanistic quest of the origin of the Volgare has been one of the greatest obstacles to a clear distinction of Bruni's civic Humanism from classicist Humanism as represented by Niccoli and many early Quattrocento scholars outside Florence. Already in the earliest modern histories of the Volgare controversy—R. Sabbadini's *Storia del Ciceronianismo* (1886) and *La Scuola di Guarino* (1896)—Bruni was judged an arch-classicist of Niccoli's stamp because he had assumed that the Latin *literati* had had a Brahmin language for themselves even in ancient Rome. Later it was discovered, especially by C. Trabalza,[1] that Flavio Biondo, in attributing the birth of the Volgare to the upheavals of the Germanic migrations, was already on the right track at the time when Bruni set forth his thesis, and that many other humanists soon accepted

1 *Storia della grammatica italiana* (1908), p. 16f., and *La critica letteraria*, esp. p. 23ff.

Biondo's views. In the light of this discovery Bruni appeared as a reactionary, whereas, as Trabalza put it, "when the opinion of Biondo, which was so well supported for its time, gradually gained the ascendency, the cause of the Italian Volgare won the day."[2] This has remained the consensus; for instance, P. Joachimsen, in a well-known survey of the phases of Italian Humanism, characterized Bruni, in view of his presumed scorn of the vernacular idiom, as the outstanding representative of the humanistic tendency toward "aristocratic purism."[3]

That this interpretation of Bruni's outlook cannot explain every aspect of his attitude has, however, been dimly felt ever since. When Sabbadini compared Guarino da Verona's practical treatment of the Volgare with Bruni's, he discovered to his surprise that Guarino, even though he subscribed to Biondo's view of the linguistic development, yet hardly ever wrote in the Volgare—and when he did use it, he wrote it badly. Moreover, in the *Politia Literaria* of his disciple Angelo Decembrio, Guarino is represented as saying that writers in the Volgare were at best fit to be read to women and children on a long winter evening, but deserved no admittance to the library of a *literatus*. As to Guarino's attitude to Dante, the *Politia Literaria* shows him adopting some of the classicist accusations known from the Niccoli of *Dialogus I* and denounced by Bruni long before.[4] Again, Trabalza, in spite of all the praise he had for the supposedly pioneering role of

2 "Col prevalere dell' opinione del Biondo così acutamente sostenuta per quel tempo, la causa del volgare italiano era vinta." *Critica lett.*, p. 23.

3 "Aus der Entwicklung des italienischen Humanismus," *Historische Zeitschrift*, CXXI (1920), 226. E. Walser, in his *Poggius Florentinus*, pp. 259-262, terms the philological observations of Biondo and Poggio (who supplemented Biondo's theory by proving the descendence of a number of Italian and Spanish words from the Latin) "admirably perspicacious" and anticipations of the results of modern linguistic scholarship, but thinks that Bruni's standpoint in the controversy did not represent any substantial step beyond Dante's medieval views of the origin of the Latin and the Volgare: "Man sieht: die Ansicht Dantes hat sich [with Bruni] kaum verändert."

4 See R. Sabbadini, *La Scuola . . . di Guarino*, p. 151f.

Biondo in the rehabilitation of the Volgare, could not conceal from himself that Biondo the writer was and remained "as much and even more of a classicist than Bruni."[5] So, finally, V. Rossi, in reevaluating the evidence in his *Quattrocento*, concluded that "in substance, the difference between the opinions [of Bruni on the one hand, and Biondo's school on the other] was after all not such a radical one."[6]

The cause for the inconclusiveness of all the arguments we have cited is the neglect of the fact that it was only one year after his controversy with Biondo that Bruni, in his *Le Vite di Dante e di Petrarca*, wrote those vigorous passages on the historical equality of the Volgare with Latin and Greek which are so well known and yet have never been weighed seriously in connection with the immediately preceding debate on the origin of the Volgare.[7] When we recall also that Bruni, a few years earlier, had composed some poems in Volgare[8]—in contrast to most of his opponents who were averse to writing in the vernacular—and that his *Vite* represented the first substantial prose work in Volgare written by a Quattrocento humanist, except the *Della Vita Civile* of his disciple Matteo Palmieri, then the only permissible conclusion is that there must be an error in the customary views as to what the adherence, or opposition, to the theory of Roman origin meant for literary and cultural appreciation of the Volgare.

5 ". . . un classico da quanto e più ancora del Bruni." *Storia della grammatica italiana*, p. 20.

6 "In sostanza la differenza delle opinioni non era poi così radicale." *Il Quattrocento*, 3rd edn., 1933, p. 112.

7 The only exception is Santini, who in his discussion of Bruni's literary production in Volgare (in *Giornale Stor. della Lett. Ital.*, LX, 1912) relates Bruni's statement in the *Vita di Dante* to the linguistic controversy with Biondo; but Santini's proposed solution—that, while Bruni intended to point to certain limitations of the Volgare, he believed them to exist only "in the treatment of profound matters, especially philosophy" (p. 295) —falls short of conclusiveness. For Bruni in the *Vita* states, with specific reference to the Volgare, that "ciascuna lingua ha . . . suo parlare limato e scientifico"; he does not make the alleged reservation.

8 See for the chronology of these poems note 12 to Chap. 15.

In this context we should not forget that our information about the course of the controversy is derived from Biondo; his description of his quarrel with Bruni as a disagreement as to what strata of Roman society had used literary Latin need not exhaust Bruni's position. At any rate, it is a fact that Bruni's short letter in reply to Biondo culminates in the assertion that the very remoteness of the Volgare from the strict rules of literary Latin gives the Volgare "qualities which commend it in its way."[9] One wonders whether the pattern of Bruni's thought on the issue of language might not have run parallel with a somewhat kindred theory on the origin of knighthood (*militia*) that he had set forth in 1421. In the treatise *De Militia*, he had tried to prove that modern knighthood-*militia* was not simply a product of medieval developments, but had its roots in ancient Rome. Here, where we have fuller information on Bruni's reasoning thanks to the treatise *De Militia*, we see that his tracing of a medieval development to ancient origins was intended to enhance its prestige. Is it not very probable that Bruni's intention was the same when in later years he thought he could trace the Volgare to Roman roots?

So much at least is obvious: Fifteenth-century humanists could use the historical theory that Latin and the Volgare co-existed in ancient Rome to support the conviction that the Volgare idiom, in addition to the sophisticated Latin speech, played a valuable and indispensable role in the education of their own time. It is quite true that Leon Battista Alberti, and others after him, agreed with Biondo and condemned Bruni's theory for the very reason that the idea of two Roman languages appeared obnoxious to their own efforts to make the Volgare the language of everybody in their own time; the assumption that there had been one language

9 "Nam et habet vulgaris sermo commendationem suam." See Vol. One, p. 305. The letter is Bruni's *Epistola VI 10*.

in Rome encouraged Alberti in his endeavours to proclaim the Volgare as the literary language of his own day. But these later uses of Bruni's and Biondo's theories do not prove that the same implications had been drawn originally, at a moment when no one had as yet dared to propose a dethronement of the Latin language and when the only moot question could be the extent to which the Volgare was to be recognized as a worthy partner beside the Latin. From the viewpoint of sound historical criticism, we are not allowed to attribute to Bruni's understanding of his thesis any overtones that are not consistent with his comments in the one surviving document on the question from his hand, the *Epistola VI 10*.[10a]

10a A counterpart to the mode of thought thus inferred from Bruni's letter is found in the notion of Benedetto Accolti, Bruni's admirer and third successor in the chancellor's office, of the coexistence of a popular eloquence and the formal art of oratory, in antiquity as well as in modern times. (See Vol. One, p. 307f.). In a chapter of his *Dialogue on the Preeminence of the Men of His Age* (edn. quoted in note 33 to Chap. 3; p. 121), Accolti argues that even Athens and Rome, among countless good council speakers, possessed only a few men capable of producing addresses in a literary, publishable form. One must not be deceived, Accolti warned, by the abundance of fine orations handed down in historical works. There was no doubt that the highly wrought Latin phraseology of the elaborate harangues quoted in Bruni's *History of the Florentine People* was the work of Bruni himself, and that the ideas expressed in them had originally been aired in Volgare ("materno sermone") and in the most diverse fashion. If such is Bruni's method, Accolti argues, then there must have been a similar contrast between the polished rhetoric of Sallust's and Livy's orations and the speeches which were actually delivered in ancient councils. Apart from a group of trained lawyers and exceptionally gifted or cultured leaders, "I deem, the rest of the citizens, in a discussion of important matters, were not dissimilar in their way of speaking from our own citizens" ("reliquos cives, dum de rebus magnis consulebant, non absimiles eloquio nostris fuisse reor"); "although they spoke to the point and with fluency, many, I daresay, did not differ from the men met during the subsequent centuries and in our own time in the city-republics of Italy" ("quanquam graves et satis eloquentes fuisse credam, tamen multos illis non dissimiles nostro aut seculis proximis in Italiae liberis urbibus fuisse dicere ausim"). "Nor do I think that it matters much in what language a man makes his speech, that is, whether he makes it in his native vernacular or in Latin; always provided that he states his opinion with appropriateness, elegance, and fluency" (see note 28 to Chap. 15). Bruni, we may assume, would, in this train of thought, have recognized the fibre of his own mind.

The reinterpretation proposed in our chapter on "Civic Humanism and the Volgare" may not tell the complete story of the complex controversy. In a definite appraisal of the Quattrocento debates on the origin of the Volgare, two further viewpoints will have to be given careful thought. One is suggested by the observation that in the sixteenth century, when Biondo's views were accepted by the majority of scholars as correct, the tracing of the Volgare to the barbarian invasions did serve as an apparent prop of their own standpoint to classicists who held the Volgare in contempt. In Sperone Speroni's *Dialogue on the Languages* (*Dialogo delle Lingue*) of 1547, the most original and open-minded Cinquecento discussion of the fitness of the Volgare as a medium for Renaissance philosophy, we find the proponent of the thesis that Latin is the only noble language and the only serviceable tool taking his stand on the general consensus that the Volgare had originated from the degeneration of Italy's ancient language under the impact of the barbaric invasions; hence, like other regrettable effects of the barbarian age, it was to be avoided as much as possible by men of culture.

Speroni tried to obviate this conclusion—which, we understand from his dialogue, had much currency—by way of three interrelated ideas. In the first place, he defended the value of variety and individuality, as against the rigid standard of Latin universalism; as he puts it, "the languages of all countries, of Arabia and India as much as of Rome and Athens, are of equal value."[10b] Secondly, he adopted the dynamic notion, well known from Machiavelli and Vasari, that nothing in history can last without change; languages too, therefore, grow up, flower, and wither away; and from this it may be concluded that with the century of Dante and Petrarch, more than half a millennium after Latin had

10b "Io ho per fermo, che le lingue d'ogni paese, così l'Arabica e l'Indiana, come la Romana e l'Ateniese, siano d'un medesimo valore." Sperone Speroni, *Opere*, Venice, 1740, vol. I, p. 193.

ceased to be spoken by the people, the time had come for a new beginning.[11] Finally, Speroni was convinced that every man's language must grow naturally from his earliest childhood on, and must take form in his social interchange in daily life, unless it is to remain artificial and "dead-letter" (*carta*).[12] Of these three basic notions of Speroni, most resolute and "modern" champion of the Volgare in sixteenth century Italy, the first had been foreshadowed by Bruni; the second had evolved logically, in the time of Machiavelli and Vasari, from Bruni's position; only the third had been completely alien to Bruni, as to all humanist and non-humanist writers of the early Quattrocento.

Once these chief lines of the historical development are redrawn, where shall we place Bruni, and where Biondo? Had the vital advance of Renaissance thought in this field really started with Biondo's theory? Or would it not be nearer to the truth to say that Bruni had been the spiritual father of the new and modern evaluation that found its definitive elaboration in sixteenth-century works like Speroni's *Dialogo*?

The other question to be answered in a final analysis, is whether, when due consideration is given to the state of factual knowledge in Renaissance scholarship, it may not be rash to look upon Bruni's assumption of an ancient Roman origin of the Volgare as nothing but a personal quirk. There were, it is true, not many humanistic scholars left in the sixteenth century who thought to discern in Bruni's theory a core of truth. But among them was Ludovico Castelvetro who, by his observations of the different effects of Gothic and Lombard rule upon the language of Italy, was able to develop Bruni's hypothesis of earlier beginnings up to a point from which a path later led on into the eighteenth century when Gian Vincenzo Gravina, one of Italy's greatest

11 *Ibid.*, pp. 175, 184. 12 *Ibid.*, pp. 174, 185, 195ff.

critics, would once more discover a positive value in Bruni's conjectures.[13] Again, among the sixteenth century continuators of Bruni's views was Celso Cittadini, who by modern literary historians has been considered "the forerunner of the theory which derives the romance languages from popular Latin."[14] Did Bruni's approach after all contain the seeds of a truth which later ages, in a different form, brought to fruition with the discovery of "Vulgar Latin"?

Whatever the answer to these broad historical questions will be, so much is certain: we must place the Quattrocento controversy on the origin of the Volgare in a wider frame than has been done so far, taking into account the fact that championship of the Volgare, and certainly no narrow-minded classicism, characterized the Humanism of Leonardo Bruni.

13 See G. Laini, *Polemiche Letterarie del Cinquecento* (Mendrisio, 1948), p. 58f., and G. Toffanin, *Il Cinquecento* (4th edn.: Milan, 1950), p. 530.

14 See the formulation, and the bibliographical references, in *Enciclopedia Italiana*, x (1931), p. 503.

APPENDIX 8

THE "*ORATIO FUNEBRIS* ON NANNI DEGLI STROZZI": ITS DATE AND PLACE IN THE DEVELOPMENT OF BRUNI'S HUMANISM

(Annex to Vol. I, p. 358)

EFFORTS to date Bruni's funeral oration for Nanni degli Strozzi—the Florentine counterpart to Thucydides' Funeral Oration of Pericles[1]—have long been under a curse. When R. Sabbadini in 1916 made the first attempt to date this oration[2] he was deceived by a note in the *Diario Ferrarese 1409-1502* according to which in the year 1426 "on the 18th day of June [*Zugno*] . . . was buried Messer Nanni de' Strozzi of Florence" with high military honors.[3] To compound the confusion, Sabbadini noted "*Luglio*" instead of "*Zugno*" [i.e. *Giugno*], 1426, and this error was repeated in his much-read

1 See Vol. One, p. 358f. In translating the title from the Latin, the name-form Nanni degli Strozzi must be used, despite the fact that even Florentine historians from the late Renaissance onward rendered the "Johannes" of the Latin title by "Giovanni"; Vespasiano da Bisticci, for instance, in his *Vite di uomini illustri del secolo XV*, lists Bruni's "Orazione nella morte di messer Giovanni Strozzi." (Ed. Frati, vol. I, p. 32.) In the eighteenth century, L. A. Muratori, in a critical digression reprinted in "Rerum Italicarum Scriptores," Nuova Ed., vol. XIX, part III, p. 419 s., first pointed out that the north-Italian form "Nanni"—sometimes "Nanne"—used in early sources is not a mere diminutive of "Giovanni," but may have a different origin. So meticulous a scholar as Flavio Biondo, as late as 1450 used the form "Nanne" when mentioning Bruni's speech (cf. *Scritti inediti e rari di Biondo Flavio*, ed. Nogara [Rome, 1927], p. 164), and the form "Nanni" is found in the two most important sources of information on the Strozzi of Ferrara—the *Diario Ferrarese* (see below note 3) which continues the Ferrarese tradition of Nanni's day, and the *Diario* of Palla degli Strozzi (see notes 39 and 40 to Chap. 16), a Florentine memoir which rests on close personal contacts with the Ferrarese Strozzi. Given this usage of the contemporaries, the hero of Bruni's Florentine eulogy will have to be cited with his dialectical name of north-Italian origin.

2 *Arch. Stor. Lombardo*, 43 (1916), 27.

3 "A dì XVIII di Zugno . . . fu sepulto messer Nanni di Strozzi da Fiorenza." *Diario Ferrarese dall' ao. 1409 sino al 1502*, in "Rer. Ital. Script.," n. s. tom. XXIV, part VII (1933), pp. 18 and 336.

Del Metodo degli Umanisti (1920, p. 84). Misled by this group of information, the present writer, in the chronology of Bruni's writings added to the edition of Bruni's *Humanistisch-Philosophische Schriften* (1928, p. 173), gave the date as "*Juni 1426*," correcting Sabbadini's indication of the month only.

In fact, however, Nanni degli Strozzi met death as commander of troops of the Este of Ferrara, who fought in alliance with Florence against Filippo Maria, in an encounter at Gottolengo on the Po River, not far from Mantua, on May 29, 1427;[4] or, more exactly, on May 29 he was found unconscious on the battlefield of Gottolengo and brought to the near-by "Ansula" (presumably Asola) where he died on June 1st in the arms of his friends, as Card. Giovanni Mercati recently established on the basis of the genuine version of the inscription for Nanni's tombstone.[5] The note in the *Diario Ferrarese* about the celebration of the funeral with military honors on June 18 in S. Domenico belongs, accordingly, in the year 1427.

Unfortunately, the first scholar who noticed the erroneousness of the date in the *Diario Ferrarese*, L. Bertalot, only replaced the earlier mistake by another, and even grosser, chronological error: he shifted the date as far forward as the year 1430.[6] Accepting at face-value a misleading statement in a Vatican manuscript of Bruni's oration (Cod. Vat. Lat. 5108, which Sabbadini had already listed in 1916, but had rightly ignored in dating the oration), Bertalot concluded

4 As noted correctly in Litta's *Famiglie Celebri Italiane*; see below note 19.

5 Contained in Cod. Ottob. Lat. 1661. See Card. Giovanni Mercati, *Codici Latini Pico Grimani Pio e di Altra Biblioteca Ignota . . . con una Digressione per la Storia dei Codici di S. Pietro in Vaticano* ("Studi e Testi," vol. 75 [1938]), p. 198f.

6 L. Bertalot, in *Historische Vierteljahrsschrift*, XXIX (1934), 396. The scribe's subscription in Cod. Vat. Lat. 5108, which Bertalot had in mind, runs: "Dixi. II. nonas Iunias. M.CCCC.XXX." (From a photostat.)

that the oration had not been composed under the immediate impress of the events it described, and was not written until three years later ("*erst drei Jahre später verfasst*"). It was Mercati who, when establishing the precise dates of Nanni's fight and death, pointed out against Bertalot that a document, already used by Sabbadini, lists a fact which precludes any attempt at placing the funeral oration such a long time after Nanni's Death.[7] According to a letter of the archbishop Bartolomeo Capra of Milan to two secretaries of the Visconti chancery, Bruni's oration was well known in Milan as early as April 9, 1429, and was then considered so formidable in its Florentine-republican attitude that the Milanese government began to look abroad for the services of a humanist capable of producing publicistic works of a like calibre.[8] There can be no doubt, as Mercati rightly concluded, that, if the oration was well known in Milan by April 1429, it must have been written by 1428.[9]

Nor do we need to depend on this inference from a casual document. The same result can be reached and supported with precise details when we examine both the oration itself and Bruni's correspondence for references to simultaneous political events and to the circumstances leading to the composition of an obituary on the dead Strozzi.

At the very beginning of Bruni's oration we find a passage mentioning the war "that our city and the Venetians are *now* waging against the Duke of Milan."[10] This implies that the war with Filippo Maria Visconti was still being fought. Later we read that for "*this* very long Milanese war"[11] more than three and one half million florins had been expended, "and yet our people are readier to pay taxes *now at the end* than

7 Mercati, *op. cit.*, p. 121.

8 See note 3 to Chap. 18, and the further references there given.

9 G. Mercati, *op. cit.*, pp. 198-199.

10 ". . . quod adversus Mediolanensium ducem civitas nostra Venetique nunc gerunt." Ed. Baluzius (see note 2 to Chap. 18 for this edition), p. 2.

11 ". . . hoc Mediolanense longissimum bellum." *Ibid.*, p. 4.

they have been since the beginning of the war."[12] The last phrase is, of course, an intimation of the introduction of the "*Catasto*" in 1427; but in addition it contains an even more precise indication of date. For the words "*nunc ad extremum*" could be used only by one who knew (as Bruni the chancellor did) that peace negotiations were underway and had reached a stage when the end of war could be expected soon. The peace between Venice and Florence on one side, and Filippo Maria on the other, was concluded at Ferrara on April 18, 1428, but was not promulgated in Florence until May 16.[13] Hence, Bruni wrote his oration either during the long-drawn out peace negotiations, that is in March and early April, or in the period between April 18 and May 16 when the peace treaty had been put to paper but had not yet been ratified. In either case, the oration for the general who had sacrificed his life for the *patria* Florence would have grown directly out of the experience of the war.

By another observation we find that Bruni's first plans had been made at an even earlier time. He had begun work on the oration in the autumn of 1427, not many months after Nanni degli Strozzi's death, but had been compelled to interrupt it soon afterwards because of the exclusive demands made on his time by his new duties in the chancellor's office. This can be inferred with certainty from what Bruni tells Feltrino Boiardo, a Ferrarese nobleman and grandfather of the famous poet, in his *Epistola X 7*. At about the same time when he was most anxious to satisfy Boiardo's demands, so Bruni writes in the letter, his entire life had been changed by the unexpected burden of a "*negocium pergrande.*" While he thought daily of Feltrino's wish, especially since a friend of Feltrino reminded him of it often,

12 ". . . et tamen promptiores nunc ad extremum in tributo sunt homines persolvendo, quam ab initio fuerant belli." *Ibid.*

13 See Perrens, *Histoire de Florence*, vol. VI, p. 303.

"and when I had already begun and was engaged in the work, lo, what I had least expected, the storm-tide of activities carried me away and cast me out upon the tossing sea. For you have heard, I believe, that against my will and although I resisted I was torn from my literary *otium* and, at the command of the City, placed at the head of the public affairs."[14] The new office of which Bruni here speaks is clearly the chancellorship which he assumed on December 2, 1427. The literary work interrupted by this office, on the other hand, can only be the oration for Nanni degli Strozzi. For, first, the addressee, like Strozzi an "*eques Ferrarensis*" and a military person at the court of Ferrara who does not appear elsewhere in Bruni's correspondence, could hardly have had any urgent literary demand on Bruni excepting that for a worthy obituary of his dead companion. Secondly, Bruni is so emphatic in acknowledging his obligation to devote to the work in question the very first moment he could spare from his official duties, that it would have been a breach of faith if the first piece of literary writing he undertook in his new office had been anything but the promised work.[15] But the first literary labor to which Bruni turned as soon as he found leisure, was indubitably the oration for Strozzi. For according to the passages of the oration already cited, the speech was written at the first approach of peace, even before greater quiet had come to Bruni with the end of the

14 ". . . cumque instituto jam operi manus admovissem, ecce tibi quod quam minime gentium suspicabar occupationum procella me corripuit et in altum undosum fluctuosumque devexit. Credo enim audivisse te literato ex ocio invitum repugnantemque me jussu Civitatis negociis publicis fuisse praefectum." *Ep. X* 7, ed. Mehus, vol. II, p. 176.

15 Bruni says in his letter: "Quas ob res licet ita impediar, ut nichil de me, utpote alieno homine, polliceri valeam, tamen, cum antecedat obligatio tua, prior enim est in tempore quam haec publica obligatio, dabo operam, ut aliquando persolvam. Interea tamen has literas tenebis, quasi chirographum promissorum meorum, ac memoriae indicem. Aldobrandinus noster est assidue mecum, ac me sedulo monet, ut promissis faciam satis. Et quia Juris consultus est, negat me legitime posse absolvi, nisi moram hanc meam cumulatiore aliquo munere purgaro." *Loc. cit.*, pp. 176-177.

war. Furthermore, his only other literary occupation during the year 1428 was the composition of the fifth and sixth books of his *Historiae Florentini Populi*,[16] which certainly was not the work whose completion the knight of Ferrara had requested.

Ep. X 7, then, allows us to ascertain that Bruni began his oration as early as the summer or autumn of 1427, and that beginning and completion were separated by one of the most decisive events in his life: the transition from the years in which he had led a private scholar's existence to his career as a Florentine chancellor. By comparing the letter, written shortly after acceptance of the office, with the oration which reflects his attitude of mind at the time when he had just become at home among Florentine statesmen and in the world of active politics, we can, therefore, gain insight into the effects of one of the profoundest changes in his life.

According to the letter cited, when Bruni assumed office he considered the chancellorship a burden placed on him against his will—a burden which destroyed his "*literatum otium*," as he termed it. The intended work on an obituary of Strozzi was to him at that time part of those activities of humanistic writers that seemed destined to be disturbed by the "*publica obligatio*" making upon his time a rival claim. There is no trace in the letter that the oration for the general fallen in the fight against the Visconti then seemed to him a patriotic work and itself a "public obligation" toward the *Respublica Florentina*. It is most improbable, therefore, that at that time he could already have been planning to write an oration which would be not only a personal eulogy for an individual (the only obituary Nanni's friends in Ferrara can have intended), but at the same time a new "*Laudatio*" on Florentine history and Florentine freedom, on the Florentine civic spirit as

16 See note 4 to Chap. 18.—That Bruni's translation of Plato's *Epistolae* does not belong in the period of his chancellorship that began December 2, 1427, is shown in note 24 to Chap. 17.

embodied in the fallen warrior, and on the role of Florence as the cultural metropolis of Italy. The tenor of the letter written on the morrow of Bruni's assumption of his office must be understood to indicate that the transformation of the personal obituary planned in the autumn of 1427 into a counterpart to Pericles' funeral oration was the result of his first few months of active service to the Commonwealth. The responsibility of public office, we must conclude, was the ultimate factor which, added to the impact of the new struggle with Visconti Milan, eventually led Bruni from the purely scholarly phase of his activities to which he had returned during the early 1420's, to the final synthesis of his civic Humanism.[17]

From 1428 on, all his literary work was to bear a new complexion. When the oration on Nanni degli Strozzi had been finished, he resumed work on the *Historiae Florentini Populi*, interrupted since 1421, as we know; carried forward by the new mood, he completed the fifth and sixth books within the same year, 1428. In the mid-1430's, when he wrote his *Vita di Dante*, he propounded the ideal of the citizen who combines his studies with the *vita politica-civilis*. In view of this significance of the years 1427-28 for the inner growth of Bruni's Humanism, it will appear justified to use his Strozzi oration (besides his *Laudatio*, the record of his youth) as the most graphic and revealing source in reconstructing the Florentine reaction to the Viscontean wars.

There is one feature of the Strozzi oration, it is true, which, at first sight, may arouse distrust against attributing so important a position to this particular work. The dead soldier who is presented as the model citizen who lived and died for the *patria* Florence was actually—though of Florentine extraction—a general and diplomat in the service of the Este of Ferrara; he had met death at the head of troops

17 See the more elaborate picture, Vol. One, p. 356ff.

that were composed mostly of Ferrarese mercenaries. Does not the presentation of this foreigner as if he were a citizen who sacrificed himself for Florence's glory cast doubt upon the honesty of the author, and does it not arouse the suspicion that much of his oration is no more than a flight of rhetoric, rather than a true expression of the Florentine sentiment of those years? This apparent incongruity, we may suspect, has indeed been mainly responsible for the complete neglect Renaissance scholars have accorded to a work that in many respects so evidently is the most eloquent expression of the Florentine civic spirit. How, it must be asked, was it possible for Bruni under such circumstances to look upon his hero as the very epitome of a Florentine patriot?

The explanation lies in an aspect of Nanni degli Strozzi's life of which the contemporary readers of the oration must have been perfectly aware. Although Nanni belonged to a branch of the Strozzi family which had made Ferrara their home since their banishment from Florence in the Ciompi revolution of 1378, and although Nanni himself had been born and bred in Ferrara, he could in one respect appear to men of Bruni's generation as a better model of the true Florentine than any member of the leading Florentine families who had remained on the Arno. At the court of the Este, Nanni had been given an opportunity that in the early Quattrocento was no longer available to a citizen in Florence: to prepare himself from early youth for a military career. When Nanni was knighted, it was not for the dubious military merits of the typical Florentine citizen-knight, but on the battlefield as an award for his help in the liberation of Verona from the Visconti. Through several decades he was the commander-in-chief of the Este troops—until he died in battle.

The life and death of this Strozzi had been in the service of a foreign prince, it is true; but in effect, and in Nanni's own intention, he had lived and died for Florence. For the State of the Este, foremost among the powers in Emilia-Romagna whose independence from Milan was the object of Florentine foreign policy, was Florence's constant ally through the whole era of the Visconti wars. From Nanni degli Strozzi's first military exploit against Milan in 1395, to his participation in the struggle for Bologna about 1402, and on to his leading generalship in the wars of the 1420's, his military and political enterprises had therefore all been undertaken as much in the interest of Florence as in that of the Este State. As to personal relations to the city of his ancestors, this Strozzi of Ferrara had from childhood on often spent short periods on the Arno; the banishment of his family had been revoked when the Albizzi aristocracy came to power. By the 1420's, Nanni had become a central figure in Florence's anti-Viscontean policy, although everything he did was still done in the service of the Este. It was Nanni who in 1424 suggested Florence's last efforts to come to a peaceful settlement with the Visconti, and who afterwards proposed the direction that Florentine war-propaganda maintained through the critical stage of the war.[18] Together with Carmagnola, the Venetian generalissimo, and the commanders of the Florentine troops, he was the leading spirit in the allied command.[19]

What, then, were Florentines to think of the meaning of this life when Nanni degli Strozzi had died for the common cause at the head of troops who fought in the alliance? Legally, this *capitano* of the Marquis of Ferrara had not been a Florentine citizen at all; he had never availed himself of

18 See Vol. One, p. 332.

19 On Nanni degli Strozzi's life, in addition to the inferences which can be drawn from Bruni's oration, cf. Litta, *Famiglie Celebri Italiane*, vol. v, disp. 68, Tabula V; and the article "Strozzi Nanne" in C. Argegni, *Condottieri, Capitani e Tribuni Italiani fino al Cinquecento* (in "Dizionari Biografici e Bibliografici Tosi"), vol. III (Rome, 1946), p. 296.

the opportunity to return to Florence and to become a citizen who shared in the offices of his state. Yet he had been one of the best-known leaders in the defense of Florence against Visconti tyranny, and his life seemed to have realized an aspect of the ideal of citizenship increasingly cherished among Florentine citizen-humanists: the revival of that citizen-soldiership which had been part of civic life in the medieval commune.

The glorification of Nanni degli Strozzi as a Florentine citizen who had lived and died for his "*patria*," with the tacit assumption that this *patria* was the Florentine Commonwealth, was, then, an historical distortion, but at the same time, in a deeper sense, a truth. It was the formulation of an ideal of the age personified in a man whom his Florentine contemporaries saw as one who had come close to what they desired and admired. How much inner truth this literary fiction did indeed possess is shown by the immediate and profound effect that Bruni's oration clearly had throughout Italy as propaganda for the Florentine concept of life.[20]

20 See Vol. One, p. 359f., and Vol. Two, p. 432.

the opportunities to [illegible] to [illegible] which [illegible] [illegible] of [illegible] had been [illegible] of [illegible] [illegible] [illegible] [illegible] [illegible] [illegible] [illegible] [illegible] [illegible] argument.

The glorification of [illegible] citizen who had [illegible] and [illegible] [illegible] the [illegible] assumption that this [illegible] was [illegible] Florentine [illegible] wealth was, then, [illegible] historical [illegible], but at the same time in a deeper sense a tribute to the formulation of an ideal of the age [illegible] in a man whom his Florentine contemporaries [illegible] one who had [illegible] what [illegible] classical and [illegible]. [illegible] from the [illegible] period [illegible] by the [illegible] found effect that [illegible] clearly [illegible] throughout Italy its propaganda for the [illegible] age [illegible].

[illegible]

Notes

DOCUMENTARY, CHRONOLOGICAL, CRITICAL

Part One

CHAPTER 1

1. Cf. the sketch of the growth of this Florentine outlook on history from Bruni and early Humanism to Machiavelli in the author's essay "Das Erwachen des historischen Denkens im Humanismus des Quattrocento," *Historische Zeitschrift*, CXXXXVI (1932), 5-20. The recognition that Machiavelli, in spite of his acrimonious criticism of his humanistic predecessors in historiography, was in vital respects indebted to Bruni's historical outlook and method may be considered an established fact today, even though the consequences for the appraisal of Machiavelli's historical place have not yet been fully drawn by Machiavelli students. Machiavelli's dependence on Bruni in its various aspects has been successively revealed by G. Salvemini, *Magnati e Popolani in Firenze dal 1280 al 1295* (Firenze, 1899), esp. p. 243; E. Santini, *Leonardo Bruni Aretino e i suoi "Historiarum Florentini Populi Libri XII"* (Reprinted from *Annali della R. Scuola Normale Superiore di Pisa*, XXII, 1910), esp. pp. 117-122; P. Joachimsen, *Geschichtsauffassung und Geschichtsschreibung in Deutschland unter dem Einfluss des Humanismus* (Leipzig, 1910), esp. p. 224; and W. K. Ferguson, *The Renaissance in Historical Thought, Five Centuries of Interpretation* (Boston, 1948), p. 15.

2. Various aspects of this transformation of humanistic thought in the civic atmosphere of early Quattrocento Florence were analyzed in the author's preface to his edition of *Leonardo Bruni Aretino, Humanistisch-Philosophische Schriften* (Leipzig, 1928), pp. xi-xxv, and in his papers, "The Historical Background of the Florentine Renaissance," *History*, n. s. XXII (1938); "Lo Sfondo Storico del Rinascimento Fiorentino," *La Rinascita*, I (1938), an enlarged Italian translation of the preceding article; "A Sociological Interpretation of the Early Renaissance in Florence," *The South Atlantic Quarterly*, XXXVIII (1939); "La Rinascita dell' Etica Statale Romana nell' Umanesimo Fiorentino del Quattrocento," *Civiltà Moderna*, VII (1935); "Cicero and the Roman Civic Spirit in the Middle Ages and the Early Renaissance," *Bulletin of the John Rylands Library*, XXII (1938); and "Franciscan Poverty and Civic Wealth as Factors in the Rise of Humanistic

Thought," *Speculum*, XIII (1938). Since then, a number of studies by Italian scholars, especially the works of E. Garin, have increasingly brought out that the ideas which had emerged at the dawn of the Quattrocento among Florentine humanists remained in the focus of humanistic thought and, indeed, were among the major attainments of the Renaissance. Cf. especially Garin's fundamental comprehensive works, *Der Italienische Humanismus* (Bern, 1947; in an Italian version as *L'Umanesimo Italiano: Filosofia e vita civile nel Rinascimento*, Bari, 1952) and *La Filosofia. Volume I: Dal Medio Evo all' Umanesimo*, in the series "Storia dei Generi Letterari Italiani" (Milan, 1947), as well as Garin's minor contributions, replete with new material from rare and inedited sources, to the problem of Humanism and civic life in *La Rinascita*, IV (1941), 409ff.; in *Atti dell' Accademia Fiorentina di Scienze Morali 'La Colombaria,'* XV (1947), 469ff.; in *Rinascimento*, I (1950), 43ff.; and *ibid.*, II (1951), 321ff.

Kindred approaches to Florentine and Quattrocento history are found in R. Stadelmann's "Persönlichkeit und Staat in der Renaissance," *Die Welt als Geschichte*, V, (1939), 137-155, and F. Schalk's "Il tema della 'vita activa' e della 'vita contemplativa' nell' Umanesimo italiano," *Umanesimo e Scienza Politica* ("Atti del Congresso Internazionale di Studi Umanistici, Roma-Firenze, 1949" [Milan, 1951]), 559-566. Like most of Garin's works, these lucid discussions were still unknown to the author during his preparation of the present book; they testify to the increasing interest in the problems with which the pages which follow deal.

3. On the Italian Peninsula, assemblies of estates or feudal parliaments developed only in Sicily, Naples, Sardinia, the Papal State, and in Friuli in the northeast, and Monferrat and Piedmont in the northwest; the whole remainder of central and northern Italy did not experience the growth of any of the representative provincial institutions characteristic of the late feudal age. Cf. the survey of *L'Istituto Parlamentare in Italia dalle Origini al 1500* by A. Marongiu, vol. IX of the "Études Présentées a la Commission Internationale pour l'Histoire des Assemblées d'États" (Rome, 1949).

CHAPTER 2

1. F. Schevill, in the chapter, "Florence Encounters the Problem of the Despot (1313-1343)," of his *History of Florence* (New York, 1936), gives the best available exposition of this earliest phase of the Florentine struggle with north-Italian tyranny.

2. For the still ecclesiastical and crusade-like hue of the fight against the early Visconti see C. Capasso, "La signoria viscontea e la lotta politico-religiosa con il Papato nella prima metà del sec XIV," *Bollettino della Società Pavese di Storia Patria*, VIII (1908), 265-317, 408-436; and G. Romano, "La guerra tra i Visconti e la Chiesa, 1360-1376," *ibid.*, III (1903), 411-432.

3. See F. Baldasseroni, "La guerra tra Firenze e Giovanni Visconti," *Studi Storici*, XII (1903), esp. 85-89.

4. According to Matteo Villani's account of the years 1361-1362 in his *Cronica*, x, 57.

5. ". . . che seguita ne' fatti del mondo la Santa Chiesa."

6. ". . . che seguitano l'imperio, o fedele o infedele."

7. ". . . fondamento e rocca ferma e stabile della libertà d'Italia e contraria a tutte le tirannie." Matteo Villani, *Cronica*, IV, 78 and VIII, 24.

8. "Universitatem Guelforum, si ad divinum respicias, cum Romana Ecclesia, si ad humanum, cum Libertate coniunctam reperies, . . . sine qua nec Respublica constare ulla potest, nec sapientissimi viri existimarunt vivendum." For Bruni's authorship, and the edition, of the *Prooemium* of the Statute of the "Parte Guelfa" see Note 18 to Chap. 17. In the preceding Statute, phrased in 1335, the "Parte e Università de' Guelfi" had been defined as the party of the Church, as identical with the "devoti di santa Chiesa." While King Robert of Naples, with his title of "king of Jerusalem and Cilicia," was mentioned in the 1335 Statute as the second chief factor which determined what "Guelphism" meant at that time, there was no suggestion as yet that Guelphism was connected with "liberty," or that the Ghibellines stood for "tyranny." Cf. the *Prologo* of the Statute of 1335 in *Giornale Storico degli Archivi Toscani*, I (1857), 4.

9. The fact of this survival and transformation of the Guelph idea in Renaissance Florence has been overlooked by many students who were led astray by the intimation of Bartolo da Sassoferrato's juridical treatise *De Guelphis et Ghibellinis*, written about

1350, that the old names of Guelphs and Ghibellines had by that time lost their ideological meaning and become pretexts for local party interests. So still quite recently L. Simeoni, in his *Le Signorie*, in the series "Storia Politica d'Italia" (Milan, 1950), p. 39f. But Bartolo's treatise does not in fact deal at all with Florence or any of the more important states of Italy; it merely draws upon experience in Umbrian and Tuscan towns which by then had sunk into second-rate positions. On the other hand, the knowledge that, contrary to Bartolo's remarks, in Florence the Guelph ideas with their inherent republicanism stayed alive throughout the Renaissance and continued as the frame of Florentine political thought, is a prerequisite for seeing the Renaissance politics of the Florentine Republic in an historical perspective. Cf. the writer's observations in his paper "Die politische Entwicklung der italienischen Renaissance," *Historische Zeitschrift*, CLXXIV (1952), 43f., 48f.

10. A change which, although basic for the political position of Florence on the eve of the Renaissance, is little known. The evidence adduced by G. Volpe (*Il Medio Evo* [Florence, 1930], pp. 362f., 368) and C. Barbagallo (*Storia Universale*, III, part 2 [Turin, 1935], pp. 1033-1036), who are aware of the altered climate in Florence's Tuscan policy after 1343, may not be sufficient to dispel the scepticism of earlier scholars still echoed in the *History of Florence* by Schevill (p. 262f.), already quoted. But a systematic reexamination of the problem of hegemony and communal confederation in medieval Tuscany made by the present writer for a paper soon to be published leaves no doubt that Florence's policy in central Italy from 1343 to the early 1380's is correctly defined in the characterization which follows in the text. For details on Tuscan city-leagues in the mid-Trecento cf. H. Baron, "A Struggle for Liberty," p. 270f. After the present chapter had been written, N. Rubinstein, in *Transactions of the Royal Historical Society*, ser. V, vol. II (1952), published an important account, largely from new archival material, of the ideas of city-state liberty in Florentine politics and propaganda between 1328 and 1390 ("Florence and the Despots: Some Aspects of Florentine Diplomacy in the Fourteenth Century"). Although he makes certain reservations—some of which would seem unnecessary when Florence's late Trecento policy is compared with her imperialism in the 1250's and 1330's—Rubinstein, too, concludes (pp. 41, 45) that in the period after 1343 the city leagues in defense of *libertas Tusciae* became an essential object of Florentine

diplomacy; "the available evidence does not seem to suggest that the Tuscan policy of the Florentines was constantly dominated by the desire for aggrandisement and hegemony." Since these conclusions are identical with those reached by a somewhat different approach in the present analysis, the author has thought it sufficient to add occasional references in our notes to some archival material discovered by Rubinstein, while leaving the text unchanged.

11. "Hic est enim ille populus, qui et intestinam tyrannidem detestatur et exterarum urbium libertatem suis operibus semper est prompta defendere. . . . Et si ex utilitate volueris hec forsitan ponderare, tanto tutior huic urbi sua videtur esse libertas, quanto latius se liberi populi circunfundant. Ex quo debet cuique facile persuaderi Florentinum populum libertatis cuiuslibet populi defensorem, in quibus et suam libertatem faciliori cura defendit." Salutati, *Ep. III 17*, in *Epistolario di Coluccio Salutati* ("Fonti per la storia d'Italia," no. 15-18, Rome, 1891-1905), ed. F. *Novati*, vol. I, p. 194f. In 1383, in a similar vein, Salutati called Florence "free and procreator of liberty on all sides [*libertatis undique genitricem*], qualities which are the highest glory of nations" (*Ep. V 17, Epistolario*, vol. II, p. 85). Another fifteen years or so later, we find Cino Rinuccini in his "*Risponsiva* to Antonio Loschi" asserting that Florence in the "War of the *Otto Santi*" had been offered, by the citizens themselves, the overlordship of several cities liberated from the rule of the Church, but had declined these offers, wishing her neighbors to "enjoy the happiness of liberty as brothers" (*che come fratelli usassono la dolcissima libertà*). *Risponsiva*, ed. D. Moreni (in an appendix to his edition of Salutati's *Invectiva in Antonium Luschum*, Florence, 1826), p. 206. For the *Risponsiva* see below, note 8 to Chap. 4.

12. See the account of Florence's role, from archival material, in G. Pirchan, *Italien und Kaiser Karl IV. in der Zeit seiner zweiten Romfahrt* (Prague, 1930), pp. 208, 222, 380ff., 404ff.

13. Our indispensable guide through the labyrinth of diplomacy in the period of Giangaleazzo is D. M. Bueno De Mesquita's *Giangaleazzo Visconti, Duke of Milan, 1351-1402* (Cambridge, 1941). This work is equally important as the sole extant summary of the results of the extensive special literature on Giangaleazzo's foreign policy, and as a source-book of many new archival documents not accessible elsewhere. But it does not advance from the reproduction of diplomatic details to a history of the profounder

tendencies of the period (see F. Schevill's critique in *Speculum*, XVI [1941], 491f.), and, because of this limitation, neglects the works of the contemporary publicists and therewith the most characteristic and revealing testimonies for the meaning of the Milanese-Florentine struggle. See the observations in Appendix 1, Vol. Two, p. 386.

14. See the account of the contemporary, Gregorio Dati, in Vol. One, p. 146.

15. See the quotations from the archival documents in De Mesquita, *Giangaleazzo*, p. 107.

16. On Venice's attitude during this period see G. Bolognini, "Le Relazioni tra . . . Firenze e . . . Venezia nell' ultimo ventennio del sec XIV," *Nuovo Archivio Veneto*, IX (1895), 3-110, and R. Cessi, "Venezia neutrale nella seconda lega anti-Viscontea, 1392-97," *ibid.*, n.s. XXVIII (1914), 233-307.

17. See the opinions of the citizens consulted by the government in the *consulte* of November 23-25, 1388, published by G. Collino in *Archivio Storico Lombardo*, XXXVI (1909), 339-349 (". . . quod omnibus Tuscis liberis comune [of Florence] se uniat, pacificet et concordet"; p. 347). During the ensuing efforts to win Siena back to the Tuscan city-league, the Florentine government on one occasion expressed its guiding motives with the words that "not only local neighborhood, but identity of the form of government, and devoted attachment to freedom" made the Florentines and the Sienese "similar, and essentially alike." ("Nos esse vobis non solum vicinitate situs, sed identitate regiminis, ac studio libertatis, et similes et conformes.") Passage in a Florentine letter of April 11, 1390, to Siena, quoted from the copy in the Florentine Archives by N. Rubinstein in the article referred to in note 10 above, p. 32.

18. See the instruction for the Florentine envoys published by De Mesquita, *Giangaleazzo*, pp. 342-345. Giangaleazzo's evasive reaction, which practically thwarted any formal commitment, has now been traced in the archival documents by N. Rubinstein in the article referred to in note 10 above, p. 43f.

19. The manifesto quoted, the Florentine rejoinder to Giangaleazzo's declaration of war, is printed in Muratori, *Rerum Italicarum Scriptores*, tom. XVI, col. 815-817: "Quid prodesse potest pacis studium, dum ille . . . pacem verbis annuntians bellum totis conatibus machinatur? Exarmavit nos, ut posset offendere. Armavit Senenses et alios, ne possent cum suis antiquis fratribus

amicitiam integrare." "Nos . . . Tyranno Lombardiae, qui se Regem facere cupit et inung[u]ere, bellum indicimus, et pro libertatis nostre defensione ac libertate populorum, quos tam grave iugum opprimit, arma movemus." (The last sentence is corrected according to the text reproduced from the original by N. Rubinstein in the article referred to in note 10 above, p. 31). For other Florentine proclamations see F. Landogna, "La politica dei Visconti in Toscana," *Bollettino della Società Pavese di Storia Patria* XXVIII (1928), 172.

Similarly, in a treaty with the Count of Armagnac, who, with a French army, was to invade the Milanese territories from the west, Florence described Giangaleazzo's policies as an "attempt to suppress and crush Italian liberty, and especially Florentine liberty" ("sepelire et contundere italicam libertatem et precipue florentinam"). Quoted in A. Visconti, *Storia di Milano* (Milan, 1937), p. 290. In a letter to the Republic of Genoa dated May 28, 1390, that is, soon after the outbreak of hostilities between Florence and Milan, the Florentine government termed the incipient war one "inter tirannidem et libertatem." Quoted by N. Rubinstein from the copy in the Florentine Archives in the article referred to in note 10 above, p. 30.

20. See the reports published by De Mesquita, *Giangaleazzo*, pp. 123 and 346.

21. Shown by L. Mirot, "La politique française en Italie sous le règne de Charles VI, 1380-1422," *Revue des Études Historiques*, C (1933), 499f.

22. ". . . cum totis gentibus . . . italicis." From a communication on the battle of Alessandria, sent by Giangaleazzo to the Pope, quoted in N. Valeri, *Vita di Facino Cane* (Turin, 1940), p. 40.

As early as a few months before the battle, in January 1391, the humanist Pier Paolo Vergerio, in view of the imminent appearance of the French army under the Count of Armagnac in Italy, and inspired by the same Italian national sentiment, had exclaimed in a letter that foreigners had nothing to seek in Italy: "Let the contemptible barbarians grow indignant and rant as much as they want: there is no room for them in Italy. If Italy must become enslaved, she shall be enslaved only by Italians." ("Indignetur et obstrepat quantumlibet despecta barbaries: illi in Italia nullus locus est. Italia si servire oportet a solis Italis vincenda est.") Vergerio, *Epistolario* ("Fonti per la storia d'Italia," no. 74, Rome, 1934), ed. L. Smith, p. 53.

23. See De Mesquita, *Giangaleazzo*, pp. 193-196, on the quarrel about Castrocaro, the intended base, and on the issuing perils for the League of Bologna.

24. On the pact and its consequences for the Italian situation see De Mesquita, *Giangaleazzo*, pp. 231ff., 238, 244.

25. ". . . la nostra difesa è la loro medesima." See the commission given to the Florentine envoys to Venice, April 7, 1400, published from the archives by De Mesquita, *Giangaleazzo*, pp. 365-370.

26. See the appraisal of the situation created by the Peace of Venice in H. Kretschmayr, *Geschichte von Venedig*, vol. II (Gotha, 1920), p. 249.

27. In the commission cited above in note 25.

28. The only comparable situation in Florence's past had occurred in 1352 when, shortly after the Florentine catastrophes of the 1340's, the Archbishop Giovanni Visconti was on the brink of invading Tuscany, and Florence promised the German king Charles IV half of his military expenses as soon as the German horsemen arrived in Italy as allies against Milan. But that deviation from Florence's Guelph traditions had amazed all Italy, as Matteo Villani tells us in his chronicle (III, 6); it was not repeated in the period of Florence's moral and material recovery during the later part of the Trecento; and last, not least, negotiations in 1352, very different from the course of events in 1401-1402, had eventually not succeeded in bringing a German army to Italy. For a significant example of the Italian national sentiment turning against Florence after the event of 1401, see the well-known humanist and educator Giovanni Conversino da Ravenna, note 44 to Chap. 6.

29. Proof that this propaganda was more than an ephemeral contrivance for diplomatic ends lies in its echo in the work of the Milanese historian Andrea Biglia, who, a score of years after Giangaleazzo's death, proudly maintained that the Visconti in general, and Giangaleazzo in particular, had restored Italy's old military virtue by building the Milanese armies up with Italian soldiers and making Italian arms triumph over northern barbarian invaders. Through the medium of this judgment of Biglia one of the key-ideas of Giangaleazzo's propaganda survived and has influenced the opinion of modern Italian historians on Gian-

galeazzo's historical role. See the reference to Biglia by G. Volpe in *Politica* (October 1926), 11f., and N. Valeri's comments, in *Nuova Rivista Storica*, XIX (1935), 464, on G. Romano who, in 1915, was the first to direct attention to Biglia's forgotten passage.

30. The most striking example is that of the "*Querelae*" of Genoa in 1396 (*Giornale Ligustico*, XIII [1886], 401-413). There Genoa is represented as imploring Giangaleazzo to come to her help by way of annexation; for Genoa knows that incorporation in the Visconti state would bring her peace and prosperity, while Giangaleazzo is shrewdly pictured as hesitating because he would incur enormous expenses solely for Genoa's benefit. For other examples of the propaganda preceding Giangaleazzo's conquests see A. Palmieri, "La congiura per sottomettere Bologna al Conte di Vertù [i.e. Giangaleazzo]," *Atti e Memorie della Deputazione di Storia Patria per le provincie di Romagna*, ser. IV, vol. VI (1916); and R. Piattoli, "Di un' ignoto tentativo di Giangaleazzo Visconti per far ribellare la terra di Prato in 1402," *Archivio Storico Pratese*, X (1931-1932).

31. The range of this pro-Visconti political poetry has been known since A. Medin's "I Visconti nella poesia contemporanea," *Archivio Storico Lombardo*, XVIII (1891), 733-795, and A. D'Ancona's "Il concetto dell'unità politica nei poeti italiani," in his *Studi di critica e storia letteraria*, vol. I (2nd edn., 1912), esp. pp. 39-45. Since then more relevant material has been added; see the good survey and bibliography in N. Sapegno's *Il Trecento* (Milan, 1934), chap. VIII, esp. pp. 462-473, and various studies by N. Valeri which are reviewed in a judicious note on the bearing of the pro-Giangaleazzo literature, in D. Cantimori's "Rhetoric and Politics in Italian Humanism," *Journal of the Warburg Institute*, I (1937-1938), 84f.

32. In 1396, in a poem addressed to Giangaleazzo, he urged him "to think of peace, accomplished through war" ("ut pacem cogitet per viam belli"). See D'Ancona, *op.cit.*, p. 40f. See also L. Pastine, "Antonio Loschi, umanista vicentino," *Rivista d'Italia*, XVIII, part I (1915), 831-879, on Loschi's activities as a political pamphleteer in general; esp. pp. 837f. and 847f.

33. ". . . che è giunto il Messia." See Medin, *op.cit.*, p. 763; D'Ancona, *op.cit.*, pp. 44f.; and Ezio Levi, *Francesco di Vannozzo e la lirica nelle corti lombarde durante la 2. metà del sec XIV* (Firenze, 1908), pp. 258ff., 262ff.

34. ". . . per parte d'ogni vero Italiano"; ". . . detestabile

seme, nimico di quiete e caritade, che dicon libertade." D'Ancona, *op.cit.*, p. 41; Sapegno, *op.cit.*, p. 472f.

35. Pastine, *op.cit.*, p. 848f.

36. This much remains true of the earlier exaggerated assertions that Mussi, as one of the first, had voiced "la parola unitaria" in Italy. See the note on a fresh discussion of Mussi's "concetto dell' unità politica italiana" in *Giornale Storico della Letteratura Italiana*, CX (1937), 179.

37. See N. Valeri, *Vita di Facino Cane* (Turin, 1940), p. 111f.

38. Personal ambitions and jealousies among the Milanese *condottieri*, to which De Mesquita prominently refers (*Giangaleazzo*, pp. 288-292), cannot possibly have caused a personality like Giangaleazzo to give up the consummation of his plans and victories for the entire remainder of the decisive year.

39. Even the Milanese official proclamations threw off the mask of caution by clamoring for a monarchy with boundaries transcending northern Italy. In 1401, Giangaleazzo himself publicly avowed "that Tuscany and Lombardy should be joined into a single whole" ("quod Tuscia cum Lombardia fiet unum et idem"); and in May of 1402, his loyal city of Pavia declared that he was held to be "full worthy to wear the crown of all Italy" ("totius Italie Diadematis non immerito digno"). Quoted by De Mesquita, *Giangaleazzo*, pp. 305 and 310.

40. The conditions after Giangaleazzo's death are well known from the excellent analysis in N. Valeri's *L'Eredità di Giangaleazzo Visconti* (Turin, 1938).

41. Bruni, in his *Historiarum Florentini Populi Libri XII* (in "Rerum Italicarum Scriptores," nuova ed., tom. XIX, parte III, ed. E. Santini, p. 288), concludes that the Florentines, before Giangaleazzo's death changed everything, "had hardly any hope of salvation left" ("vix ullam salutis spem reliquam habebant").

42. The testimony of the documents is discussed by Valeri, *op.cit.* The contemporary Florentine opinion is known through Gregorio Dati (see Vol. One, pp. 155-156) and Giovanni di Paolo Morelli in his *Cronica* (edn. in the appendix to Ricordano Malespini, *Istoria Fiorentina* [Firenze, 1718], p. 315), who, like Gregorio Dati, expressly ascribes Giangaleazzo's inaction after Bologna's fall to his financial calamity.

43. Giovanni Morelli, *op.cit.*, p. 313. For other testimonies see F. T. Perrens, *Histoire de Florence*, vol. VI (Paris, 1883), p. 94.

44. Extracts, from the "Liber Consiliorum secretorum Comunis

Florentie," are published in the *Commissioni di Rinaldo degli Albizzi per il Comune di Firenze dal 1399 al 1433*, ed. C. Guasti (3 vols., Florence, 1867-1873), vol. I, p. II.

45. "Quod in adversitatibus virtus probatur: et ideo, licet adversa sint ex parte Bononie, sumenda est tamen audacia atque vigor." "Quod licet profligate sint gentes nostre, que erant Bononie, audendum tamen est."

46. "Quod nemo expavescat, sed forti animo resistat." "Non submergatur animus, sed elevetur." "Diu habuimus bellum cum Vicecomitibus Mediolani; nec unquam poterit esse concordia, nisi una partium deleatur: et ideo forti et magno animo resistatur."

47. See R. Piattoli, "Il problema portuale di Firenze . . . 1402-5," *Rivista Storica degli Archivi Toscani*, II (1930), esp. pp. 159-61, where the cutting off of all Florentine roads and ports in Giangaleazzo's last years is shown to have made it possible for him to hope for "the economic and, in consequence, the political break-down of his opponent" ("il tracollo economico e per logica consequenza politica della rivale").

48. See the extracts from the dispatch of the Florentine envoys from Rome, in De Mesquita, *Giangaleazzo*, p. 370f.

49. See De Mesquita, *Giangaleazzo*, p. 285.

CHAPTER 3

1. Whenever Bruni's *Dialogi* is cited in the present work, page references will be to two editions: *Leonardi Aretini ad Petrum Paulum Istrum Dialogus*, ed. Th. Klette in his *Beiträge zur Geschichte und Litteratur der Italienischen Gelehrtenrenaissance*, vol. II (Greifswald, 1889), pp. 39-83; and the reissue of Klette's text by E. Garin in his *Prosatori Latini del Quattrocento* (vol. 13 of the series "La Letteratura Italiana. Storia e Testi," Milan, 1952), pp. 39-99. Garin, besides adding an Italian translation, has revised Klette's punctuation and has occasionally corrected the text on the basis of Florentine manuscripts. We have followed this greatly improved version in our quotations.

The other major work of Bruni's youth, the *Laudatio Florentinae Urbis* has never been published in extenso in its original text. Accessible in print are merely extracts published by Klette in an appendix to his edition of the *Dialogi* (pp. 84-105). Since a complete and reliable text of the *Laudatio* is indispensable, a critical text has been reconstructed from the following five manuscripts: *G* = Laur. 90 inf. 13, Florence, early part of the Quattrocento; *L* = Laur. 65 c. 15, of mid-Quattrocento Florentine origin; *C* = Vat. Chig. J VI 215, second half of fifteenth century; *O* = Vat. Ottobon. Lat. 1901, second half of fifteenth century; *P* = Vat. Palat. Lat. 1598, from Giannozzo Manetti's library. The text thus revised—as a rule following either *G* or *L*, according to the guidance given by the other manuscripts consulted—leaves no alternative readings of any consequence undecided, and provides a satisfactory basis for the critical discussion of all problems of content, structure, and chronology. In all references to the *Laudatio*, throughout the present book, the text is given in accordance with the reconstruction made on the basis of these manuscripts. The added letter *L*, and indication of folios, refer to the manuscript Laur. 65 c. 15. Klette's extracts are also quoted with page reference whenever they include the part of the text under discussion. For descriptions of the five *Laudatio* manuscripts consulted, as well as for more details on the existing editions of the *Laudatio* and the *Dialogi*, see this writer's *Humanistic and Political Literature*, note 1 to Chapter IV, section 1, and note 3 to Chapter VI, section 1.

2. Dante, *Inferno* XXXIV, 31ff. Bruni, *Dialogi*, ed. Klette, p. 61f.; ed. Garin, p. 68f.

3. "An to putas Dantem, virum omnium aetatis suae doctissimum, ignorasse quo pacto Caesar dominium adeptus fuerit? Ignorasse, libertatem sublatam et ingemiscente populo Romano diadema a M. Antonio capiti Caesaris impositum? Credis tantae virtutis fuisse ignarum, quanta M. Brutum praeditum fuisse omnes historiae consentiunt? Nam illius iustitiam, integritatem, industriam, magnitudinem animi quis non laudat? Non ignoravit haec Dantes, non, sed legitimum principem et mundanarum rerum iustissimum monarcham in Caesare finxit; in Bruto autem seditiosum, turbulentum ac nefarium hominem, qui hunc principem per scelus trucidaret; non quod Brutus eiusmodi fuerit; nam si hoc esset, qua ratione a senatu laudatus fuisset tamquam libertatis recuperator? Sed cum Caesar quocumque modo regnasset, Brutus autem [Garin: enim] una cum amplius sexaginta nobilissimis civibus eum interfecisset [Garin: interfecissent], sumpsit poeta ex hoc fingendi materiam. Cur ergo optimum et iustissimum virum et libertatis recuperatorem in faucibus Luciferi collocavit? Cur Virgilius castissimam mulierem, quae pro pudicitia conservanda mori sustinuit, ita libidinosam fingit, ut amoris gratia seipsam interimat? Pictoribus enim atque poetis quidlibet audendi semper fuit aequa potestas." (The last sentence is a quotation from Horace, *Ars Poetica* 9-10, as Paul O. Kristeller reminds me.) To this vindication of Dante as well as Brutus, Bruni's Niccoli still adds one collateral argument which, however, does not change the weight of what he had said: "Quamquam non improbe fortasse, ut equidem puto, defenderetur M. Brutum in trucidando Caesare impium fuisse. Non desunt enim auctores, qui, vel propter affectionem illarum partium, vel ut imperatoribus placerent, factum illud Bruti scelestum atque impium vocent. Sed ad illam quasi parificationem Christi atque Caesaris prima defensio probabilior mihi videtur: idque sensisse poetam nostrum nullo modo ambigo." *Dialogi*, ed. Klette, p. 76f.; ed. Garin, p. 88f.

4. "Era conveniente chosa che chome lucifero tormentava Iuda traditore dello imperadore divino, chosi [Dante] anchora punissi chi havessi tradito lomperadore et monarca humano." "Io in nessun modo lo [Dante] riprendo: Ma ho voluto dimostrare la sua sententia: accioche nessuno per falsa opinione stimi che lui vogli

dannare Bruto." Landino, *Comento Sopra la Comedia di Danthe Alighieri* (1st edn.: Florence, 1481), fol. s 5v.

5. "Et perche di comune consenso del nome christiano e' instituto che el romano imperadore sia chosi chapo delladministratione temporale di tutta la christiana rep., chome el papa nella administratione spirituale, pone Cesare primo non per Cesare, elquale non essendo giusto non potea essere giusto imperadore, ma per lomperio. Et Bruto et Cassio, equali luccisono, non pone per Bruto et Cassio, ma perchi uccide el vero monarca." "Non niego Cesare essere stato ornato dimolte varie et excellentissime virtu. Ma subito che in lui nacque si efferata impieta che per speranza doccupare la tirannide passo el fiume Rubicone, dhuomo excellentissimo divenne immanissima fiera. Et con questa sola scelerateza sobmerse et extinse tutti ebeneficii dequali Roma si confessava allui debitrice. Adunque non uccisono Bruto et Cassio quel Cesare elquale con . . . gravissimi pericoli acquisto al popolo romano tutta la Gallia, tutta la Germania, et la Brithania. . . , non uccisono quel Cesare nel quale fu somma liberalita. . . , ma quello elquale contro alla sua patria ingratissimamente volse le forze che da quella havea ricevuto; quello che scelleratissimamente tolse la liberta a quella alla quale ladovea difendere. Et certamente qual puo essere maggior virtu che vendicare le ingiurie della patria, per laquale ogni buono cittadino e' tenuto non perdonare alla roba, non a figluoli, non alla propria vita." *Ibid.*

6. "Et certamente sarebbe stato inaudita crudelta et altutto aliena dalla doctrina et equita di tanto poeta porre in eterno et si grave supplicio quegli equali per ardentissima carita si missono alla morte per liberare la patria dal giogo della servitu; per laquale, se fussino stati christiani, harebbono honoratissima sedia nel suppremo cielo acquistato." "Legghinsi tutte le leggi di qualunque rep. bene instituta; et troverremo che a nessuno si propone maggior premio che a chi uccide el tyranno." *Ibid.*

7. ". . . dannare Bruto: Del quale non me difficile a credere chome Troiano [Trajan] commosse per sua iustitia a tanta compassione Gregorio che co prieghi gia innanzi preveduti di dio lo riduxe dalla dannatione alla somma felicita. Chosi alchuno altro accepto a dio habbi facto quel medesimo di Bruto." *Ibid.*

8. *Dialoghi de' giorni che Dante consumò nel cercare l'Inferno e 'l Purgatorio*; discovered, and first published, as late as 1859; critical edition by D. Redig de Campos ("Raccolta di Fonti per la

Storia dell' Arte," vol. II, Florence, 1939). Redig de Campos in his preface suggests persuasively that these dialogues are based on actual conversations between Michelangelo and Giannotti which took place during the first half of the year 1546 (pp. 25-29). The twilight atmosphere of these conversations, held after Florentine freedom and active citizenship had come to an end, is strikingly expressed in the first dialogue, in a passage where Michelangelo relates an anecdote of the "Great Council" of Florence which until 1530 had been the center of the Florentine life under the republic. Other exiles in the group check him with the melancholy words: "Let's let them be—the Great Councils, the Senates, the laws, the civic customs and thoughts—where God has taken them, He to whose will all good and prudent men must submit themselves." ("Lasciamo stare . . . i Consigli Grandi, i Senati, le leggi, i costumi et pensieri civili, dove Dio gli ha condotti, alla cui volontà ogni buono et prudente si debbe accomodare." p. 40). Still, the memory of civic freedom breaks through once more in the quarrel between Michelangelo and Giannotti at the end of the second dialogue—this time in the form of an offense taken at Dante's judgment on Brutus, Cassius, and Caesar (pp. 88-98 in Redig de Campos' edition).

9. Michelangelo: "Che Bruto et Cassio meritino quelle lodi, . . . consento io insieme con voi." But Dante, "seguitando l'opinione cristiana, vuole che per speciale providentia di Dio, l'imperio del mondo fusse redotto in potestà de' Romani et poi degli Imperatori; gli pare che, qualunche tradisce la maiestà dell' Imperio Romano, debbe esser punito . . . con quelle pene istesse che chi tradisce la maiestà divina. . . . Egli haveva bisogno d'esempi famosissimi, et non trovava altri di maggior fama o di pari, che Bruto et Cassio; et non gli parve far loro ingiuria, non ve li mettendo per Bruto et Cassio, ma per coloro che tradiscono la maiestà imperiale, la quale egli intendeva per Cesare, non per ciò liberandolo dall'infamia dell' haver ridotto la patria in servitù e dell' esser tiranno." Giannotti: "Ditemi un poco, quando Dante dice haver veduto nel Limbo, tra gli huomini escellenti, 'Cesare armato con gli occhi grifagni', perchè lo mette egli nel Limbo? Mettelo egli per Cesare o per la maiestà imperiale?" *Ibid.*, pp. 90f., 95f.

10. Giannotti: "Io . . . credo che Dante per Bruto et Cassio non significhi Bruto et Cassio, ma coloro che tradiscono la maiestà imperiale, et per Cesare non intenda Cesare, ma la maiestà im-

periale, come havete detto; tutto questo vi credo. Ma che Cesare sia nel Limbo et Bruto et Cassio nelle bocche di Lucifero, troppo mi dispiace; talchè io vorrei volentieri potervi metter lui da dovvero, se già egli non vi è, chè altro non merita per questo peccato solo!" *Ibid.*, p. 96.

11. As in the case of most historiographical themes of the Florentines, this page might be concluded with a Venetian epilogue. Trifone Gabriele, Venetian citizen and well known writer in the early sixteenth century, connected with the Florentine school through his friendship with Giannotti (Gabriele is the main speaker in Giannotti's dialogues on the *Repubblica de' Viniziani*), rewrote the Quattrocento criticism of Dante without the patriotic respect of the Florentines for their great compatriot. "He was greatly wrong," Gabriele comments in his *Annotazioni*, "to place Brutus and Cassius into the Inferno . . . because of Caesar's death; for in truth, as Landino says, on this account they should have been put on the highest seats in Paradise; but he was too much a partisan of the Empire, and too intent on flattering that party" (". . . ma fu troppo imperiale e troppo vuol adular a quella parte"). Quoted in M. Barbi's *Della Fortuna di Dante nel secolo XVI* (Pisa, 1890), p. 245, n. 1.

12. *Dialogi*, ed. Klette, p. 68f.; ed. Garin, p. 76f.

13. For the fact that Ptolemy himself called his annals by the characteristic title of *Gesta Tuscorum*, see B. Schmeidler in his edition of *Tholomei Lucensis Annales*, "Monumenta Germaniae Historica, Scriptores," n. s., tom. VIII (1930), p. 243.

14. *De Regimine Principum*, III, 6: "Quod inter praesides romanos nemo portabat diadema, nec induebatur purpura, ut magnificaretur in ea . . . Ubi attendendum, quam ordinatum erat tunc temporis regimen politicum in Urbe . . ."; III, 12: ". . . ipsorum potentia ad omnes mundi plagas videbatur diffusa, sub consulibus tamen: quia superstitibus regibus cum finitimis sollicitabantur regionibus, et modicae adhuc erant virtutis"; II, 9: ". . . [regionem Romanam] rexerunt usque ad tempora Iulii Caesaris sub consulibus, dictatoribus et tribunis . . . In quo quidem tempore . . . tali regimine multum profecit respublica." (Ed. J. Mathis [Turin, 1948], pp. 44, 53, 29).

15. "Nostri libertas incipit evi"; "florida . . . viris . . . armipotentibus etas." *Africa*, ed. N. Festa ("Edizione Nazionale delle Opere di Petrarca," vol. I, 1926), II, 138; III, 773f.

16. *Africa*, liber II.

17. "O felix si forte modum sciat addere ferro!/ Nesciet heu! noletque miser; sed turbine mentis/ Victrices per cunta manus in publica vertet/ Viscera, civili fedans externa cruore/ Prelia et emeritos indigno Marte triumphos;/ Me tamen infami tam multa decora furore/ Commaculare pudet. Quam turpiter omnia calcat/ Ambitus, ut totum imperium sibi vindicet unus." *Africa*, II, 228-235.

18. ". . . nam sceptra decusque/ Imperii tanto nobis fundata labore/ Externi rapient Hispane stirpis et Afre./ Quis ferat has hominum sordes nostrique pudendas/ Relliquias gladii fastigia prendere rerum?" *Africa*, II, 274-278. "Vivet honos Latius, semperque vocabitur uno/ Nomine Romanum imperium; sed rector habenas/ Non semper Romanus aget. . ./ . . . tandem cadet ista potestas/ In Boream: sic res humanas Fata rotabunt." *Ibid.*, 288-293.

19. This statement needs emphasis because of its sharp contrast to the well-known works of F. Ercole which for a long time have been the chief guides to the political ideas of the late Trecento and early Quattrocento. According to Ercole (cf. his *Da Bartolo all' Althusio. Saggi sulla storia del pensiero pubblicistico del Rinascimento italiano* [Firenze, 1932], pp. 225-232, and his sketch "Coluccio Salutati e il Supplizio Dantesco di Bruto e Cassio," *Bullettino della Società Dantesca Italiana*, ser. nuova XXI [1914], 127-135), the republican interpretation of Roman history and the criticism of Caesar that were to reach their climax with Machiavelli, had been "solidly" ("saldamente") established at least one generation before Bruni: the "sentimento repubblicano" of "many contemporaries and predecessors of Coluccio Salutati" had been offended by Dante's condemnation of Caesar's assassins, and "in fact nearly all the old and recent commentators on Dante agreed in adjudging Caesar a tyrant, and Brutus and Cassius the liberators of the *patria* and the restorers of her freedom," in spite of their adherence to the medieval idea of Empire, and, consequently, defense of Dante's verdict (*Bullettino*, p. 129; *Da Bartolo*, p. 225f.). The truth is that most of the sources which Ercole cites on the occasion of this statement belong to the Quattrocento, or even to the early sixteenth century; the remainder of his references are Dante commentaries of the Trecento, but none of them—neither those referred to by Ercole, nor any others—ever tried to

vindicate Brutus and the *Respublica Romana* against Caesar and the imperial monarchy. Even the commentary of the so-called "Anonimo Fiorentino" (*Commento alla Divina Commedia d'Anonimo Fiorentino* . . . in "Collezione di opere inedite o rare," vol. 13-15 [1866-74], ed. P. Fanfani)—a work particularly revealing of the Florentine outlook toward the end of the Trecento because it originated around the year 1400 and made extensive use of Florentine sources, among them Boccaccio's *Commento* on Dante—even this last product of the Dante tradition of the Florentine Trecento makes itself merely a herald of Dante's idea of Caesar and the Empire, and shows not the slightest disposition toward criticism. In order to characterize the atmosphere that must have predominated among commentators on Dante as late as 1400, we may refer to the explanation in the "Anonimo Fiorentino" why Dante, in *Inferno* XXXIV, described the murder of Caesar as "one of the world's greatest sins." "This can be demonstrated with many reasons: it was Caesar who more than any other man made the Roman community great. . .; Caesar was the first of those emperors under whose reign Christ chose to be crucified; . . . and under the same Empire the Holy Church and the Catholic Faith expanded and grew." (". . . uno de' maggiori peccati del mondo." "Et questo si può mostrare per molte ragioni, però che Cesare fu quelli che più alzò il comune di Roma che niuno altro. . . . Cesare fu il principio degli Imperadori, sotto la cui signoria volle essere Cristo crocifisso; . . . et sotto quello medesimo [imperio fu] aumentata et cresciuta la santa Chiesa et la fede cattolica.") Ed. Fanfani, vol. I, p. 711ff. As to the composition of the commentary of the "Anonimo Fiorentino" as late as 1400, and regarding its sources, see the reexamination, virtually confirming K. Hegel's earlier conclusions, by D. Guerri, *Il Commento del Boccaccio a Dante* (Bari, 1926), p. 33f. The only one among the Dante commentators of the Trecento who raised the question of the justice of the deed of Brutus and the other slayers of Caesar seriously was Benvenuto Rambaldi da Imola, who did so because he was more deeply than any other Trecento commentator influenced by early Humanism, and therefore more familiar with the views of the ancient authors. But Rambaldi's historical considerations resulted in just the opposite to any vindication of the role and right of the *Respublica Romana*, as will be seen in due course (Vol. One, p. 127f.).

20. "Nam posteaquam res publica in unius potestatem deducta est, preclara illa ingenia (ut inquit Cornelius) abiere." *L*, fol. 144v; ed. Klette, p. 93f. Bruni's quotation is not precise, Tacitus actually having said "magna illa ingenia" (not "preclara illa ingenia") "cessere" (not "abiere")—proof that Bruni was quoting from memory. See note 23 below.

21. Whether Boccaccio himself had "stolen" the Tacitus manuscript from Montecassino, or had been using a derivative while the original was removed from Montecassino at the request of Niccolò Acciaiuoli, is still an unsolved question. See C. C. Coulter, "Boccaccio and the Cassinese Manuscripts of the Laurentian Library," *Classical Philology*, XLIII (1948), 217-230. The descent of the manuscript from the first half of the eleventh century has been established by E. A. Lowe, "The Unique Manuscript of Tacitus' 'Histories'," *Cassinensia*, I (1929), 265f.

22. R. Sabbadini, *Le Scoperte dei Codici Latini e Greci ne' Secoli XIV e XV* (two vols., Florence 1905 and 1914), vol. II, p. 254. On the rapid spread of familiarity with Tacitus during the first decades of the Quattrocento see the summary of the available information in G. Zippel's *Giunte e Correzioni* supplementing his translation of Voigt's *Il Risorgimento dell' Antichità Classica* (Florence, 1897), p. 11f.

23. "Postquam bellatum apud Actium atque omnem potentiam ad unum conferri pacis interfuit, magna illa ingenia cessere." Tacitus *Historiae* i 1.

24. See notes 20 and 23 above.

25. Bruni, *Historiae*, p. 14f.

26. Dante in the famous passage, *Paradiso*, VI, 55ff.; for Petrarch cf. Vol. One, pp. 46, 86f., 126.

27. See Vol. One, p. 123ff. and note 11 to Chap. 7.

28. "O Cai [*variant* Gai] Cesar, quam plane tua facinora Romanam urbem evertere! Sed comprimam ipse me. Sunt enim qui Lucanum, doctissimum et sapientissimum hominem, vera de te scripsisse permoleste ferant. Nec fortasse carent ratione. Etsi enim multa ac magna in te vitia erant, multis tamen ac magnis virtutibus obumbrabantur. Quamobrem de te silere tutius erit. Et simul filium tuum eadem illa ratione preteribo. . . . Fuerunt enim in illo, ut in patre quoque fuerant, vestigia quedam virtutum que vitia quoque tolerabiliora faciebant. At hec monstra, quibus imperium tradidistis, nulla virtute redempta erant a vitiis, nisi forte

virtus est omni conatu rem publicam delere nec ullo flagitio quantumvis maximo abstinere. Quare etsi cetera vestra obliviscar, illud tamen neque oblivisci neque ut vobis non succenseam adduci possum, quod viam tantis malis tantisque sceleribus [*variant* malis sceleribusque] patefecistis quanta successores vestri omni genere impietatis nequitieque ediderunt." *L* fol. 144r-144v; ed. Klette, p. 93.

29. "Hec igitur splendidissima Romanorum colonia eo maxime tempore deducta est quo populi Romani imperium maxime florebat, quo potentissimi reges et bellicosissime gentes armis ac virtute domite erant, Carthago, Numantia, Corinthus a stirpe interierant, omnes terre mariaque omnia in potestatem eius populi venerant. Nichil calamitatis populo Romano ab ullis hostibus inflictum erat. Nondum Cesares, Antonii, Tiberii, Nerones, pestes atque exitia rei publice, libertatem sustulerant. Sed vigebat sancta et inconcussa libertas, que tamen non multo post hanc coloniam deductam a sceleratissimis latronibus sublata est. Ex quo illud evenire arbitror quod in hac civitate egregie preter ceteras et fuisse et esse videmus: ut Florentini homines maxime omnium libertate gaudeant et tyrannorum valde sint inimici. Tantum, ut opinor [*variant* Tantum opinor], odii adversus invasores imperii et rei publice eversores iam ex illo tempore Florentia concepit ut nec hodie quidem videatur oblita, sed si quod illorum vel nomen vel vestigium adhuc superest id hec res publica dedignatur et odit." *L* fol. 142v-143r; ed. Klette, p. 91f.

30. E. G. Parodi, "Le storie di Cesare nei primi secoli della letteratura italiana," *Studj di filologia romanza*, IV (1889), 496f. The wealth of Florentine manuscripts was later surveyed in P. Santini's *Quesiti e Ricerche di Storiografia Fiorentina* (Florence, 1903), pp. 61-87.

31. The best analysis of these medieval legends—with emphasis that according to them "Cesare, Augusto, gl'Imperatori sono i fondatori, difensori, restauratori di Firenze"—is still that contained in P. Villari's *I Primi Due Secoli della Storia di Firenze* (Florence, 1893), vol. I, pp. 52-60, esp. 59. See also the recent critical revision of the whole group of sources by A. Del Monte ("La storiografia fiorentina dei secoli XII e XIII," *Bullettino dell'Istituto Storico Italiano*, LXII [1950], 175-282), who, p. 182, defines as the core of the medieval legend that here "Florence became the daughter and heir of Rome—estab-

lished by Caesar, the founder of the Empire, . . . destroyed by the barbarians, and rebuilt by the Romans and by Charlemagne, the restorer of the Empire"; and the similar comments by N. Rubinstein, "The Beginnings of Political Thought in Florence. A Study in Mediaeval Historiography," *Journal of the Warburg and Courtauld Institutes*, v (1942), esp. pp. 208, 215f.

32. Giovanni Villani, *Cronica*, I, 38 and 39.

33. ". . . Florentiae civitas per Caesarem conderetur." *De Origine Civitatis Florentiae et Eiusdem Famosis Civibus*, in the collection, ed. G. C. Galletti, *Philippi Villani Liber de Civitatis Florentiae Famosis Civibus . . . et de Florentinorum litteratura principes fere synchroni scriptores* (Florence, 1847), p. 8. The passage remained unchanged in the revised version of 1395/96. See the confrontation of the two versions in *Le Vite di Dante, Petrarca e Boccaccio scritte fino al secolo decimosesto*, ed. A. Solerti (Milan, 1904), p. 83; cf. p. 82. For more details cf. *Humanistic and Political Literature*, notes 7-11 to Chapter I, section 2.

34. Begun, in the version (or versions) we have, after 1379 and completed before 1383, the year in which Rambaldi sent a copy of his *Commentary* to Salutati. See D. Guerri, *Il Commento del Boccaccio a Dante. Appendice all' Edizione* (Bari, 1926), p. 36. On Rambaldi's personality and work we have the careful study *Di Maestro Benvenuto da Imola, Commentatore Dantesco* (Pergola, 1889) by L. Rossi-Casè; for supplementary information see L. Frati in *Giornale Storico della Letteratura Italiana*, LXXII (1918), 90ff. Rambaldi's thorough knowledge of Florence's sagas and traditions is explained by the fact that in Florence he spent the time of his boyhood studies in 1357-1360, and later again a part of 1373-1374; during both stays he was in close contact with Boccaccio whom he called "venerabilis praeceptor meus." See Rossi-Casè, *op. cit.*, pp. 36f., 70f., and also P. Toynbee's rediscussion of Rambaldi's Florentine sojourns in his *Dante Studies and Researches* (London, 1902), pp. 218, 222f.

35. "Est ergo . . . sciendum . . . quod multi dicunt hic multa falsa, sequentes chronicas florentinorum, quae ponunt multa magnifica ficte ad exaltationem suae patriae. Nec miror, quia simile dicunt chronicae quasi omnium civitatum, quas viderim, sicut Ravennae, Januae, Venetiarum, et Neapolis. Quanto magis ergo florentini eloquentissimi hominum studuerunt laudibus suae terrae? Dicunt ergo, in commendatione antiquae originis, quod civitas

Faesularum olim fundata fuit a rege Atlante. . . . Ulterius dicunt, quod Caesar cum duodecim principibus romanis . . . aedificavit Florentiam partim ex romanis, partim ex faesulanis ad similitudinem Romae: et quod florentini fuerunt in favorem Caesaris in bellis civilibus. Et quod sine risu scribere non possum, dicunt, quod Lucanus hoc dicit, cum facit mentionem de Sarno: quae omnia quantum sint vana unusquisque intelligens videat. Nam quomodo Caesar poterat vacare constructioni nobilissimarum civitatum tempore illius coniurationis pestiferae, cum fuerat accusatus de coniuratione, et ipse se purgavit per testimonium Quinti Ciceronis, qui erat frater Marci Ciceronis tunc consulis? Quomodo etiam romani expendidissent tantum tempus ad capiendam civitatem Faesularum illo tempore, quo Roma erat in tanto potentatu, quod per tempus ante in spatio quatuor annorum tempore belli socialis, omnes fortes populos Italiae reduxerant viribus armorum sub jugum romanum, quia juraverant contra Romam? Quomodo etiam florentini fuerunt de auxiliatoribus Caesaris, quia tantum tunc Florentia nascebatur?" *Comentum super Dantis Aldigherij Comoediam*, ad *Inf*. cant. xv, ed. J. P. Lacaita, vol. 1 (Florence, 1887), pp. 509-511.

36. "Hoc scio, quod aliquis dicet: Dic ergo tu mihi, quis fuerit fundator Faesularum, quae sic dicta est, quasi fiat sola? Dico, quod *truffa* est, et quod nescio, quis fundaverit eam, nec quando, quia principia maximarum civitatum saepe ignorantur. . . . Quis ergo aedificaverit primo Florentiam, ignoro; nec credo, quod a Florino nobili cive romano fuerit sic denominata, nec a Campo Florido, sicut etiam isti dicunt, cum dicat Plinius, quod Florentia olim habuerit ortum a Faesulis; sed quando, quomodo, vel per quem fateor me nescire." *Ibid.*, pp. 510-511.

37. The formation of this theory around 1400, and Salutati's leading part in it, will be discussed later, especially in Vol. One, pp. 61 and 132.

We may note that F. Lanzoni's comprehensive work, *Genesi, Svolgimento e Tramonto delle Leggende Storiche* ("Studi e Testi," no. 43; Rome, Tipografia Vaticana, 1925), entirely ignores this Florentine chapter of early Renaissance historical criticism, despite the promise of its title to deal with the "waning" of medieval legends. It does refer to Renaissance criticism of the legends about the founding of Milan, and in this context mentions the historians Merula and Calchi (p. 249). But Milanese criticism did not reach that stage until two to three generations after the achievements of the Florentine humanists that are analyzed in the present book. A reference to Florentine criticism during the transition from the Trecento to the Quattrocento is one of the several essential features needed to complement Lanzoni's work.

38. These various aspects of Bruni's mature historical thought are today well known. After E. Fueter's rather disparaging views of humanistic historiography, and especially of Bruni (in his *Geschichte der Neueren Historiographie* [Munich, 1911], p. 16ff.), there has gradually come about a marked revaluation of Bruni as an historian through the studies, cited in note 1 to Chap. 1, by G. Salvemini, E. Santini, P. Joachimsen, H. Baron, W. K. Ferguson (first in an article "Humanist Views of the Renaissance," *American Historical Review*, XLV [1939], esp. p. 8ff.), and recently through the paper on "Leonardi Bruni and Humanistic Historiography" by B. L. Ullman (in *Medievalia et Humanistica*, IV [1946], 45-61), which is the best-rounded presentation of the new appraisal.

39. For the Florentine authors after Bruni see E. Santini, "La Fortuna della Storia Fiorentina di L. Bruni nel Rinascimento," *Studi Storici*, XX (1911), 177-195, a rich collection of the material to which must be added, as one of the most significant statements of the Bruni school on Rome's fate under the Empire, Matteo Palmieri's introduction to his *De Captivitate Pisarum* (ed. Scaramella in "Rerum Italicarum Scriptores," n. ser., tom. XIX, parte 2, p. 4f.), presumably written in the 1440's. (*Ibid.*, p. xi). For the Florentine influence on non-Florentine historical writers, see E. Santini, *Bruni e i "Hist. Flor. Pop.,"* p. 46ff., and the first chapter of Ferguson's *The Renaissance in Historical Thought*, passim; but the theme has not yet been exhausted.

40. The various contributions to this controversy are listed in in E. Walser's *Poggius Florentinus. Leben und Werke* (Leipzig, 1914), pp. 164-176, and in R. Sabbadini's commentary to the "Epistolario di Guarino Veronese," *Miscellanea di Storia Veneta*, 3. ser., vol. XIV (Venice, 1919), pp. 323-327.

41. Poggio in his *Defensiuncula Contra Guarinum Veronensem*; in Poggio's *Opera* (Basel, 1538), pp. 365-390. After quoting as witnesses to the decay of Roman culture Cicero, from *De Officiis* ii 1.2, and Seneca, from the preface to *Controversiae* (actually not a work of Seneca the philosopher, but a writing

of Seneca the Elder, as Poggio did not yet know), Poggio goes on: "Accipe tertium quoque [after Cicero and Seneca] gravissimum historici doctissimi Cornelij Taciti testimonium, qui vel solus Guarinum deijciat ex arce utputa Minervae." After a full quotation from *Historiae* i 1, Poggio goes on: "Cum ergo et Senecae verbis, quibus illa praeclara ingenia Ciceronis aetate nata esse, deinde in deterius decrevisse affirmat, et Taciti testimonio asserentis [edn. 1538: asserentes] magna illa ingenia post imperium ad unum delatum defecisse apertissime constet quanta iactura sit secuta in literis latinis libertate amissa, rectissime scripsisse me dico . . . latinam eloquentiam corruisse." (*Defensiuncula*, p. 372f.). Poggio's use in this passage of the words "praeclara ingenia" is definite evidence that he had Bruni's *Laudatio* in mind; for the expression in the Seneca passage to which Poggio refers actually runs "omnia ingenia" (as Poggio had correctly quoted from Seneca previously), while Tacitus speaks of "magna ingenia." It had been Bruni in his *Laudatio*, as we have noted (note 20 above) who, inadvertently transforming Tacitus' statement on the disappearance of talents in historiography into a general judgment on the disappearance of intellectual brilliance, also altered Tacitus' "magna ingenia" to "praeclara ingenia."

42. Poggio states explicitly that his thesis—"Caesar was the parricidal murderer of the Latin language and of the literary arts as much as of his *patria*, because, after the destruction of the republic, Latin eloquence had collapsed"—had been treated by Guarino as "the very core of the entire dispute." (". . . tanquam robur fortissimum totius disputationis"; *Defensiuncula*, p. 370. Poggio's formulation in his preceding letter had been: "Non enim magis patriae quam latinae linguae et bonarum artium extitit parricida. Una enim cum libertate corruit latina eloquentia, et studia literarum quae in ipso flore prius fere quam inciperent extincta sunt. Erat in culmine eloquentia; erant caeterarum bonarum artium incrementa, quae statim prostrata re publica defecerunt. Erant complures viri doctissimi simul eloquentissimi, quos civilis clades absumpsit. Vigebant studia philosophiae et caeterarum liberalium artium tempore libertatis; quam nisi delevisset Caesar, crevissent latina ingenia, neque Graecis ullo doctrinarum genere cessissent. At vero libertate extincta, subsecuta sunt imperatorum portenta nepharia, qui et doctos semper ac virtutem oderunt, et adversati sunt literarum studiis et doctrinae." *Opera*, 1538, p.

365). Guarino, Poggio goes on to say in his *Defensiuncula*, had objected that many of the great works of Roman literature were written after Caesar's victory; but this difficulty could be overcome. "Virgil, Horace, Livy, and Seneca were born and bred while the republic was still in its vigor ['orti et nutriti sint vigente (?) (edn. 1538: ingente) republica']; for Livy was in his sixteenth year when Caesar was slain, Seneca (as he himself states) could still hear Cicero's speeches, Virgil was twenty-four when the battle of Pharsalus between Caesar and Pompey was waged; Horace was seventeen. Thus all the learned and eloquent men who lived later either were born in the days of liberty and nursed on that earlier eloquence, or they were born soon afterwards, while some seeds of that earlier eloquence still survived." ("Itaque quot [edn. 1538: quod] docti et eloquentes postea extitere, aut libertatis tempore orti illam priorem eloquentiam hauserunt, aut paulo post, cum aliqua prioris eloquentiae semina superessent." *Ibid.*, p. 371). The intrinsic significance of this central issue of the controversy should alone be sufficient to occasion a reappraisal.

43a. For an example of a sceptical appraisal, cf. the somewhat ironical and cavalier manner in which the Poggio-Guarino debate is presented in Walser's much-consulted book on Poggio (see note 40 above). More recently, the seriousness of the controversy has been denied entirely in Fr. Gundolf's *Caesar. Geschichte seines Ruhms* (Berlin, 1925, pp. 133-136; also in English, French, and Italian translations), a work which draws a sympathetic picture of the Caesar cult of Quattrocento princes like Alfonso of Naples, Federigo da Urbino, Sigismondo Malatesta, and Cesare Borgia, but is entirely blind to the approach to Caesar and the *Respublica Romana* found among the citizen-humanists of Florence and Venice. The controversy between Poggio and Guarino, says Gundolf, is "the characteristic evidence" which proves "that almost all of the humanists' praise for Cato and Brutus, and their reproof of Caesar which is merely rhetorical, draw their nourishment from Roman literature and not at all, as is sometimes supposed, from a genuinely political aversion of modern city-state republicans against tyranny." According to Gundolf, the motives of the humanists were "aesthetical and literary, not moral and political," and "Poggio would have championed the opposite opinion with equal dash" ("mit gleichem Schick"). Seen against our reconstruction of the continuity of the republican tradition among the Florentine humanists, the rashness and partiality of Gundolf's assertions are obvious. So deep, indeed, was the effect of this tradition on the historical outlook of the members of the Florentine group that the opinion that Roman literature decayed after the loss of political liberty, was shared (so Poggio tells us in his *Defensiuncula*, p. 372) even by Niccolò Niccoli who, as we shall see (Vol. One, pp. 292f., 320, 352), in his practical political conduct was among the Florentine humanists the least faithful to the republican ideals. How it happened that Poggio—who in many respects was in his intellectual make-up a chancery humanist at the Curia despite his Florentine origin—could by the 1430's become a mouthpiece of the Florentine political convictions and historical ideas, is a question which will become intelligible when the picture of the Florentine development has been fully redrawn, and with which we shall deal in the chapter on "Niccoli and Poggio in the 1420's and 1430's" (Chapter 17). Perhaps the most devastating refutation of Gundolf's assertions may be found in the frank words of the Venetian, Pietro del Monte, discussed in Appendix 2.

43b. Decembrio's *Panegyricus* has been published by G. Petraglione in *Archivio Storico Lombardo*, ser. IV, vol. VIII (1907), 27-45, though in an apparently slightly altered version from Decembrio's last years (around 1473); the version of 1436 seems not to have been preserved in its Latin original.

44. "Pene oblitus es: Ciceronem, Livium et in primis Maronem, divina ingenia, Cesaris et Augusti temporibus . . . floruisse. Quo igitur illa preclara ingenia, ut Cornelius inquit, abiere?" *Ibid.*, p. 40.

45. *Ibid.*, p. 41.

46. *Ibid.*, p. 32f.

47. See *Arte della Guerra*, historical excursus at the end of lib. II (in Machiavelli's *Tutte Le Opere Storiche e Letterarie*, ed. Manzoni e Casella [Florence, 1929], pp. 301-302), and *Discorsi*, II 2, II 4, II 5, for Machiavelli's views of the pernicious consequences of the subjection of all city-republics and independent states under the empire of Rome; *Discorsi*, I 10, and the discussion in O. Tommasini, *La Vita e le Opere di Machiavelli*, vol. II 1, p. 159 ff., for Machiavelli's criticism of Caesar.

48. Bruni, *Historiae*, p. 5f.

49. The Anonymus, presumably a colleague of Bruni in the

Florentine chancery, in his *Laudatio Leonardi historici et oratoris* on Bruni's death, ed. in E. Santini's *Bruni e i "Hist. Flor. Pop.,"* p. 152. Poggio Bracciolini, *Historia Florentina*, in *Rer. Ital. Script.*, tom. XX, col. 194. Cristoforo Landino, in his poem *De Primordiis Urbis Florentiae*, in A. M. Bandini, *Specimen Literaturae Florentinae Saeculi XV* (Florence, 1747), vol. I, p. 166ff., now in a critical edition in Landino's *Carmina Omnia*, ed. A. Perosa (Florence, 1939), p. 86ff.; and in his *De vera nobilitate*, Bibl. Corsiniana (Rome), Ms. 433, fol. 74. ("Estis gente autem Romani, a Sylla, invictissimo duce, deducti coloni.")

50. See note 33 above.

51. "Florentiam . . . a Sillanis militibus . . . conditam." Giannozzo Manetti, *Vita Dantis*, in *Le Vite di Dante, Petrarca e Boccaccio scritte fino al secolo decimosesto*, ed. A. Solerti (Milano, 1904), p. 113.

52. Flavio Biondo, *Italia Illustrata*, under "Secunda Regio, Etruria," states with reference to Bruni that Florence had been founded by Sulla, whose soldiers were settled there. ("Florentiae urbis inclytae originem gestasque res abunde complexus est in historia clarissimus Leonardus arretinus. Quod autem ad nos attinet eius urbis origo refertur in Syllanorum militum quibus is ager a Sylla assignatus fuit adventum. . . . Unde initium Florentia habuisse videtur ante Christi dei nostri adventum annos circiter octoginta tres." Ed. Verona, 1482, fol. A VIIIv). Lorenzo Valla, in a letter to Pier Candido Decembrio, 1435 (". . . a pessimo mortalium Sylla, qui primus tyrannus Romae fuit"), ed. in R. Sabbadini's *Cronologia della Vita del Panormita e del Valla* (in "Pubblicazioni del R. Istituto di Studi Superiori in Firenze," Florence, 1891), p. 75; reprinted and dated, by G. Petraglione, *Arch. Stor. Lomb.*, ser. IV, vol. VIII (1907), 7-12. Apparently, Valla, when reading the *Laudatio*—which asserts Florence's origin under the *Respublica Romana* without naming Sulla—was not quite clear about the role assigned to Sulla in the Florentine theory; he seems to have thought that Sulla established a Roman colony in Fiesole, thus indirectly causing an influx of Roman blood into the later Florentine population. In any case, the letter proves that Valla, in 1435, knew of the Florentine theory connected with the name of Sulla, and that he accepted it as true.

53. Decembrio, *Panegyricus*, *loc. cit.*, p. 39.

54. The sources for the history of Renaissance opinion on

the founding of Florence are gathered in an excursus in book IX of Benedetto Varchi's *Storia Fiorentina* (in the edn. Florence 1838-1841: vol. II, pp. 52ff.). Whether the information contained in the *Liber coloniarum*, whose value, according to our present knowledge, is "problematical" and whose contents is largely "distorted" in the preserved versions (see Schanz-Hosius, *Geschichte der römischen Literatur*, vol. II, part II [4th edn., 1935], p. 803), is really the last word, is still *sub judice*. The sources that might be weighed against the authority of the *Liber* are even today essentially those once collected by Salutati; see the list of authorities in a recent attempt to revive the theory of the Sullan foundation by N. Rubinstein in a note on "The Date of the Foundation of Florence" in the *Journal of the Warburg and Courtauld Institutes*, IV (1940-1941), pp. 225ff.

55. This is a recurrent motif of Verino's work; see foll. 6, 8f., 11, 17 of the 1483 edition. That on a more popular level the early Quattrocento opinion lived on throughout the sixteenth century, is shown by the fact that the note "Fiorenza Città nobilissima, et della Toscana, innanzi l'avvenimento di Christo 90. anni fù edificata da gli soldati di Silla Romano" appears in a pamphlet *Fioretti delle Croniche del Mondo, . . . con la dechiaratione della origine delle piu notabile città di tutta Italia*, published in Venice ca. 1540 (fol. B III; a copy is in the Newberry Library, Chicago), and is found also in a much consulted compilation from the latter part of the century, *L'Origine di molte città del mondo ed in particolare di tutta Italia*, by Giulio Cesare de Solis (in the edition Milan, 1591, on p. 20).

56. "Necesse id quidem Leonardo fuit, inquit Colucius, ad causam huius civitatis, quam susceperat, exornandam, ut in Caesares ipsos aliquanto inveheretur." Ed. Klette, p. 68; ed. Garin, p. 78.

57. "Sed quorsum hec? dicet fortasse quispiam. Utriusque videlicet gratia: primum, ut ostenderem non iniuste hanc civitatem eiusmodi partes suscepisse; et simul intelligeretur eo tempore hanc coloniam deductam fuisse quo urbs Romana potentia, libertate, ingeniis, clarissimis civibus maxime florebat . . .: ut plurimum intersit tunc an inferiori tempore colonia hec fuerit deducta, cum ita iam omnis virtus ac nobilitas Romane urbis extirpata erat ut nichil preclarum neque egregium qui ex ea migrabant secum possent efferre." *L* fol. 144v; ed. Klette, p. 93f.

58. "Le véritable patriotisme n'est pas l'amour du sol, c'est

l'amour du passé, c'est le respect pour les générations qui nous ont précédés." Fustel de Coulanges, *Questions historiques* (Paris, 1893), p. 6.

59. For Salutati's *Invectiva*, and its editions, see below, note 8 to Chap. 4.

60. For the details of Salutati's reconstruction of the origin of Florence see *Humanistic and Political Literature*, Chapter I, section 1, esp. note 13ff., and Chapter IV, section 3, esp. note 5ff.

61. For Rinuccini's *Risponsiva*, and its edition, see note 8 to Chap. 4.

62. "Hai mai letto, come Roma sotto i Re poco crebbe, sotto il Senato in poco tempo acquistò lo imperio del mondo, sotto gl'Imperadori quasi al nulla è ritornata?" Rinuccini, *Risponsiva*, p. 220.

63. "Come Cicerone testimonia, la temerità di Caio Cesare, perchè per oppinione si fisse nell' animo essere più degno che gli altri di principare, le cose umane e le divine rivolse, e di Roma le svelse; perocchè, come di sopra è narrato, uno nelle cose umane non può essere perfetto, e presupposto che uno ne sia assai idoneo, come fu Ottaviano, non poi i susseguenti, come Nerone. . . ." If Rome had remained "nell' ordine Senatorio costituto, anzi insino al mio tempo sarebbe durato con accrescimento in gloria, come già fe' in quella Repubblica. Intendi adunque, o servo, quanto sia il frutto della bella libertà, per la quale non dubitò morire quello esquisitissimo Cato posteriore, il quale Lucano di raggione agguaglia agli Iddei, dicendo: 'la cagione vincitrice piacque agl' Iddei, ma la vinta a Catone.' " *Ibid.*, p. 247f.

64. For Dati's *Istoria*, and its editions, see note 2 to Chap. 8.

65. "Fu . . . che gli antichi Fiorentini che vennono in grandezza, seguitavano la parte imperiale e signorile, e la moltitudine gli ebbe in odio per sospetto di non venire sotto tiranno, come venne Roma sotto Cesare per lasciarlo fare troppo potente; e per detta ragione sempre hanno tirati a terra [*Manni*: drieto] i grandi e i potenti, acciò che e' non trapassassino il modo comune [*Manni*: comune e civile]; hanno fatto come il buono ortolano che pota e ricide i rami degli arbori che si distendono troppo, acciò che durino più e facciano migliore frutto e non dieno uggia e non facciano danno alla terra e all' altre semenze, e a quelli che sono magri mettono dappiè dell' umore che gli conforti, e questa natura ha quel populo per ragione che sono nati e discesi [*Manni*: perocchè

sono discesi] di que' romani che, con reggimento di libertà, avevano acquistata la signoria del mondo e posta Roma in pace e riposo e onore [*Manni omits* e onore] più che mai fusse; i quali, se ora tornassono al mondo, sarebbono i nimici di Cesare e d'ognuno che guastò quello stato e reggimento popolare e ridusselo a tirannia. E però questi Fiorentini, nati di que' Romani liberi, seguitando la natura loro, hanno sempre sospetto di chi potesse occupare e tôrre loro la libertà del loro reggimento popolare comune [*Manni*: e civile *instead of* comune] e per questo sono nimici e contrari d'animo [*Manni omits* e contrari d'animo] di chi studia occupare per tirannia e superbia la libertà. . . ." *Istoria*, ed. Pratesi, p. 120f.; ed. Manni, p. 112f.

As for the Quattrocento theory of the origin of Florence, Dati, lacking a critical humanistic approach, strangely coordinates the traditional legend with the new idea that Florence was founded prior to the monarchy of the emperors—an idea that forms the basis of the whole paragraph, just quoted, on the role of liberty in Florentine history. He adopts the account on Florence's foundation found in Giovanni Villani's chronicle, but omits all reference to Caesar; in this way he manages to make the origin of Florence, though recounted in Villani's fashion, appear to have taken place in republican times, an impression enhanced by his depreciation, in the new manner, of the empire: "Passati poi dugento anni o circa, venne Roma in imperio sotto Cesare e poi Ottaviano, . . . e da Ottaviano in qua venne Roma sempre mancando così di virtù come di potenzia, intanto che passati poi doppo Cesare anni quattrocento o circa [*Manni*: anni quattrocento dopo lo'mperio di Cesare] molti potenti di istrane nazioni vennono con isforzo di gente in Italia per farsi imperadori pigliando Roma." Ed. Pratesi, pp. 112-113; ed. Manni, p. 106.

Part Two

CHAPTER 4

1. *Il Paradiso degli Alberti. Ritrovi e ragionamenti del 1389. Romanzo di Giovanni da Prato.* Ed. A. Wesselofsky (Bologna, 1867) in the series *Scelta di curiosità letterarie*, vols. 86^{I}-86^{II}, containing Wesselofsky's introduction (henceforth quoted as "Wesselofsky, I" and "Wesselofsky, II") and vols. 87-88, containing the text of the *Paradiso* (henceforth quoted as "*Paradiso*, I" and "*Paradiso*, II"). With this work, and the various problems it poses, we shall become more familiar in the second section of this chapter, and in Chapters 13 and 15.

2. The datings, accepted today, of Bruni's *Laudatio* and *Dialogi* are discussed in Chapters 10 and 11. For the accepted datings of Loschi's, Rinuccini's, and Salutati's invectives, see the discussions in *Humanistic and Political Literature*, Chapter II, "Publicists During the Florentine Struggle with Giangaleazzo Visconti of Milan (1397-1402)."

3. Except his brief occasional guide for searchers for old manuscripts in German monasteries, the *Commentarium in peregrinatione Germanie*, published in Sabbadini's *Storia e Critica di Testi Latini* (Catania, 1914), pp. 4-7. Republished in a considerably improved version, by R. P. Robinson, in *Classical Philology*, XVI (1921), 251-255.

4. These embarrassing implications of the accepted chronology are examined in *Humanistic and Political Literature*, Chapter V, "Bruni's Development as a Translator from the Greek (1400-1403/04)."

5. Cf. the survey of the appraisals of the *Paradiso*, from Wesselofsky and Voigt to recent scholars, in *Humanistic and Political Literature*, Chapter I, section 1, note 5.

6. This examination has been made in *Humanistic and Political Literature*, Chapter I, "Giovanni da Prato's *Paradiso degli Alberti*," and Chapter II, "Publicists During the Florentine Struggle with Giangaleazzo Visconti of Milan (1397-1402)."

7. See Chapter 10.

8. *Invectiva Lini Colucci Salutati in Antonium Luschum Vicentinum*, ed. D. Moreni (Florence, 1826). A few sections of

the *Invectiva* have been reedited and translated into Italian by E. Garin in the volume, cited in note 1 to Chap. 3, *Prosatori Latini del Quattrocento* (pp. 1-37); they include some important paragraphs on the nature of the "libertas Florentina" which lie outside the scope of the historiographical themes discussed in the present book, but are essential for a rounded picture of the political outlook of the *Invectiva.* Garin has collated the two Florentine manuscripts used by Moreni and found that Moreni's edition had been done with great care (cf. Garin's "Nota Critica," p. 1127). A critical edition of the *Invectiva*, by N. Rubinstein, is in preparation.

Loschi's work is still available only through its inclusion in Salutati's *Invectiva* where Loschi's entire text is reproduced to serve as the basis for a running commentary against it. But at least two separate manuscripts have recently been discovered by N. Rubinstein and Paul O. Kristeller (according to kind information from Prof. Kristeller) and will become accessible through Rubinstein's edition. Cino Rinuccini's *Risponsiva* is preserved only in an unsatisfactory, in several places incomplete, contemporary translation into the Volgare; published together with Salutati's *Invectiva* by Moreni, *op. cit.*, pp. 199-250.

9. For all these conclusions cf. the chapters of *Humanistic and Political Literature* cited in note 6 above.

10. "Quis non videt hunc nostrum populum tueri communem causam libertatis Italiae, qui non fateatur victo populo Florentino libertatem stare non posse, qui non agnoscat nobis servitute subactis totam Italiam sine remedio . . . servam fore?" Salutati, *Invectiva*, p. 88f. "Nos obex, nos obstaculum soli sumus, ne cursum perficiat per omnem Italiam ille tyrannicus dominatus, qui tot urbes, tot castra, totque oppida miserrima conditione subegit. Hanc pacem dominus tuus optabat . . . Huius autem pacis . . . , fateor, Florentinos semper hostes et obstaculum extitisse." *Ibid.*, p. 189.

11. Salutati was born in 1331, Cino not long after 1350 (according to Aiazzi in the work quoted in note 1 to Chap. 5), Bruni in 1370. The recent widely accepted hypothesis that Bruni was born as late as 1374 is not in harmony with several facts known from Bruni's life. This problem will be rediscussed in the revised edition of the chronology of Bruni's works referred to in note 4 to Chap. 10. In this writer's opinion, G. Calò's scepticism (*La Rinascita*, II [1939], 227f.; reprinted in Calò's

Dall' Umanesimo alla Scuola del Lavoro [Florence, 1940], vol. 1, p. 38f.) regarding the reliability of Bruni's occasional comparison of his age with that of Vergerio—the only substantial reason for doubting that Bruni was born in 1369/70 as is attested otherwise—points in the right direction. For the literature on Cino Rinuccini see the first note to the next chapter.

CHAPTER 5

1. The facts of Cino's life were gathered as early as 1840 by G. Aiazzi for the appendices of his edition of the memoirs (*Ricordi*) of Cino's sons and grandsons. (*Ricordi storici di Filippo di Cino Rinuccini dal 1282 al 1460 colla continuazione di Alamanno e Neri suoi figli fino al 1506*, ed. Aiazzi [Florence, 1840], p. 126f.). On this material were based A. Reumont's sketch of Cino's personality in his *Beitraege zur italienischen Geschichte*, vol. v (1857), p. 360f., and also the article by F. Flamini "Gli imitatori della lirica di Dante e del *Dolce Stil Nuovo*," in his *Studî di storia letteraria italiana e straniera* (Livorno, 1895), where Cino is appraised as a Volgare poet.

2. His Latin writings (*Risponsiva* and *Invettiva*) have in fact come down to us only in Volgare translations. See note 8 to Chap. 4 and note 32 to Chap. 13.

3. The Florentines had already been the saviors of "la libertà in Italia" when Mastino della Scala, "grandissimo tiranno in Lombardìa, la fiorente Fiorenza in libertà desiderò inghiottire, sottilmente veggendo, che se avesse tagliato il capo della libertà, arebbe veduto il resto del corpo morto, e agevolmente sarebbe tutta Italia soggiogata." Although all Lombardy, "sempre . . . notissima di tiranni," was subservient to Mastino, Florence resisted. (*Risponsiva*, ed. Moreni—see note 8 to Chap. 4—p. 200.) "Siamo adunque di così ottimo et unico bene [i.e., the *libertà*, for which Cato died] non solo conservatori, ma accrescitori." And, indeed, Florence had stood the decisive test already when the Duke of Athens was forced by the citizens to resign his tyranny after only eleven months. "Fu e sarà questo a noi continuo esemplo di non solo conoscere, ma onorare, adorare, conservare la libertà." *Ibid.*, p. 248f. On Florence's resistance against Giovanni and Bernabò Visconti, see *ibid.*, p. 203f. For Cino's new emphasis on the Roman Republic, see Vol. One, p. 61f.

4. *Risponsiva*, pp. 226-47.

5. See above note 33 to Chap. 3.

6. ". . . perchè non solo l'arme, ma la mercanzia amplificano la Repubblica. . . ." *Risponsiva*, p. 245f.

7. See the "Apologia nella quale si difende Danthe et Florentia da falsi calumniatori," which introduces Landino's *Commentary* on Dante, and includes in its list of great Florentines a group

of merchants "perchè sempre fu havuto in prezo in ogni città la mercatura, pure che sia exercitata con degnità." (Edn. Florence, 1481, fol. [Vv].)

8. *Risponsiva*, ed. Moreni, p. 247.

9. Cf. still quite recently C. Angeleri in an important volume on the historiography of the Renaissance problem (*Il Problema Religioso del Rinascimento. Storia della Critica e Bibliografia* [Florence, 1952], p. 148): "For one must not forget that Humanism was born in Florence, and precisely in the gatherings around Marsili in the monastery of Santo Spirito." See also above Vol. One, p. 68. For a criticism of the role ascribed to Marsili, cf. *Humanistic and Political Literature*, Chapter I, concluding pages of section 2, "The *Paradiso* as Anachronistic Fifteenth Century Fiction." For the differences between the school of Marsili and civic Humanism cf. also note 64 to Chap. 14.

10. Since there was no Florentine-French alliance any more after the middle of 1398, all of the long sections of Salutati's *Invectiva* dealing with Florence's relationship to France may be ascribed to the original draft of the winter of 1397-8.

11. See Comines, *Mémoires*, Book VII, chapter IX, where this observation is made on the occasion of the unexpected delivery of Sarzana, a fortress with which Florence might have stemmed the French expedition for an indefinite period, as Comines believed. Burckhardt, in this connection, speaks of the "direful naïveté" and the "Guelph superstition of the Florentines" (*Die Kultur der Renaissance in Italien*, ed. W. Goetz, 1922, p. 67f.); but his assertion that Comines had said the French were received "comme saints" seems to be a mistake.

12. "Loro stessi dicono che, se fosse aperto il cuore a ciascun Fiorentino, se gli troverebbe in mezzo un giglio d'oro, tanta è la connessione loro con i Francesi." Marco Foscari, in his *Relazione* of 1527, in E. Albèri, *Relazioni degli ambasciatori veneti al Senato*, ser. II, vol. I (Florence, 1839), p. 78f. Only at that late period is the first voice of protest heard among the Florentine citizens: Giannotti's proposal, in his *Discorso sopra il Fermare il Governo di Firenze*, to abolish the old name of "Parte Guelfa" because Florence should be no more Guelphic than Ghibelline (*Opere politiche e letterarie*, vol. I [Florence, 1850], p. 14)—she should not invariably hang on to France, but "variare gli accordi secondo che richiede la qualità de' tempi e degli uomini,"

as Giannotti was to term this program in his *Della Repubblica Fiorentina* (*Opere*, I, 226).

13. On Bruni's critical refutation of the medieval Florentine legends about Totila (or Attila) and Charlemagne, see the excellent discussion in Santini's *Bruni e i "Hist. Flor. Pop.,"* pp. 34-38. Cf. also Appendix 6, esp. notes 4-6. Poggio, in the introduction to his *Historia Florentina* (Muratori, tom. XX, col. 195), already failed to accept Bruni's criticism of the alleged rebuilding of Florence by Charlemagne, and in the second half of the Quattrocento Charlemagne was commonly celebrated in Florentine literature as the second founder of the city. Especially well known is Donato Acciaiuoli's *Vita Caroli Magni*, dedicated to Louis XI of France in 1461, and in 1470 honored by its inclusion as a complement in the first printed Latin edition of Plutarch's *Vitae Parallelae*. (Cf. V. Rossi, *Il Quattrocento*,[3] p. 390, and E. Fueter, *Geschichte der Neueren Historiographie* [2nd edn., 1936], p. 103). Charlemagne appears in the same role in an official oration, also of 1461, by the Florentine ambassador Filippo de' Medici before the French king (cf. E. Garin in *Rinascimento*, I [1950], 93f.); and even in diplomatic documents (see that of 1494, referred to by Santini, *op. cit.*, p. 37, note 3). So deeply was this legend ingrained in Florentine opinion that in the sixteenth century it was maintained stubbornly by Machiavelli (*Ist. Fior.* II 2), and more than four generations after Bruni's bold pioneering attack had passed when the historical criticism of Florentine scholarship—with Varchi (*Stor. Fior.*, lib. IX, ed. Milanesi, vol. II [Florence, 1858], p. 47ff.), G. B. Gelli, about the middle of the sixteenth century (*Letture* on Dante's Comedy, ed. Negroni, 1887, vol. II, p. 44), and V. Borghini, a generation later (in his *Discorso "Se Firenze fu spianata da Attila e riedificata da Carlo Magno"*)—came finally to grips with this last remaining bulwark of Florence's medieval city-legend.

14. See Vol. One, p. 14f.

15. Salutati, *Invectiva*, pp. 163-174, and passim.

16. For this aspect of Boccaccio's political views, see F. Macrì-Leone, "La Politica di Giovanni Boccaccio," *Giornale Storico della Letteratura Italiana*, XV (1890), esp. p. 98f.

17. See Vol. One, p. 22.

18. See Vol. One, p. 77.

19. See Vol. One, p. 51.

20. See Vol. One, p. 61.

21. Talking in September 1403 to Turchi about his hesitations in publishing his *Invettiva*, Salutati addresses himself as follows: you, "qui neminem hucusque tuo nomine nisi iocose leseris, incipies, discedens ab habitu tam longe consuetudinis, insanire? tune privatum stilum tuum, qui neminem hactenus offendit, ad invectionis mordacitatem translaturus es?" *Ep. XIII 10, Epistolario*, vol. III, p. 637.

22. In the process of composition during the summer of 1400; for on June 27th (according to *Ep. XI 18, Epistolario*, vol. II, p. 398) Salutati was making inquiries about a critical problem which in the treatise he is able to solve to his satisfaction. On August 30, a copy of the treatise was sent to Francesco Zabarella in Padua (*Ep. XI 23, Epistolario*, vol. III, p. 422), but publication —and possible addition of some last touches—did not occur before March 1401; for on February 21st, 1401 (*Ep. XII 4, ibid.*, p. 479) the copy mentioned was still in Zabarella's hands, and the work unpublished. Salutati told Zabarella on that day "to revise and correct" the manuscript before returning it, while he (Salutati) would wait with publication, so that the text "could be modified in the archetype according to your opinion and correction," provided Zabarella advised publication at all. See Ercole's discussion of Salutati's relevant letters, in Ercole's introduction to his edition of the treatise, reprinted in his *Da Bartolo all' Althusio* (Firenze, 1932), pp. 219ff.

23. See Vol. One, p. 44ff.

24. In the last analysis it would even require a consideration of the character of the Trecento in general; for the repeated restrengthening of strongly marked medieval convictions and sentiments during the two generations which preceded the Quattrocento is a phenomenon that is not limited to political thought nor to the slowly growing world of Humanism. The observation that, after the 1340's, there was a reversal of many a step toward a new outlook on life that had been made in the early Trecento applies likewise to art and Volgare literature and to the attitude of men in all social groups to the values of the earthly life. To mention merely the major causes, one may perhaps say that during the crucial period of the 1340's the beginning departure from medievalism in various fields of culture had been arrested by the simultaneous operation of three agonizing experiences: the po-

litical disappointment following the collapse of Cola di Rienzo's attempt at a federal reconstruction of Italy under the leadership of the city of Rome; the financial breakdown of the Italian banking houses throughout Europe, which ruined nearly all the great fortunes and the middle-class wealth of the time of Dante; and the destruction of countless human hopes by the Black Death. In many ways the psychological consequences of these catastrophes continued to be felt until, toward the end of the century, their memory was dwarfed by the new challenges discussed in the present book. To understand how novel the responses to these challenges were, one must consider the retarding forces which had characterized the period from the 1350's to the 1390's. Even in painting and literature—in the choice of iconographic themes as well as in artistic expression—the spiritual climate of the time of Giotto had been transformed in a fashion sometimes approaching the emotion and attitude toward man found in medieval phases prior to the Trecento. This has been excellently demonstrated, particularly for the time from 1350 to 1375, in a recent work by Millard Meiss on *Painting in Florence and Siena After the Black Death* (Princeton, 1951). Prof. Meiss's book appeared too late for an inclusion of its results in our appraisal of the background of the subsequent crisis, but, since it arrives at a similar awareness of the deflection of many Renaissance-bound tendencies during the later part of the Trecento, this reexamination of the art of the period complements and reaffirms the interpretation which we propose in the chapters which follow.

25. On Salutati's pioneering role in this respect see L. Borghi, "La dottrina morale di Coluccio Salutati," *Annali della R. Scuola Normale Superiore di Pisa*, ser. II, vol. III (1934), esp. 93ff.; E. Garin, *Der Italienische Humanismus* (Bern, 1947), p. 21ff.; and E. Garin, *La Filosofia*, vol. I (Milan, 1947), p. 204ff. Salutati's twilight position in the transition from Medievalism to the Renaissance, which will attract our attention in the next few chapters, was already clearly observed by the first modern student of Salutati's *Weltanschauung*, Alfred v. Martin. The somewhat odd result was that v. Martin, in a monograph published in 1913 (*Mittelalterliche Welt- und Lebensanschauung im Spiegel der Schriften Coluccio Salutatis*) portrayed Salutati as the representative of a medieval outlook—and three years later (in *Coluccio Salutati und das Humanistische Lebensideal*, 1916)

discussed him in another monograph as a mouthpiece of Humanism. More recently, E. Garin, in a brief but notable article "I Trattati Morali di Coluccio Salutati" (*Atti dell' Accademia Fiorentina di Scienze Morali 'La Colombaria,'* 1943, 53-88), has emphasized the persistent basic notions of Salutati's philosophy that allowed him to express himself in so widely different ways on different occasions—especially his conception of life as a constant "tension" and field for ceaseless activity, a conception which gained its energy precisely from the fact that Salutati, as his medieval-minded treatises prove, was so acutely aware of human depravity and sin. While it is entirely true that recognition of these and similar unchanging convictions is one of the tasks requisite for bringing unity into our picture of Salutati, there are two other questions that must be asked also: cannot the variations of Salutati's thought be explained largely as successive phases of his intellectual development—a form of explanation in which v. Martin has led the way with regard to some important details? And cannot the question to what extent Salutati's apparent inconsistencies were genuine, most easily be solved by looking on Salutati, more than has been done so far, as a member of his generation, and by comparing the harmony or discordance of thought characteristic of him and his contemporaries with the outlook of the generation after him? The analysis of Salutati's thought given in various chapters of the present book will show that, once we explore these questions earnestly and, moreover, include Salutati's political outlook and historical ideas in our exploration, the puzzle of the discord of his *Weltanschauung* merges into the wider problem of the struggle of the forces which produced an intellectual crisis on the eve of the Quattrocento.

26. So Salutati in his *Ep. III 9*, January 21, 1372, *Epistolario*, vol. I, p. 156.

27. ". . . utilem ad detestationem negotiosae vitae, qua bonis temporalibus implicamur, . . . ad fugiendam caducam exhortans . . ." Filippo Villani, *De Origine*, ed. Galletti, p. 19.

28. This attitude of Filippo Villani and other cultured Florentine citizens on the eve of the early-Quattrocento crisis is an essential factor in the historical appraisal of the transition from the Trecento to the Quattrocento; we shall have to give detailed attention to it when we weigh the effects of the crisis on civic thought and conduct. See Vol. One, p. 287ff.

29. Salutati, *Ep. I 12*, June 20, 1366, *Epistolario*, vol. I, p. 32. The device cited, "non posse simul uxori et philosophie servire," came from St. Jerome's *Adversus Iovianum*, and had often been repeated by medieval humanists and writers.

30. *Ep. VIII 3*, July 23, 1392, *Epistolario*, vol. II, p. 365-374—a letter attacking many arguments against matrimony, both of the medieval ascetic tradition and of Petrarch.

31. "Nam quanvis solitaria putetur tutior, non est tamen; et honestis et honeste vacare negociis, nisi sanctum forte et sanctius quam solitarium ociari. Sancta quippe rusticitas solum sibi prodest, ut ille [St. Jerome] ait. Negociosa vero sanctitas multos edificat . . ." *Ep. VIII 18*, July 22, 1393, *Epistolario*, vol. II, p. 453. Similarly *Ep. IX 4*, Oct. 24, 1392-4, vol. III, p. 50f., with the question put to a friend: Why do you think "solitudo" to be superior to active life? "Negociosi fuerunt patres nostri et omnes, quos vulgato nomine dicimus, patriarchas." The same was true of the kings of Israel, and later of bishops and popes. "Crede michi: . . . non produxisset nos natura politicos, hoc est associabiles, si conversatio prorsus non dirigeret ad salutem."

32. The above is an extract from *Ep. XII 20*, September 21, 1401, addressed to Frà Giovanni da Samminiato. The chief passages referred to run: "Tu, quod sancte rusticitatis est, solum tibi prodes; ego michi prodesse conor et aliis. Tu forte confratres et socios tuos sanctitate vite mones exemplo; ego proximos meos invito iuvoque quod discant . . ." "Tutius est, fateor, a mundi rebus quantum possumus elongari . . . Nam, quanvis ubique Deus presto sit, nos tamen, in quibus agi debeat illa coniunctio, remotiores simus in dispositione mentis, quam habeamus aliis occupatam." "Non est, ut forte putas, tanta vivendi differentia, quod qui religionem elegit non aliquando, et utinam non multotiens!, longinquior sit a Deo quam qui videntur inter hec secularia periclitari. Mens est que Deo coniungitur et de quocunque statu vite clamaverit, quoniam ipse nusquam abest, invenit illum . . ." ". . . ut aliis et posteris, sicut alii nobis suisque temporibus profuerunt, sic aliquid et ego prodessem; quod michi videtur scientibus non minus debitum, quam agricolis arbores serere, que pervenire debeant ad nepotes." *Epistolario*, vol. III, pp. 541-542.

33. See E. Garin in his introduction to the edition quoted in the next note, p. xlvi ff.; and Garin's volume *La Disputa delle Arti nel Quattrocento. Testi Editi ed Inediti*, vol. IX of the

same series (Florence, 1947), where the major literary sources of the controversy in the period after Salutati are collected—a survey of Quattrocento opinions which shows that Salutati's standpoint must not be overrated, and in any case did not represent the only argument consistent with the ideas of the Quattrocento; see Garin's own balanced statement in his introduction to *La Disputa*, p. xvi. As for the diversity of the possible reactions, see also the history of the controversy in L. Thorndike's *Science and Thought in the Fifteenth Century* (New York, 1929), chapter "Medicine Versus Law at Florence," esp. pp. 24ff., 45ff.

34. *De Nobilitate Legum et Medicinae*, ed. E. Garin in vol. VIII of the series "Edizione Nazionale dei Classici del Pensiero Italiano" (Florence, 1947); cf. esp. pp. 28, 36-39, and also Borghi's comment, *op. cit.*, p. 94, upon Salutati's defense of "*vita activa*" in his *De Nobilitate Legum.*

35. Cf. Borghi, *op. cit.*, p. 100f., and E. Garin, *Der Italienische Humanismus* (Bern, 1947), p. 24ff.

36. See Vol. One, p. 270ff.

37. Also circulated through Orosius; but Salutati refers directly to *Civitas Dei* in *Ep. XII 4*, 1401, *Epistolario*, vol. III, p. 472.

38. See the quotations from the *Declamatio Lucretiae*, and the bibliographical note on the *Declamatio* by Novati in *Epistolario di Salutati*, vol. IV, p. 253f.

39. The effect of their heroic deeds is that whoever hears of them "is spurred to a like daring by the thrill these virtues give him" ("titillante quasi quodam virtutum pruritu, ad idem audendum . . . animetur"). *Ep. II 18*, 1369, vol. I, p. 105.

40. *Ep. IX 13*, 1396, vol. III, p. 116; *Ep. XII 4*, 1401, vol. III, p. 471; *Ep. XIV 22*, 1406, vol. IV, p. 164.

41. A. v. Martin, *Salutati und das Humanistische Lebensideal*, p. 263f. There, and *ibid.*, p. 125f., one finds quotations from Salutati's earlier and later writings contrasted with each other.

42. ". . . Suum Brutus utraque tulit etas. Tres iam hinc ex ordine celebrantur Bruti: primus qui Superbum regem expulit; secundus qui Iulium Cesarem interfecit; tertius qui nostri temporis tyrannos et exilio et morte persequitur." Petrarch to Rienzo from Avignon, middle of June 1347. Ed. K. Burdach, *Vom Mittelalter zur Reformation*, vol. II, part III (Berlin, 1912), p. 68. See also the verses on Brutus in *Africa*, II, 150-152: ". . . animosaque

pectora Bruti / Ante oculos habeo, stupeoque ubi condere ferrum / Audeat."

43. *De Remediis*, lib. II, dial. 118: Why try to flee from the rule "viri omnium non tyrannorum modo, sed principum clementissimi atque mitissimi. . . . ?" The real motive of Cato probably was not flight from Caesar, "quam ut Stoicorum decretis obtemperaret suumque nomen grandi aliquo facinore clarificaret. . . . Et tibi alia praeter invidiam causa moriendi vanitas stulta?" In his *Hist. Caesaris* (ed. Schneider, p. 292) and in *Ep. Var. 33*, Petrarch notes that his criticism of Cato had been stimulated by Augustine's censures.

44. That is, since Petrarch's enthusiastic epistolary exchanges with Emperor Charles IV during the 1350's. As far as Petrarch himself is concerned, the reappearance of imperial monarchism was not tantamount to a reappearance of the medieval religious arguments in justification of the Empire—the arguments on which Dante's thought had been built. But such an identification was to take place again among Petrarch's pupils and friends, who soon believed to see full harmony between the view of Petrarch in his later years, and Dante's medieval idea of Empire.

45. Petrarca, *Epistolae Seniles*, *Ep. XIV 1*, end of 1373; sometimes copied and printed as a separate pamphlet with the title "Qualis esse debeat, qui rempublicam regit." The references to Caesar in Fracassetti's edition of the *Ep. Sen.*, vol. II, p. 342f.

CHAPTER 6

1. The significance of the Cicero controversy in the Trecento for the rise among humanists of a civic attitude to life was pointed out years ago by this writer in his paper "Cicero and the Roman Civic Spirit in the Middle Ages and the Early Renaissance" (*Bulletin of the John Rylands Library*, XXII [1938], 84-89). But the same controversy also represents an important episode in the history of the humanistic rediscovery of the *Respublica Romana*, and of the Renaissance revolt against the medieval notion of Universal Empire. It is from this viewpoint that the following narrative has been planned, and despite some duplication with the pages just quoted it is different in scope and based on wider source material.

2. "O inquiete semper atque anxie, . . . quid tibi tot contentionibus et prorsum nichil profuturis simultatibus voluisti? Ubi et etati et professioni et fortune tue conveniens otium reliquisti? Quis te falsus glorie splendor senem adolescentium bellis implicuit et per omnes iactatum casus ad indignam philosopho mortem rapuit? . . . Ah quanto satius fuerat philosopho presertim in tranquillo rure senuisse, de perpetua illa, ut ipse quodam scribis loco, non de hac iam exigua vita cogitantem, nullos habuisse fasces, nullis triumphis inhiasse, nullos inflasse tibi animum Catilinas." *Ep. XXIV 3, Le Familiari*, ed. V. Rossi, vol. IV (Firenze, 1942), p. 226f.

3. "Accendit ergo viri illius ingenium solitudo, et quod miraberis odiosa; quid putas factura esset optata, aut quantum putas optanda est, quae vel nolentibus tantum prodest?" *De Vita Solitaria*, II, tr. 8, c. 4 (in the older editions, c. 2); ed. A. Altamura "secondo lo pseudo-autografo Vaticano 3357," Naples 1943, p. 131. Cf. also the polemical passages against Cicero in *De Vita Solitaria*, I, tr. 3, c. 2, and II, tr. 10, c. 7 (in Altamura's ed. c. 6); and in *Rerum Memorandarum Libri*, lib. I, c. 4 and 15, lib. III, c. 43 (according to the numeration of the chapters in the edition by G. Billanovich, in "Edizione Nazionale delle Opere di Petrarca," Firenze, 1943).

4. "Sed quis te furor in Antonium impegit? Amor credo reipublice, quam funditus iam corruisse fatebaris." *Ep. XXIV 3*; ed. Rossi, vol. IV, p. 226. "Neque tamen in vita tua quicquam preter constantiam requiro, et philosophice professioni debitum quietis studium et a civilibus bellis fugam, extincta libertate ac

sepulta iam et complorata republica." *Ep. XXIV 4*, ed. Rossi, p. 228.

5. *Historia Julii Caesaris*, ed. C. F. Chr. Schneider (Leipzig, 1827), p. 292f. *De Remediis*, lib. II, dial. 118.

6. He had asked Milanese friends for a manuscript of Cicero's *Ep. ad Atticum*, but received from the treasures of the old Cathedral library at Vercelli a manuscript of the *Ep. familiares*. See Sabbadini, *Le Scoperte*, vol. I, pp. 34, 75, vol. II, p. 214, and especially Novati's fundamental note in his edition of Salutati's *Epistolario*, vol. II, p. 340.

7. Adherence to the conjecture that Cicero's *De Republica* had been purposely destroyed by the Roman emperors, "qui non ad rempublicam sed ad tyrannidem principatus potentiam convertebant, ne aliquando salutaribus Arpinatis nostri preceptis quis animaretur ad rempublicam liberandam." *Ep. I 20*, 1368, *Epistolario*, vol. I, p. 51. "Caesar ipse, qui nefas rempublicam invasit." *Ep. III 17*, 1374, *Epistolario*, vol. I, p. 197. ". . . omnes Cesares Augustos atque tyrannos . . ." *Ep. VII 11*, 1392(?), *Epistolario*, vol. II, p. 299.

8. "Vidi . . . bellorum civilium fundamenta et quid caput illud orbis terrarum de libertate populica in monarchie detruderit servitutem." *Ep. VIII 7*, 1392, *Epistolario*, vol. II, p. 389.

9. This emerges from Salutati's answers.

10. *Ep. IX 3* and *IX 4*, *Epistolario*, vol. III, pp. 25f., 50.

11. For Vergerio's life see Vol. One, p. 104ff. As to the early role of Padua for Humanism, see Vol. One, p. 4.

12. See the *Epistolario di Pier Paolo Vergerio*, ed. L. Smith ("Fonti per la Storia d'Italia," vol. 74, Rome, 1934), introduction p. xiv f., p. 53, note 2, and the letters nos. xxxi ff.

13. *Ibid.*, *Ep. XXVIII*, p. 55; *Ep. XXXI*, p. 62; *Ep. XXXIII*, p. 66.

14. The first to draw attention to Vergerio's rejoinder seems to have been B. Ziliotto, *La Cultura Letteraria di Trieste e dell' Istria* (Trieste, 1913), p. 40f., but he saw in it nothing but "un' innocente esercitazione rettorica." The text is now available in an "Appendice" to Vergerio's *Epistolario*, ed. Smith, pp. 436-445. See also below note 2 to Chap. 7.

15. "Nunquam . . . tantum corruerat libertas quin manu et consilio erigi posset." *Ibid.*, p. 442.

16. "Ea enim michi matura semper et prestans philosophia visa

est, que in urbibus habitat et solitudinem fugit. . ." Ed. Smith, p. 444. "Et scripsi enim crebro in libris nostris, et ita semper visum est, prestare omnibus vel genere vel vita quisquis ad administrandam rempublicam impertiendosque saluti omnium labores se accommodasset." *Ibid.*, p. 439f.

17. "Neque enim spectatam eius clementiam placebat plus legibus aut senatu valere; nam, ut in libera civitate nomen ipsum crudelitatis odiosum est, ita et clementie invidiosum, nec facile solemus quenquam clementem dicere, nisi qui et crudelis impune esse possit." *Ibid.*, p. 441.

18. ". . . eversa libertate, ut esset tyrannus, qui princeps civis esse, florente urbe, poterat. . ." "Non enim amicior dominus quam iustior michi civis querebatur." *Ibid.*, pp. 443, 442f. See p. 441f. for the preceding passages referred to above.

19. The dates for Vergerio's later life are now established by L. Smith's fundamental "Note Cronologiche Vergeriane," in *Archivio Veneto-Tridentino*, x (1926), 149-157, and *Archivio Veneto*, ser. v, vol. IV (1928), 92-141.

20. For the completion of *De Ingenuis Moribus* by June, 1402, see L. Smith in his edition of Vergerio's *Epistolario*, p. 254, and G. Calò in *La Rinascita*, II (1939), 228, 232, reprinted in *Dall' Umanesimo*, pp. 40, 43. That Vergerio was tutor of Ubertino da Carrara has been denied by Smith, *Epistolario*, p. xxii ff., but the counter-arguments proposed by G. Calò in order to show that this traditional assumption has not yet been convincingly refuted (*Rinascita*, pp. 243, 245f.; *Dall' Umanesimo*, pp. 56, 58f.) are strong.

21. See H. Baron in *Bulletin of the John Rylands Library*, XXII (1938), 91.

22. In 1446 or 1447, according to the observations of A. Segarizzi in his edition of the *De Laudibus Patavii* in *Rerum Italicarum Scriptores*, n. ser. tom. XXIV, parte XV (1902), p. viii.

23. For this tendency of the *Vitae Principum Carrariensium* and for the reference to Caesar, see B. Ziliotto, *La Cultura Letteraria*, p. 59.

24. As has been established in the careful "Ricerche intorno al *De principibus carrariensibus et gestis eorum liber* attribuito a Pier Paolo Vergerio seniore" (*Università di Padova, Pubblicazioni della Facoltà di Lettere e Filosofia*, vol. XXIII, Padua,

1946) by Carmela Marchente, who also definitely proves Vergerio's authorship.

25. See Vergerio's *De Monarchia* in his *Epistolario*, ed. Smith, pp. 447-450. The only date proposed by Smith is the span of time spent by Vergerio in Padua, 1390-1404. But the fragment must be younger, and in fact considerably younger, than 1394. For on p. 449, line 4, it speaks of Francesco the Elder of Carrara, who died 1394 as Giangaleazzo's prisoner, as of someone "remembered" by Vergerio ("nostre memorie"), i.e. as dead, and the tone of the passage suggests that Francesco's death was not a recent event. Since Vergerio's attitude in the mid-1390's can be inferred from the fact that in 1394 he composed his defense against Petrarch of Cicero as a champion of the *Respublica Romana*, and since from 1397 to 1400 Vergerio was away from Padua in Bologna and Florence, we may take it as certain that *De Monarchia* was written after his return from Florence to Padua—between 1400 and 1405, when he was the tutor of a young prince of the Carrara family, to whom he dedicated his *De Ingenuis Moribus*. This more precise delimitation of the time in which *De Monarchia* must have been written makes it possible to reconstruct the development of Vergerio's political outlook: From an enthusiastic republican sentiment in the time of his contacts with the Salutati of the early 1390's, Vergerio's path led to the monarchical ideals of the tyrant court at the very time when a new republican outlook on history was being built up among the citizen-humanists of Florence.

26. *Epistolario*, p. 448.

27. "Illud michi ante omnia certum videtur, monarchiam, id est unius principatum, multitudinis imperio prestare, et ad similitudinem huius machine mundane, que tam firma pace, tam certis legibus iuncta constat, mortales homines regi, atque ad regulam illius summi imperatoris, qui cuncta solus arbitrio suo moderatur, vitam nostram conferri. Namque, ut est in omni natura unum primum a quo cetera defluant, ita et in communione viventium esse decet unum qui ceteros dirigat. Quid enim esse potest similius Deo et illi perpetuo celorum consensui quam princeps bonus et bene composita civitas?" *Ibid.*, p. 447.

28. N. Festa, *Saggio sull' "Africa" del Petrarca* (Palermo, 1926), pp. 40-46; on the date—1380-96—*ibid.*, p. 42. For the

appraisal of Vergerio's work on the *Africa*, see also G. Billanovich, *Petrarca Letterato*, vol. 1 (Rome, 1947), pp. 381-384.

29. For a correction of the accepted information on Vergerio's relations with Florence after 1400, see *Humanistic and Political Literature*, Chapter IV, section 5, "A Letter of Pier Paolo Vergerio (*Epistola LXXXXVI*) and Bruni's *Laudatio*."

30. Conversino, whom Lehnerdt was the first to distinguish from Malpaghini—both had originally been known under the name of 'Giovanni da Ravenna'—has become for us a living personality through Sabbadini's reconstruction of his life and works in *Giovanni da Ravenna. Insigne Figura d'Umanista (1343-1408)* (Como, 1924). Sabbadini reproduces extracts from most of Conversino's writings, but confines himself to paragraphs that contain data on Conversino's life. An analysis and historical appraisal of Conversino's humanistic ideas, his moral philosophy, and political attitude, are still a desideratum. As to the *Dragmalogia*, a critical text would have to be based on the two extant manuscripts, both considerably corrupt at many points, Paris, Bibl. Nat. Ms. lat. 6494, and Venice, Fondazione Querini-Stampalia Ms. IX 11. Some extensive passages from the text of the Paris manuscript are reproduced in the notes and appendices of M. Korelin's work, written in Russian, on the early Italian Humanism (Moscow, 1892; see note 18 to Appendix 3). The present writer could consult the Querini-Stampalia manuscript. The following quotations are partly from photostats the author was kindly permitted to take of portions of the Venetian manuscript, and partly from extracts which he copied many years ago and cannot recheck at present. For a survey of the chief contents of the work see Sabbadini, pp. 105-107. The unusual term of "Dragmalogia," by which the work is conveniently cited, seems characteristic of the transitional position of Conversino's Humanism. It represents an effort without a future to find, with medieval-traditional means, a name for the literary genre which was going to be called by the name "Dialogus." Since the disappearance of the ancient theatre, from the early Middle Ages onward, the meaning of the term "drama" had become obscured and in medieval literature "Dragma" or "Dragmaticon" had become identified with "interrogatio and responsio"—what we should call "dialogue." (See P. Lehmann, "Mittelalterliche Büchertitel," *Sitzungsberichte der Bayerischen Akademie der Wissenschaften, Philos.-hist. Klasse*, 1948, Heft 4,

p. 54f., and W. Cloetta in his *Beitraege zur Literaturgeschichte des Mittelalters und der Renaissance*, vol. I [Halle a. S., 1890], p. 24ff., 49, where a number of examples and references to the dictionaries are given. Lehmann and Cloetta do not seem to know the form "Dragmalogia".) Conversino, the humanist of the late Trecento, we may say, continued the medieval misinterpretation of the traditional term, while trying to give it a more classical appearance by making it look Greek.

31. This advice is mentioned in a letter of Conversino to Vergerio, written in 1406, and published by Sabbadini, *op. cit.*, p. 229.

32. The cessation of payments to the Paduan scholars, and Conversino's indignation about this action, are described on the introductory pages of the *Dragmalogia*. For the precise date of the treatise see Sabbadini, *Giovanni da Ravenna*, p. 105.

33. ". . . et civitas calcatis potencium motibus tirampnica potestate respiravit." Fol. 18v.

34. Fol. 19r and 20r.

35. "Unius non modo optimi (tunc velut numen esset in terris), sed mediocriter boni eligibilius esse regimen arbitror." Fol. 16b. ". . . tute fatebere unius etate regentis quam seculo populi urbi felicitatem magis adolevisse." Fol. 18v.

36. "Ludovicus Rex Hunnorum regnum illud discis[s]um, inhumanum, sine lege, sine more cultuque divino, erexit, composuit, ampliavit, . . . subque disciplina ac lege vite racionalis reformavit." Fol. 19r.

37. "Haud me tempero quin alium, vestris affinem aquis, principem Estensem, Nicholaum (non hunc ephebum, sed penultimum ex germanis) subiiciam. Nam ceno inmeabilem et gravem odore Ferariam illimem [MS: illimen] ac salubrem reddidit, vicos lateribus ac saxo stravit, domos assericias lapideas dimisit, castra et turres erexit, opida munivit. Sic denique prudencia et circumspectione augmento urbis ornamentoque indulsit, ut pro mensura nulla vicinarum opulencior neque frequencior specciosiorque visatur." Fol. 19r.

38. One need not hesitate, "senioris Francisci urbanas laudes supponere, qui suscepto Padue sceptro menia urbis suplevit, vacua spacia domibus constructis ornavit, artes auxit, lanificinam induxit, civium facultates promovit, studia literarum unice excoluit. Quid loquar pontes, aquarum ductus [MS: devotus], amnes [MS: annes] circumactos, vales exhaustas in arvaque versas, siccos [? MS:

doctos] montes uvis fluere peregrinis, turres opidaque constructa, alia fossis murisque munita, tot denique et tanta fecit, ut minime etatis unius hominis sed multorum opera nescius iudicaret; brevique, nondum senex, eo decoris et amplitudinis rem provexit Euganeam, ut populus toto seculo non implesset. Num ambigis, ad vos parumper oculum retrahe et intueberis turrim Cluse a magnificencia Venetica, omni cessante obice, lustro non exactam, claustraque pelagi lustris pluribus coherceri cepta adhuc [MS: ad hec] infecta spectari. Adeo lenta sunt populorum negocia, solicita dominorum. Comunitates presentibus estuant malis, torpenter asurgunt [MS: asurgant] ad futura." Fol. 19r. On the comparative affinity of oligarchic Venice to efficient monarchy: Venice, though a republic, is free of some of the evils of a republican regime because she is an oligarchy. "Oligarchicus [MS: olingarchius] principatus est diligenti pene tirampnidi compar, propter quod Franciscus prior [Venice] tirampnorum urbem nominare solebat . . ." Fol. 18v. Conversino's description of the beautification and modernization of Padua and its countryside by Francesco *il Vecchio* of Carrara (1355-88) may serve as a precious matter-of-fact commentary on the picture of the ideal prince that Petrarch had drawn for Francesco in his *Ep. Sen. XIV 1* in 1373. (See for this "Mirror for Princes" Vol. One, p. 96.)

39. Princes, "quippe amplissima orti fortuna magnificeque educati, magnis eciam assueti, proni redduntur ad magna. Item maiorum imagines nec non proprie estus glorie tum ad magnifica tum ad liberalia factaque clementer calcar aditur. Hinc rursus facilius donant, remittunt facilius, quia nec in acquirendo laborant, nec paciuntur iacturam largiendo." Fol. 17r-17v.

40. "Novissime omnium in hac virtutis laudibus Johannes Galeacz liberalitatem supergressus est, non dico poetas et oratores, qui rarissimi comparent, sed medicos eciam iuris consultos qui predicarentur ad eliciendum fruendumque indiscussa erogatione [MS: erragacione] munificus." Fol. 17v. A similar reference to Giangaleazzo's patronage is found in the introduction to the work, fol. 4r.

41. "Multitudo autem surda et pene inflexibilis ad beneficium, ad veniam. Nam nisi consonent universi, frustra postulabis. Quod ferre desideras, inhibebit alius. . . . Amplo alter animo dona et largitiones magnificas suadebit. Contra, qui angusto singula digerit, publicis facultatibus censebit esse parcendum. Quid multa? Dum

sua quisque passione raptatur, dificile est plures habere concordes ac per hoc et impetrari quod cupitur." Fol. 17r.

42. One finds that monarchs like Giangaleazzo have encouraged outstanding men in every branch of intellectual activities, "quod, ubi imperet multitudo, raro leges factum, rarius cernes. Profecto nonquam poetica, oratoria, philosophia, cronographia, ceteraque sublimis opere studia, dempta principancium liberalitate et cura, eo decoris incrementique pervenissent. . . . At dominans multitudo nullius virtutem gratis respicit, mercenarias recipit, ociosas aspernatur. Dum enim quisque vel stringit nummum, vel extra limen gloria[m] non licetur, poetas ut non sapit ita contempnit, et mavult canes alere quam philosophum aut lectorem. Quod quam officiat gloriae silencio choercere non possum. Vestra res publica, florens et magnifica, quam nulla Europe felicitate rerumque amplitudine equiperat, uno dumtaxat urbis nomine pervagatur. Cum autem clarissimis viris speciosissimisque exemplis fulxerit, per tot secula domi ac milicie illustria facinora quis novit? quis legit? quis meminit? Suis nota temporibus, obducta nunc oblivionis nube, laudibus vacant." The Venetian: "Inficiari nequit et absque nota ruboris audiri quod [? MS: que] res publica terra marique totum orbem gestarum rerum gloria eo usque maximis editis operibus percensuit, memoratuque digniora tum pace tum bello gessit. Quorum quidem si florerent historie, vix peno romanoque cederemus. Verum magis [MS: *m*] studemus suam quisque domum auro locuplectare quam fama; quamquam minime desunt, arbitror, qui gesta analibus cogant." Whereupon the Paduan answers: "Caduca profecto . . . predicacio. Nam maternis aut nudis vocibus al[l]igantur. Quo fit ut, quemadmodum rudes picture spectentur, ac illicet pretereantur. At vero scita ac dives oracio splendorem indit rebus et imprimit magiestatem, efficitque ut ex lectione voluptas, ex voluptate laus, ex laude fama prodeat. Illud preterea meritis laudibus officit quod, eam si qui luccubracionem capessunt, . . . vestrigene sunt et abrogant [MS: abrogam] rerum fides. Nam sicut propria laus indecenter exprimitur, sic proprie gentis honor sine mendacii suspicione aut culpa iactancie non extolitur. Unde Roma ab externis scriptoribus gestarum rerum gloriam plurimum mutuata est, quorum ocia princeps, fortuna vel animo, plenis favoribus aluit [MS: aluerunt]; quippe rarum ac celeste munus eloquencia non est negocii et indigencie, sed quietis et opulencie. . ." Fol. 17v-18r. On Venice's commercial spirit, there is also a special, extensive

excursus, full of bitter complaints of Conversino, on fol. 29v[I]-30r[II].

43. The Venetian interlocutor and defender of the Venetian Republic introduces the section dealing with the relative merits of Tyranny and Republic with the words: "Tuus iste sermo de gubernatoris officio in hanc me coniecturam divertit, uniusne principis an plurium dominatu *ceu nostra ceu Thuscha* [apparently a reference to Florence] felicius urbs regatur." (Fol. 16v). Beyond this, he does not cite Florence in the course of his argument.

44. In the introductory words of the work: "Quid enim ignominiosius Cesaree magiestati, quam si mercenarius agnoscitur. Hunc, inquam, elatio florentina stipendio allexit in Latium. . . . Pudor Italice probitatis accire barbaros, quo preda barbaris pateat Italia."

45. For the details of this relationship, see *Humanistic and Political Literature*, Chap. v, Excursus "The Date of Salutati's *Epistola XII 10*," esp. notes 8-10.

46. Cf. already Loschi's modest denial when, on Salutati's death, he was told he was expected to take Salutati's position in the humanistic movement: "How could I, who was born in the region . . . settled by the Cimbri whom Marius had conquered, how could I ever exclude from the heritage of their compatriot and master the Florentines who are born to eloquence?" (See Loschi's letter to Giovanni Tinti da Fabriano, Oct. 25, 1406, in Salutati's *Epistolario*, ed. Novati, vol. IV, p. 477). For another example of involuntary admission that the Humanism and historiography of the Florentine school were superior, see the letter of Bartolomeo della Capra discussed in Vol. One, p. 359f., and Vol. Two, p. 432.

47. This feature of Florentine historiography, which has not always been sufficiently taken into account, is excellently brought out by Sabbadini in his *Il Metodo degli Umanisti* (Florence, 1920) with the following words: In Venice, Milan, Genoa, and Naples, "the historians were commissioned by the Republic or by the Court, in whose interest and for whose greater glory they had to slant their writings. The only exception are the Florentine historians, who, although they tend to extol their own city, set to work out of a personal urge and of patriotic feeling." (p. 84f.)

48. See the letter of Bartolomeo della Capra mentioned in note 46 above.

49. "Libertatem utique probo et tecum pariter . . .; tirampnidem fonditus odio, set eam libertatem quam unius, non multorum, iusticia dispenset, quoniam solidior quidem et tranquilior. Nam ubi unus dominatur, suo quisque negocio prorsus publici securus vacat. In multitudinis autem imperio dominus quisque haberi vult. . . ." (Fol. 19v.) Fol. 23f. asserts that true liberty can be obtained only in a life of leisure in country surroundings, unencumbered by social and political burdens; and the long section fol. 31ff. is to prove that the freedom obtainable in a life of scholarship and independence of mind is more genuine than political liberty.

50. "Porro quam uno principe rerum protendatur felicitas, hinc latissime claret quod ingenia philosophorum, poetarum, oratorum, historias describentium [MS: describen̊] alumnata [MS: alonata], fota provectaque a principibus animumve principis gerentibus reperies. Augusto orbis domino, Maro, Flachus, Naso, ad nostra usque tempora cellebres, aliique incelebres non pauci, indulgencia liberali vacacionem et facultates ociis habuerunt. Deinde orbem Justiniano moderante, formam et ordinem iuris civilis utilitas cepit." Fol. 17v. "Urbem Romam Cesar Augustus—taceo signa ab hostibus recepta, victas gentes, ultroque deditos reges, directos legibus populos, ab incendiis restauratas urbes, stratas scilicibus vias—principibus et facultatibus exauxit [MS: exausit] illustravitque ornamentis, ut obiens gloriaretur, invenisse latericiam, marmoream relinquere." Fol. 19r.

51. "Per reges romanum fundatum est et vires cepit imperium. Deinde, ubi regi superbo superbi cives parere contempserunt, populariter res acta est, deus bone quanto fluctu et turbine civitatis, primo tribunis [MS: tribunus] plebis, deinde militaribus, mox insolencia decemvirali populum urbemque vexantibus. Inficiari non possumus romanum populum sub consulibus magna gessisse, licet despectum sepe atque derisum. Sed quantulum est ad eam collata magnitudinem imperii et dignitatis, ad quam sub cesaribus sublimatum exauctumque [MS: exauctam, sublimatam exauctamque] legimus." Fol. 18v.

52. "Atque Atheniensium et Lacedemoniorum predicata res publica opesque et bellis externis et civili sedicione semper turbulentissime fatigate sunt, sub regibus respirarunt." Fol. 18v.

"Plus glorie magiestati Romane Augusto moderante, quam multis ante seculis, acrevisse memoratur." Fol. 19r.

53. ". . . quod omnis creature status, quo similior conditori, hoc pulcrior, ordinacior et perfectior existit; quare cum rerum auctor et rector unus sit, unius gubernationem [MS: gubernamen], quoniam universi conformius, melius esse iudico." Fol. 16v.

54. "Conducibilius ac divinius urbes ac regna mecum fateare oportet unius quam multitudinis ducatu componi, quod . . . creator, nempe deus, hominem continuo sub obediencie lege constituit. . . ." Just as it is in every family and house, "unum gubernatorem, cui pareatur ad nutum, navigancium salus efflagitat. In officina vulgarium unus ministeria sortitur, obtemperant singuli. Ecclesia militans reverenciam uni et obedienciam profitetur. Claustrales unius discipline, quatenus fructuosior existat tranquiliorque spiritualis religio, subduntur. Quoniam dampnabiliter superbiret impenderetque ruine, si moderamen superioris . . . contempnens propria usurparet vivere libertate, omnis prope Theutonis plaga, velut Italia [MS: Italie], Romanum Imperatorem veneratur. . ." Fol. 19r-v.

CHAPTER 7

1. We have no less than three Latin, one Italian, and one English editions of *De Tyranno*. The Latin text was edited by A. v. Martin, *Coluccio Salutati's Traktat vom Tyrannen* (Berlin, 1913), and by F. Ercole, *Der Tractatus de Tyranno von Coluccio Salutati* (Berlin, 1914); both editions have fundamental introductions; Ercole's text is founded on a more complete manuscript basis. Ercole's introduction has been republished in Italian in his volume *Da Bartolo all' Althusio. Saggi Sulla Storia del Pensiero Pubblicistico del Rinascimento Italiano* (Florence, 1932, pp. 219-389), and the text of his edition—used in the following quotations—is reprinted in *Coluccio Salutati. Il Trattato 'De Tyranno' e Lettere Scelte*, ed. F. Ercole ("Scrittori Politici Italiani," vol. IX, Bologna, 1942), pp. 1-38. The latter volume, on pp. 153-184, also includes an Italian translation. An English translation, with a discussion of the political conditions of the late Trecento interpreted in the light of Salutati's treatise, is found in E. Emerton's *Humanism and Tyranny. Studies in the Italian Trecento* (Cambridge, Mass., 1926), pp. 25-116.

2. If we could be sure that the letter was written in Florence, as L. Smith originally assumed (*Archivio Veneto*, ser. V, vol. 4, [1928], 97), the probability that it did not escape Salutati's attention, would of course be great. But Smith himself, in his edition of Vergerio's *Epistolario* (Rome, 1934), p. 436, later assumed the letter to have been written at Padua—though he added a question mark. All we really know is that Vergerio from 1390 to 1397 lived at Padua, and that once during that period, some time around 1394, he travelled to Florence. (Cf. Smith's own statement in his "Prefazione" to the *Epistolario*, p. XV.) As a consequence, the letter, which to judge from the manuscripts preserved was transcribed only in a few copies, may never have circulated in Florence and come to Salutati's notice. Bruni did not know Vergerio's letter while he was in Florence, but discovered it many years later during a stay at Arezzo, as he tells in his *Ep. IV 4* of January 2, 1416: ". . . ego nuper Aretii epistolam quandam eiusdem [M. Tullii] reperi, quem te [i.e. Poggio] nunquam vidisse certo scio. In ea non sine stomacho Tullius noster Petrarchae respondet." (*Leonardi Bruni Arretini Epistolarum Libri VIII*, ed. L. Mehus [Florence, 1741], vol. I, p. 111).

3. "Primo [i.e. in the first chapter] docebimus quid tyrannus, . . . ne forsitan in equivoco fluctuemus." In chapters II to IV "discutiemus an tyrannum occidere liceat," and "disseremus . . . an Caesar inter tyrannos rationabiliter . . . debeat numerari" and "numquid iure fuerit an iniuria . . . occisus." "Ultimo vero probabimus divinissimum Dantem civem et compatriotam meum, quod eos in inferni profundum demerserit, non errasse." Prefatio, §5.

4. Since Conversino visited Florence early in 1400 and had conversations on literary subjects with Salutati at that time (see above note 45 to Chap. 6 and the references there given), it is even probable that some of the ideas of Conversino with which we have become familiar were then discussed directly between Salutati, already occupied with his *De Tyranno*, and his north-Italian friend who was to compose his *Dragmalogia* only four years later.

5. "Nullusne est rei publice status in monarchia? Nullamne Roma rem publicam habuit, donec sub regibus fuit? Nullamne post Cesarem habitura fuit sub alicuius quamvis [Edn.: quemvis] sanctissimi principis dominatu?" *De Tyranno*, cap. IV, §14.

6. "Quod si nichil divinius et melius quam mundus regitur uno solo presidente deo, tanto melius est humanum regimen, quanto propinquius ad illud accedit. Illi vero similius esse non potest, quam unico principante." IV, 15-16.

7. V, 4.

8. "Verum cum autor iste doctissimus christianus videret ex rerum effectibus, qui divine voluntatis verissimi testes sunt, deum decrevisse res hominum sub una Romanorum redigere monarchia, nonne debuit eos, qui conati sunt huic ordinationi, qua ratione potuerunt, obsistere, velut dispositioni Dei contrarios, inter damnatos et reprobos deputare?" V, 6.

9. IV, 10-11.

10. IV, 12-13.

11. "Potuit, imo debuit vos docere Sillanorum temporum vastitas proximaque dissensio, ad illa tollenda necessarium fuisse monarcham in quem ordine debito totum corpus rei publice dirigeretur. Nam in illa, quam diligebas, politia vel aristocratia, malorum remedium, vel esse non poterat dissidentibus animis, vel tam difficulter et periculose, quod nichil minus tempori conveniret. Sicut, occiso Cesare ruptaque monarchici principatus

armonia, rerum experientia clarum fecit: mox enim ad bella civilia fuit reventum; ut nedum utile, sed necessarium fuerit ad unum devenire principem, in cuius manibus tot rerum motus et animorum contrarietates iustitia et equitate regnantis simul discerent convenire atque coalescere. Quod si factum in Octavio non fuisset, numquam romana rabies quievisset. . ." IV, 17-18.

12. ". . . quando quidem non omnino ne quisquam, sed uter regeret et rerum summam et moderamen assumeret, certabatur. . . . Utrimque par impietas, par furor et equalis ambitio, par votum opprimendi concives, tollendi leges, et illud equum ducere, quod placeret prodessetque victoribus. Non tuende rei publice, sed opprimende certamen illud fuit. Quis iustius induit arma, scire nefas, ut ille ait." III, 9. The source of inspiration for this objective estimate of the guilt existing on either side is, doubtlessly, Petrarch's *Historia Julii Caesaris* and particularly those sections of it referred to below (notes 19 and 22). One may admit that Salutati, in taking Petrarch as his model, was not a slavish imitator; with the help of Petrarch's appraisal of the characters of the leading Roman statesmen, he produced an analysis of the political situation of Rome—an historical task not yet performed by Petrarch. But in spite of this relative originality of Salutati's treatise, the failure of recent students to weigh at all Petrarch's predecessorship in respects vital to Salutati's approach must be said to have distorted and over-magnified the significance of *De Tyranno*.

13. Ercole, in the introduction to his edition of *De Tyranno*, p. 172f., and in *Da Bartolo*, p. 379f.; A. v. Martin, in his edition of *De Tyranno*, pp. 40f., 59f.

14. Both Ercole and v. Martin, encountering these surviving medieval elements in the treatise, judged them carry-overs of negligible significance; the relevance of the work was to be sought exclusively in its new realistic method. It is not until near the end of the treatise—thus both argued—that the medieval theological arguments appear and Caesar is considered as creator of the imperial dignity; up to that point, Caesar is visualized realistically as if he were one of the *signori* of the Trecento (cf. Ercole, in the introduction to his edition, p. 14; *Da Bartolo*, pp. 228f., 266ff.) and Caesar's assassins are discussed and condemned according to "natural" political standards (cf. v. Martin, p. 42). The weakness of this appraisal is that the late appearance in the treatise of the arguments derived from medieval tradition does

not mean that they are of small significance to the author; the section in which they are taken up is the chapter which deals with the verdict on Caesar given by Dante—the climax of the entire discussion, and the logical context for acceptance or rejection of the medieval teaching of Universal Monarchy. The point that matters is not frequency or place, but the function of the surviving medieval notions in the web of Salutati's argument: the question whether the realism found in the treatise extends to those fields where the medieval tradition could be vitally endangered, or whether the mainsprings of Dante's thought—the medieval ideas of Universal Empire and of the likeness of Monarchy to the divine order of the world—have remained intact.

15. See Vol. One, p. 46f. and 86f.

16. See Vol. One, p. 119.

17. See notes 19 and 34 to Chap. 3.

18. See Vol. One, p. 51.

19. "Sic adeo mors illa indignissima visa est displicuisse Deo et hominibus." *Benvenuti de Rambaldis de Imola Comentum super Dantis Aldigherij Comoediam*, ed. P. Lacaita (Florence, 1887), vol. II, p. 560. Rambaldi's whole description, pp. 560-561, of the hostile reaction of the Roman people against the assassins is nothing but a repetition—a plagiarism, according to modern standards—of what Petrarch had dramatically narrated at the end of his *Historia Caesaris* (ed. C. E. Chr. Schneider, Leipzig 1827, pp. 334-335), where the final conclusion had also been: "ut evidenter ostenderetur caedem illam nec Deo nec hominibus placuisse."

20. "Nota etiam quod Caesar visus est dignissimus tali morte; quia qui totam terram civilis sanguinis fusione resperserat, suo sanguine totam curiam debuit inundare. . ." *Benvenuti . . . Comentum*, vol. II, p. 561.

21. "Unde nota, quod pulcerrima pars sapientis est nullius esse partis, sicut scriptum est in Inferno." Comm. on *Par.* canto XVII. Vol. V, p. 195.

22. ". . . sed uterque petebat regnum, uterque ingratus patriae. . ." IV, p. 447. To be compared with Petrarch, *Historia Caesaris*, ed. Schneider, p. 217f., ". . . ut utriusque partis merita non usque adeo, ut putantur, imparia et utrumque . . . regnare voluisse . . . constaret."

23. ". . . quod romanum imperium a Deo habet universalem

gubernationem orbis." "Et hic nota bene quod monarchia romani imperii facta est sub Caesare, ampliata sub Augusto, sub Traiano reparata, sub Constantino justificata, sub Justiniano ordinata, sub Theodosio sustentata, sub Karolo adiuta." *Benvenuti . . . Comentum*, IV, pp. 423, 418f.

24. IV, p. 423.

25. ". . . ut, sicut unus est princeps in summo coelo, a quo dependent omnes, . . . ita esset unus princeps in terra." IV, p. 435.

26. "Dei dispositione factum est, ut victor Caesar fuerit." *De Tyranno*, III, 10.

27. Cf. this writer's references to the general historical interest in the interpretation of early Renaissance art in such works as M. Dvořák, *Geschichte der Italienischen Kunst im Zeitalter der Renaissance* (2 vols., 1927-8), and G. Weise, *Die geistige Welt der Gotik und ihre Bedeutung für Italien* (1939) in *Archiv für Kulturgeschichte*, XXI (1930), 106-112, and in *American Historical Review*, XLVI (1941), 621ff., and his discussion of the problem of "Realism" in the art and in the intellectual life of the Renaissance in *Journal of the History of Ideas*, IV (1943), 45-48, and *ibid.* XI (1950), 503-505.

28. In the chapter "Republicanism Versus Dante's Glorification of Caesar," Vol. One, p. 40f.

29. See Vol. One, p. 82ff.

30. See Vol. One, pp. 61 and 84.

31. For the details of Salutati's and Bruni's attitudes to the Sulla theory, see the references in note 60 to Chap. 3.

32. We can here only mention, but not discuss in detail, a related aspect of *De Tyranno* which must not be entirely forgotten when we weigh our findings concerning Salutati's cautious reserve toward all the new trends of thought that were potentially dangerous to the medieval tradition. Even in the introductory juridical part of Salutati's treatise, we find no bold and forthright contributions from the perspective of the Italian city-state republic, but rather the same cautious manner, and the same attempts at solutions that would leave intact the early-Trecento conceptions of the supremacy of imperial power. F. Ercole—in the preface to his edition of *De Tyranno*, and in his *Dal Bartolo all' Althusio*—has made a detailed comparison between the juridical discussions in *De Tyranno* and the earlier doctrines of the great Guelph jurist Bartolo da Sassoferrato set forth in his *De Tyrannia* (about

1355). Ercole's studies reveal that Salutati not only failed to modify the teachings of Guelph jurisprudence on the relation between Italian city-states and imperial power in favor of the sovereignty of the city-state *populi*, but that he in fact produced a theory which in some respects enhanced the role of the Empire as the source of all public law. For whereas Bartolo had made a theoretical distinction between cities "acknowledging a superior" (*superiorem recognoscentes*) where public authority was to proceed from the emperor as the overlord, and autonomous cities (*civitates superiorem non recognoscentes*) where the government rested on the will and the explicit consent of the citizens, Salutati was practically satisfied that for all governments in central and northern Italy concerted action by both these final authorities was needed in every case—public acclamation of the rulers by the citizens as well as bestowal of the office of imperial "vicar" on the city-state government by the Emperor. In view of what we have observed about the general mood and tendency of Salutati's treatise, the ultimate purpose of these juridical comments, too, may be interpreted as an effort to reinforce the crumbling foundations of the idea of Empire because these were needed for the preservation of Dante's medieval thought.

33. The close affinity between the underlying juridical definitions of Tyranny in Salutati's *De Tyranno* and in Bartolo's *De Tyrannia* was first noticed by Ercole. In spite of this affinity, Ercole did not believe that Salutati had known Bartolo's work, but thought it more probable that Salutati found his way to the same argument by working independently from the same ancient and medieval sources. (Introduction to Ercole's edition, p. 112ff.; *Da Bartolo*, p. 315ff., esp. p. 320.) Emerton, on the other hand, (*Humanism and Tyranny*, p. 120f.), reviewing the facts established by Ercole, concluded that "there can be no doubt whatever that Salutati knew Bartolus' treatise"; and in 1942 Ercole, in his reedition of *De Tyranno*, seems to have come nearer to this view, since he conceded that Salutati's distinction of two types of Tyranny was "*perhaps* taken over from Bartolo" ("forse desunta da Bartolo"; p. xxxv). It is important to recognize Salutati's dependence on Bartolo, if we are to avoid overmagnifying the originality and significance of the introductory juridical chapter of Salutati's treatise. The purpose of *De Tyranno* was to defend Dante's politico-historical philosophy with intellectual weapons

taken from Petrarch's Humanism, and the first chapter merely was to present some clear definitions, and proper terminology, from current legal theories that could aid this purpose. *De Tyranno* cannot be adequately appraised as being in any way an original contribution to the ideas of public law in the Renaissance; its historical place depends on how much or little it contributed to the growth of politico-historical thought.

34. Ercole, who assumed that censures of Caesar and Dante from a republican standpoint had been wide-spread in the fourteenth century (see note 19 to Chap. 3), saw in Caesar's vindication by the chancellor of the Florentine Republic a sign of the "independence of Salutati's historical criticism and of the originality of his thought," a triumph over blind adherence to "traditional" standards. (Ercole's edition, p. 193; *Da Bartolo*, p. 226ff.) But since Ercole's assertion that Caesar and in particular Dante's glorification of Caesar had been attacked before Salutati's time is completely unfounded, this argument does not hold. (See the note just quoted.) To A. v. Martin, Salutati's rejection of the criticism of Caesar seemed to be tantamount to a great advance toward modern thinking because in Martin's eyes the mark of modern political realism is relativism—the realization that the problem of Republic versus Monarchy is incapable of an absolute decision. Now if this realization is thought to imply that the modern historian who deals with the contest between Caesar and the last advocates of the *Respublica Romana* ought to consider Caesar's monarchy an historic necessity, and to criticize those who resisted that historical trend—if this is the implication, then we should be compelled to adjudge the entire historiography of the Quattrocento and the early Cinquecento, including Machiavelli, as less "modern" than Salutati's treatise. And this indeed is the consequence drawn by v. Martin: Salutati's historical appraisal of Rome's development from the *Respublica* to the *Imperium*, says v. Martin, is less prejudiced and more realistic than that of the doctrinaire Machiavelli who displays a "fanatical cult" of the republican ideal and "shows himself incapable of forgiving the founding of a monarchy even to a Caesar"; in this respect, Salutati, whose thinking was otherwise medieval in many ways, is a "genuine Renaissance personality" ("eine echte Renaissance-Persoenlichkeit") and "incontestably more modern than Machiavelli" ("unstreitig moderner als Machiavelli." *Op. cit.*, pp. 66, 74).

It is hardly necessary to point out that v. Martin's standards are proved unsound by the very absurdity of these their consequences. A considered historical criticism of the *Imperium Romanum* and its founder Caesar, based on a sympathetic understanding of the role of civic freedom, was one of the essential traits and achievements of politico-historical thought in the Florentine Quattrocento and early Cinquecento; no adequate appraisal of the new and the old in Salutati's *De Tyranno* is possible unless we succeed in drawing a picture of the period which leaves room for that basic fact.

35. "Nonne politicum est, et omnium sapientum sententiis diffinitum, monarchiam omnibus rerum publicarum conditionibus preferendam, si tamen contingat virum bonum et studiosum sapientie presidere? Nulla libertas maior quam optimo principi cum iusta precipiat obedire." *De Tyranno*, IV, 14.

36. "Quare concludamus illos Cesaris occisores non tyrannum occidisse, sed patrem patrie et clementissimum ac legitimum principem orbis terre, et tam graviter contra rem publicam erravisse, quam grave et detestabile potest esse in quiescente re publica civilis belli furorem et rabiem excitare. Nec illis imponere volo superbiam spiritus, qua nedum meliorem supra se perpeti non poterant . . . Non imponam et ambitionem, qui . . . sperabant . . . inter summos Rome . . . principes numerari: hanc optabant: hanc intendebant gloriam. Sed ea non parricidio, non scelere, non superbia, non ambitione paranda fuit." IV, 19-20.

37. "Tot quidem calamitates sequi solent totque scandala concitari, cum status rei publice commutatur, quod omnia satius tollerare sit, quam in mutationis periculum divenire. . . . Quarum rerum metu, tolleranda potius hominis vita fuit, non Cesaris solum, qui tanta clementia sicut legitur utebatur, sed etiam Sille vel Marii, qui non poterant civili sanguine satiari." IV, 9-10.

38. See for instance more recently S. Frascino in *Civiltà Moderna*, II (1930), 871, and E. Emerton, *Humanism and Tyranny* (see note 1 above), pp. 56-58, 63. Since Emerton's small but thoughtful and well-written book has served English-speaking students for more than twenty-five years as a cicerone to the political problems of the early Renaissance, it should be noted that his picture of "Humanism and Tyranny . . . in the Italian Trecento" is basically derived from this reading of Salutati's *De Tyranno*. In Emerton's interpretation, the struggle

for survival in which the local states of medieval Italy were engaged throughout the second half of the Trecento, was bound to lead to the obsolescence of republican liberty and to the emergence of powerful families and individuals everywhere (pp. 46ff., 58f.); in Florence, "Salutati, the practical man, must have felt it [this calamity] coming and, however much he may have disapproved, in theory, of every form of tyranny," he must have realized the benefit and necessity of "a single directing will" (p. 56). This, says Emerton, is the only possible explanation of "why a man of Salutati's type should have thought it important, toward the close of a long life, to put into literary form his views as to the nature of despotic government, and why he should have shown so much consideration for a kind of rule which he himself characterizes as the worst plague of human society" (p. 58). This inference is also the only way to explain Salutati's vindication of Caesar. "He saw the empire of Rome torn, like his beloved Italy, by furious party warfare and brought back to comparative unity and peace by the successful if unconstitutional usurpation of one man, and he had come to believe, after a lifetime of intimate knowledge of affairs, that the salvation of his country lay along the same road" (p. 63). When Emerton wrote these words, Mussolini had just been erecting his dictatorship in Italy, and Emerton, as he himself expounds (pp. 59-63), was using the events of his time to explain, by analogy, the situation around 1400. According to his reasoning, republican freedom and a monarchical establishment of order have always been alternating in Italian history as by necessity, the last wave of reorganizing dictatorship, in Emerton's own day, having been ridden by Mussolini. In the late Middle Ages, the republican phase of the Italian city-states, characteristic of the thirteenth and the first half of the fourteenth century, was giving way to an era of tyranny from the second half of the fourteenth century onward, and the acceptance by the Florentine mind of this inevitable fate is evidenced in the political teachings and historical views of Salutati's *De Tyranno* (pp. 47f., 58). Today, almost a generation after Emerton's attempt to interpret the development of the early Renaissance as a parallel to that of Italy in the beginning of the Fascist era, the time has come indeed for reconsideration.

39. Even in the famous humanistic controversy on true *nobilitas* and how it can develop—whether a man must have a

great *patria* to reach personal greatness, or needs only individual talent—Salutati was the first to defend the civic point of view against the individualistic pride of the *literati*, and influenced Bruni's convictions, as we shall see in the chapter on "Florentine Sentiment in Bruni's pre-Curial Period," note 13 (Vol. Two, p. 536f.).

40. See the references in Vol. One, p. 28.

CHAPTER 8

1. In all probability in 1407/08, except that the appended analysis of the Florentine constitution, in the ninth book, may have been added in 1409/10. See *Humanistic and Political Literature*, Chapter III, "The Date of Gregorio Dati's *Istoria di Firenze 1380-1406*."

2. Gregorio Dati, *L'Istoria di Firenze dal 1380 al 1405*, ed. L. Pratesi (Norcia, 1904). As to the limitations of Pratesi's edition, which make it necessary also to consult the edition published by G. Manni, Florence, 1735, see "The Date of Gregorio Dati's *Istoria*," just quoted, passim. In general one may say that, although Manni's manuscript basis is at many points corrupted or incomplete, Pratesi's text, constructed as it is with the help of late manuscripts, can in many instances not be accepted without suspicion. Our quotations follow Pratesi's text, but refer also to Manni's version in places where the divergence of the two editions affects the meaning of the text and the genuine reading is not obvious.

3. See. Vol. One, p. 62.

4. See F. Flamini's survey (though not complete) of Dati's public activities, with references to archival documents, in *Giornale Storico della Letteratura Italiana*, XVI (1890), 2f.

5. As early as 1404, his name was entered in the list of those entitled to the office of "Gonfalonieri di compagnie," and drew a lot for 1412. In 1405, he was one of the "Ten of Liberty" ("Dieci della libertà") appointed during the war against Pisa. See Dati's *Libro Segreto*, ed. C. Gargiolli ("Scelta di Curiosità Letterarie," vol. 102, Bologna, 1869), pp. 79, 82.

6. "La storia della lunga e grandissima (*Manni* grande) guerra di Italia che fu a questi nostri dì tra il tiranno di Lombardia, duca di Milano, e il magnifico Comune di Firenze." *Istoria*, ed. Pratesi, p. 11; ed. Manni, p. 1f.

7. Given Bruni's custom not to name his sources, but to make free use of them in his narrative, his dependence on Dati's account is difficult to establish; so far it has not been proved in literal details. (Cf. E. Santini in his introduction to the edition of Bruni's *Historiae*, p. x f.) But the similarity of the politico-historical categories employed by the two authors is striking, and it is hard to believe that Bruni, who is known to have exploited the extant literature of Florentine political memoirs, and who must have

been in frequent personal contacts with Dati when he himself was chancellor and Dati one of the most active statesmen during the late 1420's and early 1430's, did not know Dati's work at all.

8. The exception is Gino Capponi, who in his *Storia della Repubblica di Firenze* (vol. I, p. 533), as early as 1875, remarked that Dati's history deserved the title of "Political Discourses concerning the State of Florence and the City's Way of Life" ("Discorsi politici intorno allo Stato di Firenze ed al vivere della città"), and that he had often consulted Dati "as a thoughtful man who observes and appraises things from the inside, penetrating and practical, and who knows well how to portray the quality and the temper of this Florentine people" ("come di uomo pensatore che guarda e giudica le cose addentro, acuto e pratico e che sa bene ritrarre le qualità e gli umori di questo popolo fiorentino"). More recently, V. Rossi in his *Quattrocento* (3rd edn.: 1933, p. 185f.), with his usual acuteness of observation, noted Dati's "relative maturity of thought" among his contemporaries, shown by his "endeavours to recognize psychological causes (*cause umane*) and the logical connection of actions." But these brief suggestions have remained sterile since no one has made a systematic effort to determine Dati's place in the growth of the politico-historical ideas of the Renaissance. This is true even of E. Santini who, in his *Bruni e i "Hist. Flor. Pop.,"* p. 102f., briefly compared Dati and Bruni from the viewpoint of historiographical method and reached the conclusion that in Dati is found "none of the true critical spirit which is the achievement of the Renaissance" ("nulla del vero spirito critico che è un portato del Rinascimento"). Now it is quite true that Dati, the citizen writing in Volgare, proves himself alien to the historical criticism which humanists like Salutati and Bruni knew how to apply to traditional legends, and that he, in the manner of earlier chroniclers, does at times find the explanation of the events he describes in the just victory of piety and faith. However, we have already seen (note 65 to Chap. 3) that these limitations of the non-humanist did not prevent him from viewing the history of the free Commonwealth of Florence and its relationship to the *Respublica Romana* in the manner of Quattrocento historiography. Moreover, the criticism of sources and the exposure of legends are not the main points of a work that is primarily devoted to the study

of the most recent past. The qualifications crucial for such a task are rather an understanding of the nature of political events, and the capacity to render an impression of the imponderables of the political attitude from which decisions have flown. The essential problem for us is to determine what role Dati has played in the development of these capacities which became as important for the historiography of the Renaissance as did the humanistic criticism of the sources. We shall observe that Dati's part in this development was considerable; Santini's assertion that Dati "is a stranger to the politics of his time" ("è estraneo alla politica del tempo"), and that his judgment on the motives of his contemporaries is therefore unreliable, simply does not correspond to the facts. Wherever we have a chance to compare Dati's presentation with other documents, Capponi's high estimate is fully borne out. A correct historical interpretation of Florentine political conduct and sentiment around 1400 depends to a considerable degree on the reestablishment of interest and confidence in this too long neglected source.

9. An illustration of Dati's use of the Fortuna concept is his remark about the destruction of the Duke of Armagnac and his French army at Alessandria—cause of the failure of all Florentine plans in the war of 1390-92: "But Fortuna had not yet decided to stop here; she wished to keep him [Giangaleazzo] in suspense still a little longer, she wished to let him rise still a little higher to make him fall all the more deeply." (Ed. Pratesi, p. 39; ed. Manni, p. 33.) Here the following observations are in order: First, that the Fortuna simile is used as an artistic device for emphasis, but not in place of causal explanation; for immediately afterwards, the disastrous defeat in the battle is traced to the fact that the French knights met their doom because of their arrogant belief that no one in the world could resist them; thus they acted "with valour rather than wisdom, with daring rather than an understanding of the Italian ways" ("più forti che savi, e più arditi che pratichi de' modi italiani"; *ibid.*). Secondly, the mood of Dati's passage is not pessimism and weariness springing from the view that the spinning of Fortune's wheel renders all human things futile; but rather a passionate interest in the rise and fall of historic greatness, already adumbrating the mood of historiography in the time of Machiavelli. This is seen clearly in the continuation of Dati's simile, when the narrative has turned to the acme of

Giangaleazzo's power in 1402 and to the sudden reversal of everything by Giangaleazzo's sudden death: "Now the Duke had reached the happiest condition, as it seemed to him, and found himself in possession of the greatest and most exalted rule that had ever existed; here is the apex, whence one is bound to descend just as far as one had risen until now; but the fall is much more vehement and furious." "Just as on the western coast, on the ocean, when the tide rises, the water in some parts covers large stretches of land with its waves, and then, when it has risen as far as it must, runs back within a short time with a quicker current, leaving the sand uncovered—just so changeable Fortuna does to some men: for a time she lets them rise high, and when she so pleases she turns and drags them down with extreme violence. Up to now, the Duke of Milan, by Fortune's favor, has covered and carried off a large territory, and has reached the top of the wheel; now she turns it and reclaims her property in order to perform her customary office of taking from some men and giving to others; beyond resistance by human wit, and with ruin in the downfall more sudden than was the rise." ("Sì come ne' liti occidentali del mare oceano, quando cresce il fiotto in alcune parti ricuopre con le sue onde l'acqua grande spazio di terra e quando è cresciuto quanto debba, in poco d'ora ritorna con più veloce corso e lascia l'arene scoperte, così fa la nobile [*Manni* volubile] fortuna a certi che per ispazio di tempo gli fa sormontare alti e quando le piace volge e ritrae abbasso con strabocchevole corso [*Manni* furore]. Insino a qui il duca di Milano per beneficio di fortuna ha ricoperta e avviluppata molta terra ed è venuto al sommo della ruota; ora quella rivuole e richiede e suoi beni per fare l'usato uficio suo, permutando di gente in gente, e oltre alla difensione de' senni umani e con più subita ruina al calare che non fe' al salire." Ed. Pratesi, p. 80; ed. Manni, p. 75; see also Pratesi, pp. 11, 54 and 76.) In passages like these, the traditional image of the Wheel of Fortune fades imperceptibly into the notion that all things are subject to a natural flux and reflux—one of the basic ideas of the later Renaissance. This is an aspect of the Fortuna discussion which the study of Dati can add to the history of "Fortuna im Mittelalter und in der Renaissance" as told by A. Doren in a much used study (in *Vortraege der Bibliothek Warburg*, II, part I [1922-3], 71-144); for Doren's narrative proceeds from Petrarch and Boccaccio directly to Salutati and

Poggio (p. 110ff.), only to find that in the early Quattrocento there were as yet no features pointing to a new stage in the Fortuna debate.

10. More accurately, between 1441 and Bruni's death in February, 1444. The chief evidence for this date lies in the fact that books XI and XII, with slight alterations, include a few passages which are already found in Bruni's *Rerum Suo Tempore Gestarum Commentarius* written between the second half of 1440 and the first half of 1441. Details will be discussed in the revised edition of the "Chronologie der Werke Brunis" referred to in note 4 to Chap. 10. See also note 37 to Chap. 18.

11. ". . . suditi sono (*Manni* sono già) tutti nati nella suggezione e fattisi naturali in quella." *Istoria*, ed. Pratesi, p. 14; ed. Manni, p. 5.

12. "E questa guerra de' detti due Signori fu un baleno sì subito e appresso il mettervi le mani il Conte che si spacciò in breve che appena in tanto poco di tempo si potè avere consiglio che fusse da fare in casi tanto dubbiosi. . . ." Ed. Pratesi, p. 27; ed. Manni, p. 19. The documentary reconstruction of Florence's politics in 1388, by G. Collino, "La guerra veneto-viscontea contro i Carraresi nelle relazioni di Firenze . . . (1388)," *Archivio Storico Lombardo*, XXXVI (1909), 11f., 15f., confirms Dati's points: the deceitfulness of Giangaleazzo's diplomacy and the inability of the Florentine politicians to grasp its scope immediately.

13. ". . . non potendo pensare che il pensiero del Conte si estendesse più oltre." Ed. Pratesi, p. 26f.; ed. Manni, p. 19.

14. Ed. Pratesi, pp. 29, 37.

15. *Ibid.*, pp. 27, and 29f.

16. "Ora comincia il Comune di Firenze a mettere le mani a' grandi fatti; ora sono chiari i Fiorentini dell' animo insaziabile del tiranno, ora seguitano i belli ordini e i grandi consigli e le magnifiche operazioni." Ed. Pratesi, p. 37; ed. Manni, p. 30.

17. Ed. Pratesi, p. 96f.

18. *Ibid.*, pp. 37, 50.

19. *Ibid.*, p. 37.

20. "Gran vantaggio ha colui nelle guerre che per sua sollecitudine e industria può sapere i portamenti e lo stato e la possa della parte contraria; e però i detti Fiorentini, che sanno tutti i pertugi d'entrare e d'uscire che sono al mondo, a un' otta spiavano ogni dì ciò che faceva il Duca e si provvedevano a' rimedi loro,

onde più salutevoli potessino vincere." Ed. Pratesi, p. 61; ed. Manni, p. 56f.

21. ". . . hanno distese le loro ali per tutto il mondo e d'ogni parte sanno novelle e hanno avvisi." Ed. Pratesi, p. 37; ed. Manni, p. 30.

22. Ed. Pratesi, p. 37ff.

23. *Ibid.* See also above note 9.

24. See Vol. One, p. 14.

25. "E finalmente sarebbe forse fatica a ritrovare la prova di chi prima rompesse. . . ." *Istoria*, ed. Pratesi, p. 47; ed. Manni, p. 41.

26. "Seguì . . . tutta la forza . . . del Conte ad assalire . . . Mantova . . . , e questo era antiveduto di provvidenza (*Manni* provveduto) con bastie e isteccati e con la gente de' Fiorentini che aspettavano di continuo quello che avvenne e a niuna cosa furono giunti sprovveduti. Il combattere fu grande . . . che a' nostri tempi non si ricorda più magnifica battaglia . . . ; e posto che le genti de' Fiorentini fussino assai meno, sì come è usanza delle battaglie che la ragione vince, . . . guadagnarono i Fiorentini maravigliosa vittoria." Ed. Pratesi, p. 53; ed. Manni, p. 48.

27. The document is cited in De Mesquita, *Giangaleazzo*, p. 222.

28. ". . . perchè i Fiorentini istimavano se ottenessino il ponte e vincessono la resistenza del Conte, che potrebbono correre in su tutte le sue terre ogni dì, nelle quali agevolmente pensavano avere parte perchè male contenti vivevano sotto loro signore veggendolo volere guerra che li disfaceva del mondo tra di gravezze e di non potere esercitare le loro mercatanzie. E così il Conte stimava che se con tutto suo sforzo vincesse il ponte, gli verrebbe vinta Mantova e levarsi via quel battifolle da presso e sanza sospetto poi delle sue terre potere rimandare sue genti in Toscana. Ciascuna parte fa conto che questo partito è quello che può dare vinto e perduto, e niuna cosa che sia di bisogno lassa fare. . . ." Ed. Pratesi, p. 52; ed. Manni, p. 46f.

29. Ed. Pratesi, pp. 51-53.

30. Dati, *Istoria*, ed. Pratesi, p. 53f.

31. *Ibid.*, p. 74.

32. This is the concluding sentence of Bruni's *Historiae* (see above note 41 to Chap. 2); almost the same wording occurs in his *Rerum Suo Tempore Gestarum Commentarius*, p. 432f.

33. "E cierto si sarebbe fatto signore d'Italia in piccolo tempo apresso, pure ch'egli ci avesse vinti. Ed era innordine di vincierci però ch'egli era signore di Pisa, di Siena, di Perugia . . . ," etc.—of all central and northern Italy, "ecietto Vinegia." Buonaccorso Pitti, *Cronica*, ed. A. Bacchi della Lega ("Collezione di Opere Inedite o rare," vol. 91, Bologna, 1905), p. 134.

34. Cf. *Istoria*, pp. 43f., 49f.

35. ". . . avevano fatta la ragione con la penna in mano e dicevano come di cosa certa: tanto può durare. . ." *Istoria*, ed. Pratesi, p. 71; ed. Manni, p. 67.

36. ". . . si distruggesse come gli intervenne, benchè e' non vedesse sua distruzione chè [editions: che] prima si morì." *Loc. cit.*

37. "E questo partito avevano preso i Fiorentini con intenzione che la guerra avesse a durare lungo tempo, perchè disposti erano di non fare più pace con lui, perchè due volte ne furono traditi e ingannati, non volevano aspettare la terza, ma col perseverare in guerra vedere lui consumare. . . Ed era veduto e conosciuto per li Fiorentini che vi aveva a scoppiare sotto." *Loc. cit.*

38. ". . . perchè molti sono amici della fortuna, e tenevano la parte di colui che pareva loro che dovesse vincere. . . ." Ed. Pratesi, p. 59; ed. Manni, p. 54.

39. Ed. Pratesi, p. 27.

40. ". . . che le forze bastassono di pari . . ." ". . . che essi rimanessero di poi i maggiori di ciascuna." Ed. Pratesi, p. 54f.; ed. Manni, p. 49.

41. ". . . parevano ammaliati da lui." Ed. Pratesi, p. 73; ed. Manni, p. 69.

42. *Loc. cit.*

43. Florence "era quella che sosteneva tutto il pondo alle altre città vicine." *Loc. cit.*

44. "I Fiorentini furono la siepe che non lo lasciarono mai passare più avanti; di certo se non fusse (*Manni* fusse stato) il sostenere de' Fiorentini non era alcuna resistenza in Italia, che gli veniva fatto che e' sarebbe stato signore di tutto e non arebbe auto pari tra' cristiani; sì che gli pareva che i Fiorentini gli dovessino tôrre (*Manni* togliessono) quello che non gli lasciavano acquistare, avendo già stimato che suo dovesse essere, e per questo non aveva alcuna temperanza inverso di loro." Ed. Pratesi, p. 72; ed. Manni, p. 68.

45. "D'essere vinti, cioè sottoposti, [the citizens of Florence]

non ebbono mai alcun dubbio perchè gli animi loro sono tanto a lui contrari e avversi che non lo potevano consentire in alcun loro pensiero, e ogni volta pareva loro avere molti rimedi—siccome fa il cuore franco e sicuro che mai non li manca via e rimedio—e sempre si confortavano con una speranza che pareva avere loro la cosa sicura in mano, cioè che il Comune non può morire e il Duca era uno solo uomo mortale, chè finito lui, finito lo stato suo. . . . Ma non si stettono mai i Fiorentini che, consumato o mancato uno rimedio, non ricorressono subitamente (*Manni* sollecitamente) all' altro." "E puossi (*Manni* E però si può) dire che tutta la libertà d'Italia stesse solo nelle mani de' Fiorentini, che (*Manni* perchè) ogni altra potenza li abbandonò." Ed. Pratesi, pp. 74, 73f.; ed. Manni, pp. 70 and 69.

Part Three

CHAPTER 9

1. "It is regrettable," says Kirner in his pamphlet *Della 'Laudatio . . .'* (1889; see note 12 below), p. 8, "in view of so many great treasures of Greek literature, that a writer who definitely belongs to the period of decay should have been the first to be imitated."

2. Bruni, *Ep. VIII 4*, 1440, ed. Mehus, vol. II, p. 111.

3. The references to the *Laudatio* in Bruni's correspondence soon after the appearance of the work are discussed in *Humanistic and Political Literature*, Chapter IV, at the beginning of section 1, "Two Versions of the *Laudatio*? A Blind Alley."

4. The *Laudatio* is composed of the following main parts which may be entitled by key-words occurring in the text, as follows: Introduction and survey of contents: *L* fol. 133v-134r; ed. Klette, pp. 84-86. "Qualis urbs ipsa est": *L* fol. 134r-141v; ed. Klette, pp. 86-90. "Quibus parentibus populus Florentinus ortus est": *L* fol. 141v-144v; ed. Klette, pp. 90-94. "Quibus artibus Florentia de principatu in Italia certavit. De virtute urbis qualis foris fuit": *L* fol. 144v-152r; ed. Klette, pp. 94-98. "Quare Florentia disciplina institutisque domesticis admirabilis est": *L* fol. 152r-156r; ed. Klette, pp. 98-105. For *L* and Klette, and for the textual basis of our quotations, see note 1 to Chap. 3.

5. That Aelius Aristides was used as a model is stated by Bruni himself in his *Ep. VIII 4*. For a survey of the rhetorical topics treated in classical city eulogies, such as were available to Bruni, cf. Th. C. Burgess, "Epideictic Literature," *Studies in Classical Philology* (Chicago), III (1902), esp. pp. 107ff., 146ff., 153f.

6. *Laudatio, L* fol. 145v-148v; ed. Klette, pp. 94-96.

7. So especially F. Novati when, in 1898, he edited the most interesting and mature of the medieval city-state eulogies, Bonvesino della Riva's *De Magnalibus Urbis Mediolani* of 1288, and, in his preface, for the first time surveyed and appraised the surviving specimens of this literary genre. (*Bullettino dell' Istituto Storico Italiano*, No. 20 [Rome, 1898], pp. 7-50). After giving high praises to the medieval *Laudes*, Novati characterized Bruni's humanistic *Laudatio* as a work "which is ready and glad to sacri-

fice the substance of things to eloquence and distinction of style, and endeavours not so much to set forth good reasons, as to give tenuous and subtle arguments" ("... sforzandosi non già di recar innanzi buone ragioni, ma di argomentare in guisa arguta e sottile"; p. 12). In a similar vein, E. Verga, republishing Bonvesino's work in an Italian translation in 1921, called Bruni's presentation "full of grace . . . , but poor in content." (*Bonvesino della Riva. Le Meraviglie di Milano.* Trans. & comm. E. Verga. Milan, 1921, p. xlix.)

8. How far from these attainments of Renaissance Humanism the medieval *Laudes* of cities had remained is seen even by a cursory comparison of Bonvesino della Riva's *De Magnalibus* with Bruni's work. In the general arrangement of the subject matter, it is true, there are similarities between the two "*laudationes*." In both cases, the eulogy begins with the geographical situation and external appearance of the city, proceeds to the character and the history of the inhabitants, and ends with the proof that the eulogized city deserves a preeminent position in Italy. But the medieval work makes hardly any effort to come to grips with individual traits; it is satisfied to ascribe to the object of its praise the greatest quantity or largest number of what it considers good or honorable for a city-state. In chapters I and II, after attributing to Milan the most favorable climate, the best rivers and fountains, and the most fertile fields, Bonvesino gives account of how many castles, city-gates, churches, convents, houses, etc., are found in Milan. The only passage in his description of the "*situs*" of Milan which goes beyond enumeration is the assertion (a classical reminiscence, no doubt) that "the city itself is orbicular in the manner of a circle whose admirable roundness is the sign of its perfection" ("civitas ipsa orbicularis est ad circulli modum, cuius mirabillis rotonditas perfectionis eius est signum"; II 4). But this claim is not made good by the presentation of any concrete evidence; it derives from an abstract, stereotyped ideal, not from a fresh ability to view and analyze the panorama of Milan.

The chapters III and IV, intended to point out the excellent qualities and the wealth of the inhabitants, are also given to statistics only—priceless statistics for the modern scholar, it is true, from the quantity of the produce, and of the grain consumed by men and animals in Milan, to the number of citizens engaged in every industry and profession, providing a survey even more detailed than the famous one for Florence included in Giovanni Villani's chronicle. But the fact remains that what is given is merely a list of figures; no effort is made to correlate causes and effects, or even tabulate relations between the industrial output and the changing number of firms, as was done in the chronicle of Villani. Chapter V, on the virtue of the citizens, contains a summary of the military deeds of the Milanese in history—their struggles with neighbor cities, their resistance to German emperors, and their resilience after every defeat. But the individual scenes, realistically told, are not set in a historical framework; there is no appraisal of the Empire, nor of the historical origin, rise, and mission of the Italian city republics. Nor is there any mention of Milan's contribution to the growth of literature and culture. Instead, the long narrative of military deeds, in the casual manner of late medieval popular chronicles, closes with the account of two Milanese "*mirabilia*": the entertaining episode of a Milanese citizen who was physically stronger than any other known man and, in proportion to his strength, an incomparably voracious eater; and the history of another citizen who, thanks to his "natural wisdom," surpassed in prudence everybody else although he had received no education. The last part of Bonvesino's book depicts the higher values for which Milan stood in Italy: According to chapter VI, her enduring loyalties had always been to the Papal Church, and to the memory of her local martyrs who exceeded in number and fame those of any other city; the greatest calamity in Milan's long history, therefore, had been the loss of the bones of the three Magi of the East, which, after the destruction of the city by Barbarossa, were sent to Cologne and never returned. In accord with these loyalties, chapter VII defines the *libertas* of Milan as independence won in the service of the Church, and by faithfulness to the tradition whose basis had been laid by those martyrs. There is no word, neither in this nor any other chapter, on the institutions and laws which had made possible, or caused, civic liberty. According to the final (VIIIth) chapter, the principal reasons for Milan's incomparable excellence are: In antiquity, Milan had held the position of a second capital of the Roman emperors; in the medieval Empire, the Archbishop of Milan had had the privilege of presenting the Kings of Italy to the Pope for imperial coronation. Given the fact, furthermore, that the Church of Milan, like that of Rome, had been founded by an apostle, Barnabas, and that Milan had enjoyed the special concession of a liturgy of her own (the "ritus Ambrosianus"), this city was not only superior in dignity to her ancient rival in northern Italy, Ravenna, seat of the Byzantine Exarch, but worthy of becoming, in the place of Rome, the home of the Papacy.

We now can see that Bonvesino's *De Magnalibus*, measured against the performance of Bruni's *Laudatio*, falls into the pattern, so often found in late medieval thought, of a keen realistic attitude in matters of local and practical concern, combined with a firm adherence to the medieval political and spiritual standards. If we, with Novati, allow ourselves to look upon Bonvesino's love of listing and counting as the only possible approach to the "substance of reality," and minimize the significance of the discoveries, made by fifteenth-century humanists, of causes, rules and structures of political and cultural conditions, we merely mistake our technical interest in rich statistical information for a genuinely historical approach to the gains and losses brought about by the mind of the Quattrocento.

9. Throughout the Chapter 3, "A New View of Roman History and of the Florentine Past."

10. See Vol. One, p. 58ff.

11. *Laudatio*, *L* fol. 139v-141r; cf. Klette's reference, p. 90.

12. See G. Kirner in the pamphlet *Della 'Laudatio urbis florentinae' di Leonardo Bruni: notizia* (Livorno, 1889), p. 13.

13. "Sedet enim media inter Tyrenum et Adriaticum mare quasi regina quedam Italie." *Laudatio*, *L* fol. 141r.

14. See Klette's introduction, p. 32f.; Kirner, *Della 'Laudatio,'* p. 13.

15. *L*, fol. 136v-139r; a few passages in Klette, p. 89f.

16. "Urbs autem media est tanquam antistes quedam ac dominatrix; illa vero circum adstant, suo queque loco constituta. Et lunam a stellis circumdari poeta recte diceret quispiam; fitque ex eo res pulcerrima visu. Quemadmodum enim in clipeo, circulis sese ad invicem includentibus, intimus orbis in umbelicum desinit, qui medius est totius clipei locus: eodem hic itidem modo videmus regiones quasi circulos quosdam ad invicem clausas ac circunfusas. Quarum urbs quidem prima est, quasi umbelicus quidam, totius ambitus media. Hec autem menibus cingitur atque suburbiis. Suburbia rursus ville circumdant, villas autem oppida; atque hec omnis extima regio maiore ambitu circuloque complectitur. Inter

oppida vero castella sunt arcesque in celum minantes. . . ." *Laudatio*, *L* fol. 139r.

17. See Vol. One, pp. 149f. and 152.

18. The relationship of the various preserved specimens, the Florentine origin of the original engraving, and its date, as yet not exactly fixed, in the 1470/80's have been gradually established by an extensive critical literature, especially the papers "Die alte Ansicht von Florenz im Kgl. Kupferstichkabinett und ihr Vorbild," *Jahrbuch der Königlich Preussischen Kunstsammlungen*, XXXV (1914), 90ff., by Ch. Hülsen; "Die ältesten Stadtansichten von Florenz (1469-1783)," *ibid.*, LI (1930), 115ff., by K. H. Busse; and "A Fifteenth-century View of Florence," *The Burlington Magazine*, XCIV (1952), 160ff., by L. D. Ettlinger. The small fragment of the original engraving, preserved in the Società Colombaria in Florence, indicates the gradual transition from city to countryside in the hill region surrounding the metropolis even more delicately than the woodcut does; see the excellent reproduction of the fragment by Hülsen, *loc. cit.*, p. 93, and its small replica by Ettlinger, *loc. cit.*, p. 166. Ettlinger's article discusses and reproduces a painted panel from the early 1490's which imitates the engraving with variations and testifies to its contemporaneous influence. Ettlinger also confronts the engraving and woodcut with a photograph of Florence taken from about the same place where the Quattrocento artist must have worked (p. 162), thereby showing in a striking fashion how much of the singular effect of the 1470/80's engraving (and, we may add, of the literary description in the *Laudatio*) is due to the specific interest and visual approach of the Quattrocento. All the known panoramic views of Renaissance Florence, together with the pictures and maps available from the later periods, are reproduced in the volume *Piante e Vedute di Firenze. Studio Storico Topografico Cartografico di Giuseppe Boffito e Attilio Mori, Dedicato al Municipio di Firenze* (Florence, 1926). This work established the basis for the subsequent discussions of chronology and authorship; but as far as Quattrocento material is concerned, it has been corrected at essential points by Busse's and Ettlinger's papers.

The woodcuts in Schedel's *Liber chronicarum* of 1493 are the work of Michael Wolgemut and Wilhelm Pleydenwurff.

19. "Dico igitur omnes homines sic esse admiratos magnitudinem contentionis et diurnitatem belli ut secum ipsi obstupescerent

unde huic uni civitati tante vires, tante opes, tante ad bellum suppeditarent (suppeditarentur *G C*) pecunie. Sed hec tanta admiratio, hic tantus stupor, tam diu apud homines est quam diu hanc pulcerrimam urbem non aspexerunt neque viderunt eius magnificentiam. Ceterum ubi illam intuiti sunt, omnis talis evanescit abitque admiratio. Videmus hoc quidem inter omnes constare, nec ullus Florentiam advenit qui non id sibi evenisse fateatur." *Laudatio*, *L* fol. 137v-138r.

20. ". . . illico omnium mentes animique ita mutantur ut non iam de maximis atque amplissimis rebus ab hac urbe gestis obstupescant. . . ." *Laudatio*, *L* fol. 138r.

21. ". . . ut sit libertas, sine qua nunquam hic populus vivendum sibi existimavit." *Laudatio*, *L* fol. 152v; ed. Klette, p. 98.

22. ". . . quasi ad quoddam signum ac portum, omnia huius rei publice instituta provisaque contendunt." *Loc. cit.*

23. Vol. One, p. 364ff.

24. Composed in 1339; published in *Stephani Baluzii Tutelensis Miscellanea novo ordine digesta et . . . aucta*, ed. G. D. Mansi, vol. IV (Lucca, 1764), pp. 117-119. The genuine title, according to C. Frey, who reedited the pamphlet in his *Die Loggia dei Lanzi zu Florenz* (1885), pp. 119-123, runs *Breve Memoria . . . del presente stato e disposizione della città di Firenze nell' anno Domini Mille X$\overset{c}{X}$XVIII d'aprile*. For the background and genesis of the *Memoria* cf. O. Hartwig, *Quellen und Forschungen zur aeltesten Geschichte der Stadt Florenz*, vol. I (1875), pp. xxix-xxxv.

25. "Quemadmodum enim in cordis convenientia est, ad quam cum intense fuerint una ex diversis tonis fit armonia, . . . eodem modo hec prudentissima civitas ita omnes sui partes moderata est ut inde summa quedam rei publice sibi ipsi consentanea resultet . . . Nichil est in ea preposterum, nichil inconveniens, nichil absurdum, nichil vagum; suum queque locum tenent, non modo certum, sed etiam congruentem." *Laudatio*, *L* fol. 152r. The same aversion to mere collection of accidental facts is seen in Bruni's description of the Florentine constitution, made in 1413 at the request of Emperor Sigismund—a counterpart from the next phase of Bruni's life that should be remembered together with the *Laudatio*. It was not enough to ask, so Bruni then explained, "whether an institution of the state rests on the authority of the ancestors; but it is necessary to understand and explain why it was instituted. For it

is by knowing its cause that we gain knowledge of a thing." ("Preterea non satis [? MS: vis] est sitne aliquid in re publica maiorum auctoritate constitutum; sed quam ob rem id constitutum, intelligere oportet atque exponere. Causa enim rei scientiam facit"). Cf. the edition of Bruni's constitutional analysis in *Humanistic and Political Literature* Chapter VIII, "An Epistolary Description by Bruni of the Florentine Constitution in 1413."

26. "Prima che particularmente alcuna imagine dipingano, tirano certe linee, per le quali essa figura universalmente si dimostra." Donato Giannotti, *Della Repubblica de' Viniziani*, in *Opere Politiche e Letterarie*, ed. Polidori (Florence, 1850), vol. II, p. 28.

27. "Prudenti architettori . . . non alterano [in] cosa alcuna i trovati fondamenti, ma secondo le qualità loro disegnano uno edificio conveniente a quelli." Giannotti, *Della Repubblica Fiorentina*, in *Opere*, vol. I, p. 70.

CHAPTER 10

1. See Vol. One, p. 173. Other unequivocal passages will be found later in the present chapter, esp. pp. 186f., 189.

2. This is the result at which we arrived by analysing the political situation around 1400, and by revising the chronology of the political literature written under the impress of the war; see Vol. One, pp. 28, 68f.

3. That is, of his development as a translator from the Greek; see Vol. One, p. 73.

4. An even remotely satisfactory chronology of Bruni's writings is wanting—perhaps the most embarrassing lacuna at present in the studies of early Florentine Humanism. One cause for this lack of an indispensable tool is that the chronology of Bruni's literary works depends largely on the information furnished by Bruni's letters, and Bruni's *Epistolario* has fared exceptionally ill in modern research. To be sure, some fifty years ago F. P. Luiso, with the help of important manuscripts, prepared a chronological rearrangement of Bruni's letters, including an edition of the pieces and passages omitted in Mehus' edition of 1741; but this work, which was to be entitled *Studî su L'Epistolario di L. Bruni*, was never published even though it had been set up in print. The fact that it has not become generally accessible and yet exists—students in Italy have now and then been able to borrow Luiso's proof sheets for consultation—has been a blight on all subsequent Bruni research. When this writer in 1926-27 prepared for publication a collection of unedited or rare works of Bruni (*Leonardo Bruni Aretino, Humanistisch-Philosophische Schriften*, Leipzig, 1928), he, like others, received the privilege to use for a few days Luiso's proof sheets, though not his critical preface and description of the manuscripts consulted. In order to make the substance of Luiso's findings accessible, the writer, in agreement with Luiso, included in his own work (pp. 189-228, in an appendix dealing with Bruni's correspondence) a checklist indicating Luiso's revised chronology and referring to the more important of his textual changes and additions. (Cf. the notes on the nature of the arrangement with Luiso in *Bruni, Schriften*, pp. 189-194, and in *Archiv für Kulturgeschichte*, XXII [1932], 353-354). This makeshift list is still the only tool available for the study of Bruni's correspondence, and will remain so until the critical edition of

Bruni's *Epistolario*, in preparation for the "Fonti per la Storia d'Italia" for half a century, is finally given to the scholarly world. As to Bruni's literary writings, the findings of Luiso and some other scholars, especially R. Sabbadini, on the chronology of Bruni's letters made it possible in 1928, to work out the first complete chronological survey of Bruni's works; it is contained in this writer's edition of Bruni's *Schriften*, pp. 159-189. Planned as a supplement to that collection, the list was not the fruit of protracted critical studies; it was intended to collect and integrate the widely scattered results that Bruni scholars had achieved by the mid-1920's. This survey, too, has still not been replaced. The only substantial supplement, published in 1932 by L. Bertalot in *Archivum Romanicum*, XV (1931), 298-301—supplying about five corrections and about five more precise indications of dates, as well as adding four minor items to the list of Bruni's works—is greatly impaired in its usefulness because it is couched in a language apparently borrowed from humanist invectives, and, like them, abounds in inaccuracies and distortions of fact. It should be consulted together with the rectifications given in the present writer's article "Studien über Leonardo Bruni Aretino," *Archiv für Kulturgeschichte*, XXII (1932), esp. pp. 368-371. In the twenty-five years that have passed since his preparation of Bruni's *Schriften*, this writer has gradually come to realize the inadequacy, and often erroneousness, of many of the chronological assumptions made in the 1920's by Bruni scholars. By 1945 he had worked out a monograph which revised a considerable number of the accepted dates and, on this basis, redrew the picture of Bruni's humanistic development. This book on Bruni has so far remained unpublished because of the need first to clear up the mystery that has always surrounded the genesis of the *Laudatio* and the *Dialogi* and, consequently, the origins of Bruni's civic Humanism. In preparing his solution of this vexed problem for discussion in *Humanistic and Political Literature* and in some of the chapters of the present book, the writer could draw upon his unpublished monograph at all places where familiarity with the later phases of Bruni's development was needed. Whenever that information is essential for the results which follow, data taken from the Bruni monograph have been explained at some length in the notes. The revised chronology of some of Bruni's works that has thus been included in the present book can easily be put together by consulting the index under "Bruni."

5. See the discussion of the relevant pieces of Bruni's correspondence in *Humanistic and Political Literature*, Chapter IV, at the beginning of section 1, "Two Versions of the *Laudatio*? A Blind Alley."

6. ". . . tandem etiam Bononiam occuparat." See note 24 below.

7. *Dialogi*, ed. Klette, pp. 67-69; ed. Garin, pp. 76-78. For Klette's and Garin's editions used here in all subsequent references, see note 1 to Chap. 3. The fact that the *Laudatio* is discussed in the *Dialogi* was already mentioned in Vol. One, pp. 44 and 164.

8. These are the conclusions reached in *Humanistic and Political Literature*, Chapter VI, section 4, "The Date of *Dialogus I*."

9. See *Humanistic and Political Literature*, Chapter IV, section 1, "Two Versions of the *Laudatio*? A Blind Alley."

10. In the only finished part of his Bruni studies, *Commento a una lettera di L. Bruni e cronologia di alcune sue opere*, in *Raccolta di studii critici dedicata ad Alessandro D'Ancona* (Florence, 1901), pp. 85-95.

11. For R. Sabbadini's quoted assent to Luiso see his *Storia e critica di testi latini* (1914), p. 80. For the assent of G. Petraglione, editor of Pier Candido Decembrio's *Panegyricus*, the Milanese reply to the *Laudatio*, see *Archivio Storico Lombardo*, ser. IV, vol. VIII (1907), 6.

12. See note 6 above.

13. Such is the gist of Luiso's argument, *Commento a Bruni*, pp. 91-92. The passage of Bruni's *Historiae* is in Santini's edition on p. 276. For possible objections to this daring reinterpretation of the reference in the *Laudatio* to Bologna's occupation, see *Humanistic and Political Literature*, note 6 to Chapter IV, section 2.

14. Bruni, *Ep. VIII 4*. Bruni, an admirer of Polybius, had undoubtedly taken his inspiration from Polybius X 21.8, where a quite similar distinction is made between ἐγκώμιον (encomium), which requires selection of facts and glorification of deeds, and ἱστορία (history), which demands sincerity and proof. See F. Leo, *Die Griechisch-roemische Biographie* (Leipzig, 1901), p. 227.

15. Luiso was obviously aware of this character of Bruni's eulogy, for he referred to it when observing some chronological irregularities in the narrative. (*Commento a Bruni*, p. 92). But he did not recognize the practical implications of Bruni's procedure.

16. See the quotation in note 25 below.

(quam plurima *G*, complura *O*) bella, contra potentissimos hostes reluctata est. Stravit crescentes et formidolosas potentias. Consilio, opibus, magnitudine animorum eos superavit quibus nec par quidem fore nec resistere posse ullo pacto credebatur. Nuperrime vero adversus potentissimum et opulentissimum hostem ita summa vi per multos annos contendit ut omnium mentes in admirationem converteret. Eum enim ducem, cuius opes atque potentiam et transalpine gentes et reliqua omnis formidabat Italia, spe elatum, victoriis exultantem omniaque miro successu quasi tempestatem quandam occupantem hec una civitas inventa (reperta *L, om. O*) est que non solum invadentem reprimeret cursumque victoriarum retardaret, verum etiam post longum bellum affligeret. Sed de rebus quidem ab hac urbe gestis paulo post erit tempus facultasque dicendi; nunc autem quod intendimus agamus. Dico igitur omnes homines sic esse admiratos magnitudinem contentionis et diurnitatem belli ut secum ipsi obstupescerent unde huic uni civitati tante vires, . . . tante ad bellum suppeditarent pecunie. Sed . . . ubi illam intuiti sunt, omnis talis evanescit . . . admiratio." (Cf. the full passage in note 19 to Chap. 9.) *Laudatio*, *L* fol. 137v-138r; omitted by Klette, p. 90.

26. In the interest of a simpler demonstration, it has seemed advisable to exclude three possible complementary inquiries from our discussion. The first concerns the question whether, besides the allusions to the experience of 1402 we have noted, there may be other passages in the *Laudatio* that can be shown to have been written after 1402. This problem is discussed in *Humanistic and Political Literature*, Chapter IV, section 4, "Salutati's *Invectiva* as a Source of Bruni's *Laudatio*." The second inquiry concerns a group of observations on the date of the *Laudatio* by which R. Sabbadini in 1930 tried to qualify his earlier approval of Luiso's theory. Since, on a closer view, these observations are implicitly refuted by the result we have now reached, they could be ignored here but are discussed in *Humanistic and Political Literature* in a critical *Excursus* to Chapter IV, section 2, "A Recent Abortive Approach to the Problems of the *Laudatio*." Finally, one can refute Luiso's assertion (cf. Vol. One, p. 181) that the earliest document referring to the *Laudatio*, Bruni's *Epistola I 8* (dated September 5th without indication of the year), must have originated in 1400 instead of after 1402. See the discussion of "The Date of Bruni's *Ep. I 8*" in *Humanistic and Political Literature*, at the beginning of Chapter V.

CHAPTER 11

1. The history of Bruni's scholarly advance after 1402, based on the sources which become available once we are no longer hampered by the apparent authority of an erroneous date of the *Laudatio*, is told in *Humanistic and Political Literature*, Chapter V, "Bruni's Development as a Translator from the Greek. (1400-1403/04)." For *Ep. I 8* and the *Laudatio*, cf. note 26 to Chap. 10.

2. As to the reliability of this date, see *Humanistic and Political Literature*, Chapter VI, section 4, "The Date of *Dialogus I*." Cf. also Vol. One, p. 180f.

3. See the discussion of the source evidence and of the available manuscripts in *Humanistic and Political Literature*, Chapter VI, section 2, "One-Dialogue Manuscripts of the *Dialogi*," and section 3, "The Title of the *Dialogi*."

4. See the edition by Carmine Di Pierro in *Rerum Italicarum Scriptores*, Nuova Ed., tom. XIX, parte III (1926).

5. See Bertalot, *Archivum Romanicum*, XV (1931), 299.

6. *Bruni, Schriften*, p. 167.

7. *Bruni, Schriften*, pp. 147, 177.

8. For this interesting parallel to what, according to our reconstruction, had taken place in the successive publication of the two dialogues, see *Humanistic and Political Literature*, Chapter VII, "The Genesis of Bruni's Annotated Latin Version of the (Pseudo-) Aristotelian *Economics*."

9. *Dialogi*, ed. Klette, p. 41; ed. Garin, p. 44.

10. ". . . sed cum semper nobis tua praesentia desideretur, . . . ut nuper, cum est apud Colucium disputatum, non possem dicere quantopere ut adesses desideravimus." *Dialogi*, ed. Klette, p. 40; ed. Garin, p. 44.

11. Ed. Klette, p. 67; ed. Garin, p. 76.

12. "Itaque ego istam defensionem aliud in tempus magis commodum differam." Ed. Klette, p. 65f.; ed. Garin, p. 74.

13. "Simulque illud teneo, et semper tenebo: nullam esse rem quae tantum ad studia nostra quantum disputatio afferat; nec si tempora haec labem aliquam passa sunt, idcirco tamen nobis facultatem eius rei exercendae ademptam esse. Quamobrem non desinam vos cohortari, ut huic exercitationi quam maxime incumbatis. Haec cum dixisset, surreximus." Ed. Klette, p. 66; ed. Garin, p. 74f.

14. "Postridie vero, cum omnes qui pridie fueramus in unum convenissemus, additusque praeterea esset Petrus Minii filius, adolescens impiger atque facundus in primis, Colucii familiaris, placuit ea die, ut hortos Roberti viseremus." Ed. Klette, p. 67; ed. Garin, p. 76.

15. "Cum solemniter celebrarentur ii dies, qui pro resurrectione Jesu Christi festi habentur, essemusque in unum Nicolaus et ego pro summa inter nos familiaritate coniuncti, placuit tum nobis ut ad Colucium Salutatum iremus. . . . Nec longius fere progressis Robertus Russus fit nobis obviam, . . . qui, quonam tenderemus percontatus, audito consilio nostro approbatoque, ipse etiam una nobiscum ad Colucium secutus est." Ed. Klette, p. 42; ed. Garin, p. 46.

16. ". . . id maxime conati sumus, ut morem utriusque [Salutati and Niccoli] diligentissime servaremus. Quantum vero in ea re profecerimus, tuum erit iudicium." "Scis enim Colucio neminem fere graviorem esse; Nicolaus vero, qui illi adversabatur, et in dicendo est promptus, et in lacessendo acerrimus." Ed. Klette, p. 41; ed. Garin, p. 44f.

17. "Nolite enim putare meas esse criminationes istas; sed cum ab aliis quibusdam audivissem, ad vos heri, qua tandem de causa scitis, retuli." Ed. Klette, p. 81; ed. Garin, p. 94.

18. Bruni, in his *In Nebulonem Maledicum* (ed. G. Zippel, in his *Nicolò Niccoli* [Firenze, 1890], p. 77): "Itaque bellum indixit scurra nepharius cunctis prestantibus ingenio viris; nec viventibus modo, sed etiam mortuis. Nam et Dantem optimum nobilissimumque poetam vituperare assidue prope convitio non cessat, et de Petrarcha ita loquitur, quasi de homine insulso et ignorantie pleno; Boccacium ita spernit, ut ne tres quidem litteras scisse illum asseveret." Francesco Filelfo, in his *Satyrarum* Decas I, Hecatosticha quinta (according to the ed. Venice, 1502): "Additur [by Niccoli to those whom he despises] huic [Chrysolorae] dius Dantes suavisque Petrarcha." In his *Orazione fatta . . . al popolo fiorentino delle laude di Dante nel principio della lettura del Poema* (December 1431), Filelfo declared that he was going to continue his explanations of Dante's *Commedia*, although there were "envious" persons who sneered at such lectures. Those who opposed Filelfo at that time were Niccoli and Marsuppini, but not Bruni. (See Voigt, *Die Wiederbelebung*, I³, pp. 355-356). About these adversaries, as late as 1431, Filelfo

made the same assertions that are familiar from the testimonies on Niccoli's attitude about 1400: "Et avvegnadiochè il leggere di questo divino poeta, chiamato da miei ignorantissimi emuli leggere da calzolai e da fornai, . . . in tanto odio . . . ha me indotto presso de' miei invidi, non però mi ritrarrò." (G. Benaducci, in his edition of *Prose e poesie volgari di Francesco Filelfo*, in *Atti e Memorie della R. Deput. di Stor. Patr. per le Marche*, v [1901], 23.)

In view of all these testimonies on the attitude of the historical Niccoli, the assertion of the second-dialogue Niccoli that he had proven his enthusiastic admiration for Petrarch by making copies from Petrarch's *Africa* on a trip to Padua, cannot be considered to refer to a very relevant historical occurrence. For whatever portion of the epic may have been copied on that occasion, Niccoli cannot have done any systematic and extensive work since not the slightest trace of his copy of the *Africa* is known among Florentine humanists. See the pertinent observations on the inacceptability of this attempted alibi of the second-dialogue Niccoli, made by G. Billanovich in his *Petrarca Letterato*, vol. I, p. 385, n. 1.

19. The similarity between the *Dialogi* and Cicero's *De oratore* was already noticed by R. Sabbadini, *Giornale Storico della Letteratura Italiana*, LXXXXVI (1930), 131f.; but he used this discovery merely to establish Bruni's imitation of certain Ciceronian words and phrases. He made no attempt to ascertain whether the two dialogues show differences in their relationship to the classical model.

20. Cicero *De orat.* ii 15ff. Some essential preparations of the Ciceronian scene already in i 99.

21. ". . . sed cum ab aliis quibusdam audivissem, ad vos heri, qua tandem de causa scitis, retuli." See note 17 above. The "causa" had been explained by Niccoli at the beginning of his recantation: "Illud tamen ante omnia certissimum habetote, me non alia de causa heri impugnasse, nisi ut Colucium ad illorum [Dante, Petrarch, Boccaccio] laudes excitarem." "Haec ego ea de causa dico, . . . ut Colucium prae indignatione ad eorum laudes impellerem." Ed. Klette, p. 72f.; ed. Garin, p. 82f.

22. ". . . neque sane quid ipse sentiret, sed quid ab aliis diceretur, ostendit." *De orat.* ii 41.

23. ". . . hoc mihi proposueram, ut, si te refellissem, hos a te discipulos abducerem; nunc . . . videor debere non tam pugnare tecum quam quid ipse sentiam dicere." *De orat.* ii 40.

24. "Nox ista te, Nicolae, . . . nobis reddidit: nam eiusmodi a te heri dicebantur, quae a nostro coetu planissime abhorrebant." Ed. Klette, p. 83; ed. Garin, p. 96.

25. "Nox te, nobis, Antoni, expolivit hominemque reddidit, nam hesterno sermone . . . nobis oratorem descripseras . . . inurbanum." *De orat.* ii 40.

26. Though the text of the second book of *De oratore*, as available about 1400, was fragmentary, Bruni may be expected to have known it from ii 19, and possibly from ii 13, on. See Sabbadini, *Le scoperte*, vol. I, pp. 100, 218; *Storia e critica* (1914), pp. 101ff.

27. From this analysis it will appear that Sabbadini's statement, *Giornale Storico*, *loc. cit.*, 131, "Bruni's *Dialogi* follow in the footsteps of the dialogues of *De oratore* everywhere" ("i *dialogi* del Bruni sono interamente ricalcati sui dialoghi del *de oratore*"), requires considerable modification. The similarities, noted by Sabbadini, between *De oratore* and the *Dialogus I* (a gathering of friends during the leisure of a holiday—the "ludi Romani" in *De oratore*, and the Easter-day in Bruni's dialogue) concern only superficialities of form and are of little consequence. In all respects of importance for the atmosphere of the conversations, Bruni at that point of his work does not follow the Ciceronian example, but evidently draws upon the reality of Florentine life, from the first casual meeting of the members of the group in a street of Florence to their visit to Salutati in his town-house, in contrast with the Ciceronian gathering in the country atmosphere of a "villa" in Tusculum. It is, therefore, misleading merely to state in general that the *Dialogi* depend on *De oratore* as a model, without considering the varying importance of these reminiscences in each dialogue.

Another possible approach to establishing the structural difference between the two dialogues could start from the observation that vocabulary and sentence-structure seem to be more elaborate in *Dialogus II* than in *Dialogus I*. A systematic comparison of the two dialogues from this viewpoint might yield valuable criteria for our argument.

The recognition of the direct derivation of some crucial features of the *Dialogus II* from *De oratore* makes it possible to refute definitively an apparently weighty argument previously used in the interpretation of the *Dialogi*. Klette, in his introductory exposition (p. 14), concluded that Niccoli's attacks in the first dialogue represent the historically essential aspect of the work because Niccoli says himself on the second day that his former theses had not been his idiosyncrasies, but had been an echo of opinions heard from (and consequently, Klette adds, spread at the time among) others. With the awareness that Niccoli's assertion is one of the literary devices of the second dialogue directly adopted from *De oratore* (cf. notes 21 and 22 above), we see the fallacy of this argument.

28. See Vol. One, p. 191f., and the full discussion of the evidence in *Humanistic and Political Literature*, Chapter VI, beginning of section 2, "One-Dialogue Manuscripts of the *Dialogi.*"

29. *Leonardi Aretini ad Petrum Paulum Istrum Dialogus*, ed. Th. Klette in his *Beiträge zur Geschichte und Litteratur der Italienischen Gelehrtenrenaissance*, vol. II (Greifswald, 1889), pp. 39-83. *I 'Dialogi ad Petrum Histrum' di Leonardo Bruni*, ed. G. Kirner (Leghorn, 1889). *Leonardi Bruni Aretini Dialogus de Tribus Vatibus Florentinis*, ed. K. Wotke (Vienna, 1889).

30. Kirner, in the introduction to his edition of the *Dialogi*, pp. xi, xxii.

31. First in a masterly treatise on the fortunes of Dante in the Renaissance ("Dante nel Trecento e nel Quattrocento," published in 1921, subsequently revised and complemented in Rossi's *Scritti di critica letteraria*, vol. I [1930], pp. 293-332), and later in the third edition of his standard work on the Quattrocento (*Il Quattrocento* [1933], pp. 105-107).

32. *Scritti di critica*, I, p. 299: "I believe my interpretation in this form to be definitive and incontestable." (". . . credo la mia interpretazione in questa forma definitiva e inoppugnabile"). *Il Quattrocento*, p. 119: "The argument is now exhausted and my interpretation of the *Dialogi* is definitive" (". . . ormai l'argomento è esaurito e . . . la mia interpretazione dei dialoghi è definitiva. *Sat prata biberunt*").

33. The last study in book form of the *Dialogi* which has come to the writer's knowledge—E. de Franco's *I dialoghi al Vergerio di Leonardo Bruni* (Catania, 1929)—merely underscores and develops Rossi's viewpoint, by attempting to minimize the importance of the parallels between the Niccoli of the first dialogue and the historical Niccoli brought out by earlier students, and to show (in line with Rossi's interpretation) that either dialogue

reveals one facet of an oscillating sentiment shared by both Bruni and Niccoli. If our thesis of a successive origin of the two dialogues and of the two views contained in them is tenable, the way in which this latest attempt at interpretation develops Rossi's thesis is *ipso facto* proved to have been built on unstable ground.

34. *Dialogi*, ed. Klette, p. 83; ed. Garin, p. 96.

35. "Verum me horum hominum suscipere patrocinium eosque a tuis maledictis tutari tempus prohibet. . . . Itaque ego istam defensionem aliud in tempus magis commodum differam." *Ibid.*, ed. Klette, p. 65f.; ed. Garin, p. 74.

36. "Nonne heri sententiam meam satis deprompsi, quid ego sentirem de summis illis viris?" *Ibid.*, ed. Klette, p. 70; ed. Garin, p. 80.

37. See Kirner's judgment, in the introduction to his edition of the *Dialogi*: "La parte, che Leonardo fa sostenere al gran cancelliere fiorentino, non è molto bella; ma non sappiamo, se si debba attribuire al difetto dell' autore o piuttosto all' intento di far figurare maggiormente il Niccoli" (p. xxii).

38. ". . . non magis Nicolai causam quam meam hoc sermone agi." *Dialogi*, ed. Klette, p. 56; ed. Garin, p. 62.

39. ". . . qui [i.e. Bruni] iamdudum non desinit a me petere, ut laudes illorum litteris mandem. Quod etsi ego facere cupio, et Leonardo morem gerere, . . . tamen nollem, mi Nicolae, tuis fraudibus impulsus videri." ". . . sed si vobis cordi est, huic Leonardo committatis; qui enim universam urbem laudarit, eundem hos quoque homines laudare par est." *Ibid.*, ed. Klette, p. 71; ed. Garin, p. 80f.

40. That Bruni was already Salutati's most intimate disciple, regular visitor in his study, and indispensable adviser in all questions connected with Greek, is attested by Salutati's letters *Ep. XII 10* (May 24, 1401), *Ep. XII 14* (August 4), *Ep. XII 17* (September 3), *Ep. XII 21* (September 25); *Epistolario*, vol. III, pp. 511-551.

41. See for this date Vol. One, pp. 226, 240, 244f.

42. Salutati, *Ep. XIV 20* (to Bernardo da Moglio), January 8, 1406 (*Epistolario*, vol. IV, p. 146): Bruni was "anime plus quam dimidium mee, imo penitus idem ego." (Cf. also *Ep. XIV 21* [to Bruni], January 9, 1406 [*ibid.*, p. 157]: "si tu alter es ego, sicut arbitror teneoque . . ."). Salutati, *Ep. XIV 22*, March 26, 1406 (*ibid.*, p. 160): Niccoli was Poggio's "alter ego."

43. For the relations between Salutati and the younger members of his group in that late period cf. also Vol. One, p. 228. The two letters of November/December 1405 and January 9, 1406, in which Bruni and Salutati violently quarrel over personal issues, are Bruni's *Ep. X 5* and Salutati's *Ep. XIV 21.*

44. See Vol. One, pp. 44, 164, 180.

45. "Itaque nec parricidam fuisse unquam putabo, nec unquam desinam Caesarem in caelum tollere pro magnitudine rerum quas gessit. Si tamen filii mei ad virtutem hortandi forent, vel a Deo id petendum, potius equidem optarem, ut M. Marcello aut L. Camillo similes essent, quam C. Caesari. Illi enim non inferiores bello fuere, et ad hanc rei militaris virtutem sanctimonia vitae accedebat, quae, an in Caesare fuerit, ego nescio; illi autem qui vitam eius describunt, contra tradunt. Itaque non ignaviter, ut mihi videtur, Leonardus causae suae inserviens, cum virtutum Caesaris meminisset, vitiorum suspicionem inseruit, ut aequis audientium auribus suam causam probaret." Ed. Klette, p. 69; ed. Garin, p. 78.

46a. ". . . non minima pars gloriae . . . huius nostrae civitatis." Ed. Klette, p. 70; ed. Garin, p. 80.

46b. See Vol. One, p. 180f.

47. Since the acceptance of our argument entails the rejection of the prevailing theory set forth by Rossi thirty years ago (see above note 31), it should be added that Rossi's interpretation of the *Dialogi* has been limping from the beginning because it was solely concerned with the memory of Dante but failed to consider the circumstance that Niccoli's charges and reactions refer to Petrarch as well. Now it is clear that the specific motive which Rossi regarded as basic for Bruni's alleged vacillation between his instinctive awareness of Dante's greatness as a poet, and the humanist's offense he took at Dante's medieval thought, cannot be applied to Bruni's attitude toward Petrarch the humanist. Yet we find the Niccoli of the *Dialogi* travelling precisely the same road, from a negative criticism to a positive appreciation, with regard to Petrarch. Here the more positive attitude in the second dialogue is based on the idea that the achievements of Petrarch, father of the humanist movement, could not be measured by the classicist's standards of the fifteenth century; his greatness lay in having "opened a road" on which those who came later could advance further. (See Vol. One, p. 236f.) Long

before Rossi, it had been pointed out by Bruni scholars (as early as 1892 by M. Korelin in his Russian work on early Italian Humanism, and later, 1912, by E. Santini in the paper "Della Produzione Volgare di Leonardo Bruni Aretino," *Giornale Stor. Lett. Ital.*, LX, p. 293f.; see also Vol. Two, p. 398f.) that this train of thought has a close parallel in Bruni's *Vite di Dante e di Petrarca* of 1436; in addition, as will be seen in Vol. One, p. 239f., this historically-minded appraisal of Petrarch was, indeed, something novel at the time of the *Dialogi* and clearly an attainment of Bruni the historian. While the views of the second-dialogue Niccoli thus turn out to be Bruni's own, the attacks made by the Niccoli of the first dialogue correspond, as has also long been known, to ideas attributed by other sources to the historical Niccoli. Consequently, it is most improbable that the two views of Petrarch found in the *Dialogi*—that still held by Bruni in his later years, and that characteristic of Niccoli—were shared by Bruni simultaneously, and that the *Dialogi* were meant to set forth a picture of how his mind was being torn with regard to Petrarch. But since Bruni in both passages speaks not only of Petrarch but also of Dante, it seems more than probable that what applies to his views on Petrarch applies with equal force to those on Dante. If this warning had been heeded, it could have led the interpretation of the *Dialogi* away from Rossi's theory even before the successive origin of the two dialogues had been established.

How greatly our verdict on the entire later course of the humanistic Quattrocento, especially in Florence, depends upon the correctness of our understanding of the *Dialogi*, can be seen from the important chapter in Rossi's *Quattrocento* (3rd edn., pp. 104-115) in which Bruni's *Dialogi* provide Rossi with the categories for his subsequent appraisal of the Quattrocento attitude toward Dante and the Volgare. Throughout the Quattrocento (thus Rossi explains the relationship) we see "arising a vacillating state of mind, of which Bruni's little work is the very picture." (". . . s'ingenera . . . uno stato d'animo titubante, di cui è imagine l'operetta del Bruni." p. 109f.) How the later history of the reputation of Dante and the Volgare must be rewritten in the light of our discovery that the two dialogues reveal an evolution from radical classicism to civic Humanism, will be discussed in the Part Four of this book, esp. pp. 261ff. and 301ff., and in Appendix 7.

CHAPTER 12

1. For the origin of *Ep. I 8* after 1402, cf. note 26 to Chap. 10.

2. See Vol. One, p. 32.

3. *Bruni, Schriften,* p. 161.

4a. This has been attempted in *Humanistic and Political Literature,* Chapter IV, section 3, "The Date of the *Laudatio*: Summer 1403 or Summer 1404."

4b. See the discussion of our information from Salutati's correspondence, *ibid.*, esp. notes 6-11.

5. See below, note 7.

6. *Dialogi,* ed. Klette, p. 39f.; ed. Garin, p. 44.

7. See *Laudatio, L* fol. 149v; ed. Klette, p. 97: To write a history of Florence would be an ambitious task, one very different from referring to a few historical examples, as in the *Laudatio,* but a task "quod nos ut spero aliquando aggrediemur, et quo pacto singula ab hoc populo gesta sunt litteris memorieque mandabimus."

8. "Omnes cives tibi habere gratias, Leonarde, debent." *Dialogi,* ed. Klette, p. 68; ed. Garin, p. 76. That this assertion was no vain self-flattery, but reflects the sentiment with which the *Laudatio* was received in Florentine circles, is shown by Salutati's remark in his letter to Bruni, Nov. 6, 1405: the "copiosissima et ornatissima oratio," which you composed "in patriae laudes," is one which "non presentibus solum, sed posteris edidisti" (Salutati, *Ep. XIV 17, Epistolario* vol. IV, p. 118). See also the evaluation in the anonymous *Laudatio Leonardi Historici et Oratoris,* written after Bruni's death: "De laudibus Florentinae urbis orationem composuit, quasi publicum quoddam munus." (Ed. Santini, in the appendix of his *Bruni e i "Hist. Flor. Pop.,"* p. 152.)

9. ". . . non minima pars gloriae sunt huius nostrae civitatis." "Nos . . . cives in laude civis nostri. . . ." "Et nescio an primus omnium lauream in nostram urbem attulerit." *Dialogi,* ed. Klette, pp. 70, 80; ed. Garin, pp. 80, 94.

10. On this exchange of letters during Bruni's stay at Viterbo see also Vol. One, pp. 213, 228, 241ff., 268.

11. *Archivum Romanicum,* XV (1931), 322.

12. The fact that the *Laudatio in Funere Othonis Adulescentuli* was composed at Viterbo in 1405, is stated in some manuscript titles. (See *Bruni, Schriften,* p. 161, and Mehus in his in-

troduction to Bruni's *Epistolae*, vol. I, p. lxii.) This information can be confirmed and supplemented from the oration itself, in which Bruni recounts that Otho, after the death of Pope Boniface IX (October 1, 1404), had rushed to Rome, lived there during the revolt of the Roman populace, and finally moved with the Curia from Rome to its present place (i.e. Viterbo): "una simul fuimus, una totum illud iter confecimus." (Ed. Santini, in *Bruni e i "Hist. Flor. Pop.,"* p. 145.)

13. "By Hercules, neither should I be *nobilis* if I were a Seriphos islander, nor would you have become famous if you were an Athenian" ("Nec hercle si ego Seriphius, nobilis: nec tu si Atheniensis esses, unquam clarus fuisses"), Themistocles had exclaimed, according to Cicero, *De senectute*, 3, 8. Bruni says in his speech: "Therefore one must attend to family and *patria*; for even Themistocles, that Athenian of the highest *virtus* and assiduity, believed that without his distinguished *patria* he could never achieve fame." ("Quare . . . genus atque patria attendenda sunt, sine cuius splendore nec Themistocles quidem ille Atheniensis summae virtutis et industriae vir claritatem se unquam adepturum putavit"; p. 143). What Bruni had in mind must have been the version just quoted, an attainment of Salutati's textual criticism (though the phrasing cited, that of Salutati, is not entirely identical with the text as established today). In contrast to Salutati, whose argument will be discussed presently, the text in most medieval manuscripts of *De senectute* had been "Neither would you have become *nobilis* if you were an Athenian, nor would I be obscure if I were a Seriphos islander" ("Neque tu, si Atheniensis esses, nobilis extitisses, neque ego, si Seripius essem, ignobilis")—a reading of the passage which would not have allowed for considering the *patria* a decisive factor. Bruni, during his stay at Viterbo, then, continued to side with the civic interpretation, giving it a place of honor in his speech.

Vergerio, on the other hand, in his *De Ingenuis Moribus et Liberalibus Studiis Adolescentiae*, had preferred to adhere to the uncorrected version because, differing from the political-mindedness of the Florentines, he could not bring himself to accept the thought that a man owed so much to his *patria*, and had to have a great *patria* in order to make himself *nobilis*. Only a few years before Bruni's oration, Salutati and Vergerio had carried on a notable epistolary discussion on the implications of the philological problem. Salutati, in a letter to Vergerio, had referred to Plato's *Politeia*, I, 329 s., as the source of the Themistocles anecdote and guide to its correct interpretation. He had added that the version of Themistocles' dictum which he preferred "branded the disputatious man from Seriphos with a twofold obscurity, that of his *patria* and that of his person, while acknowledging that all of his own [Themistocles'] *nobilitas* was due to his *patria*. This is the wise reply of a philosopher; this is the modesty and the frank confession of a citizen who has deserved well of his *patria*" ("duplicem . . . Seriphio iurgatori ignobilitatem inussit, patrie scilicet et persone, totamque nobilitatem suam a patria recognovit. Hec docta philosophi responsio; hec civis de patria benemerentis humilitas atque confessio"). To this interpretation Vergerio had objected "that it is proper neither for the *virtus* nor for the self-reliance of a man like Themistocles" ("quod neque virtuti Themistoclis neque fiducie convenit") to attribute so much to external conditions, "for we see men of superior *virtus* becoming famous even if they come from the peasantry and the socially lowest place" ("cum videamus meliori virtute homines ex agro atque infimo loco natos illustres evadere").

Salutati's and Vergerio's letters which contain this controversy were first published by Novati in *Epistolario di Salutati*, vol. IV, pp. 83f. and 366ff.; they have been reprinted with corrected dates (1402 or 1403) by L. Smith in *Epistolario di Vergerio*, pp. 253-262 (the quoted passages on pp. 255 and 259).

14. See the information in Poggio's letter to Niccoli, May 15, 1406, from Rome: "Audio insuper in successione officii [Colucii] multos esse competitores et in his Leonardum nostrum, pro cuius honore, ut soles, labora." Ed. by Novati, in Salutati's *Epistolario*, vol. IV, p. 474, with Novati's comment. Bruni had left Viterbo for Rome in early April, and, from the end of April into the early summer, was serving as a Papal commissioner in the northern parts of the Church State, as follows from his letters *Ep. I 11-I 14* and the documentary evidence listed by Novati, *op.cit.*, p. 470.

15. "Hic ego michi vivendum puto, atque eo magis, quod bona spes habetur, hanc pestiferam divisionem e medio sublatum iri." *Ep. II 4*, ed. Mehus, vol. I, p. 35.

16. "Arretina civitas, quam nonnulli contemnendam putant, judicio omnium palmam tulit." *Ibid.*, p. 36. The significance of this attitude is seen in its full light when it is added that Bruni

in later years, when he had returned to Florence and had definitely become a Florentine citizen both by status and attitude, in his *Historiae* (book IX) had nothing to say about the end of Arezzo's independence and her incorporation into the Florentine territorial state but the following few words of satisfaction with the course of events: "Ita Aretium . . . in Florentinorum potestatem, tamquam in portum aliquem deveniens, a longis iactationibus et acerbissimis tempestatibus requievit." (Ed. Santini, p. 239.)

17. As has already been mentioned briefly in Vol. One, p. 213f.

18. August 17 of 1405, not 1404, despite some indications that on the surface might seem to point to the latter year. See Novati, in his edition of Salutati's *Epistolario*, vol. IV, p. 127, and Walser, *Poggius Florentinus*, p. 32. Salutati's letter (from which Poggio's preceding one can be reconstructed in fragments) is *Ep. XIV 19* (December 17, 1405), *Epistolario*, vol. IV, pp. 126-145. On Poggio's anonymous companion see *ibid.*, p. 131.

19. Salutati, *Ep. IV 20*, July 13, 1379, *Epistolario*, vol. I, pp. 334-342. About the inclusion of this letter in manuscripts containing collected works of Petrarch, see Novati, *ibid.*, p. 334, and vol. IV, p. 130.

20. Salutati, *Ep. III 15*, August 16, 1374, *Epistolario*, vol. I, p. 177ff. *Ep. III 25*, December 24, 1375, *Epistolario*, vol. I, p. 227. (Petrarch and Boccaccio are here called such Florentine lights ["lumina"], "qualia modernis obicere non potest antiquitas").

21. Somewhat sneering and over-bearing: for Salutati said in October with regard to Poggio's letter that he would answer in such a way "quod discat parcius male dicere; nec voluntatem reputet rationem discatque iuvenis parcere seni." Salutati, *Ep. XIV 14*, *Epistolario*, vol. IV, p. 105.

22. The two letters of Salutati are *Ep. XIV 19* and *Ep. XIV 22*, *Epistolario*, vol. IV, pp. 130-145 and 158-170. It should be noted that A. v. Martin, in an excursus in his *Coluccio Salutati und das humanistische Lebensideal* (Leipzig, 1916), pp. 291f., denied Poggio's reasoning, which we have called his "recantation," to have been in the nature of "concessions" ("Zugestaendnisse") or attempts at reconciliation; he therefore objected to the comment of Novati, who (especially p. 161 n. 2) had emphasized the *rapprochement* to Salutati's standpoint in Poggio's second letter. The following observations will make clear the significance and

novelty of at least some of Poggio's arguments in January/February 1406, though without upholding Novati's entire argument. For Novati's comment, too, missed the mark by failing to note that the new element in Poggio's answer was largely not of Poggio's own making, but, as will be seen presently, derived from another source.

23. See Walser, *Poggius*, p. 32, n. 2.

24. For Poggio's stay at Viterbo see Walser, *ibid.*, p. 22.

25. See note 21 above.

26. See Vol. One, p. 213.

27. *Dialogi*, ed. Klette, p. 63f.; ed. Garin, p. 72.

28. Salutati, *Ep. IX 9*, August 1, 1395, *Epistolario*, vol. III, p. 84. R. P. Oliver has drawn attention to this statement of Salutati, in a recent excellent study of "Salutati's Criticism of Petrarch," in *Italica*, XVI (1939), pp. 53-54; it is not noted in Walser's exposition of the phases of Salutati's attitude in the "Petrarch controversy" (*Poggius*, p. 29ff.). Oliver's assumption of Salutati's later inconsistency in 1405-06 must be modified in the way suggested above.

29. Salutati, *Ep. XIV 19*, *Epistolario*, vol. IV, p. 135.

30. *Ibid.*, pp. 134f., 144.

31. As can be gathered from Salutati's subsequent letter to Poggio, of March 26, 1406. See the passages in question in Walser, *Poggius*, p. 36, n. 3.

32. Nelli to Petrarch, about 1355: You have succeeded in what none of the Greeks and Romans succeeded in doing; for one knows that Nature, in Rome, "brought forth two different men, one who is our model in verse, the other in prose" ("duos peperisse diversos, alterum . . . , quem ligatis frenatisque, alterum quem solutis passibus imitemur"), but none who were sufficiently able in both fields. Petrarch, however, was great in both fields, so that Nelli could say in his praise: "If I read you alone, I seem to read both Virgil and Cicero" ("te solum legens, Maronem Ciceronemque legam"). See E. Cochin, *Un Ami de Pétrarque. Lettres de Francesco Nelli* (Paris, 1892), pp. 115, 218. For a later example, prior to Bruni, of this train of thought compare Cino Rinuccini, in his *Risponsiva* (ed. Moreni, p. 229): Petrarch, "il quale universalissimo così fiorito di cetera l'altezza di Vergilio colla dolcezza d'Ovidio accompagnò, e il quale in ogni istilo così

volgare come latino, così metrico come prosaico, scrisse elegantissimamente."

33. *Epistolario*, vol. I, pp. 181ff., 342.

34. *Ibid.*, vol. IV, pp. 143f., 166f.

35. Bruni, in his *Vita di Petrarca*: "Ebbe il Petrarca nelli studi suoi una dote singolare, che fu attissimo a prosa ed a verso. . . . E questa grazia . . . è stata in pochi o in nullo fuor di lui, perchè pare che la natura tiri o all' uno o all' altro. . . . Onde addiviene che Virgilio, nel verso eccellentissimo, niente in prosa valse o scrisse, e Tullio, sommo maestro nel dire in prosa, niente valse in versi," and so with all other poets and orators. "Il Petrarca è solo quello che per dota singolare nell' uno e nell' altro stile fu eccellente . . ." (*Bruni, Schriften*, pp. 66-67). Manetti, in his *Vita Francisci Petrarcae*, following Bruni's example, recast the very same ideas in full-sounding Latin phrases, adding Homer and Demosthenes to Vergil and Cicero. (Ed. Solerti, in his volume *Le Vite di Dante, Petrarca e Boccaccio* [Milan, 1904], pp. 306-307.)

36. *Dialogi*, ed. Klette, p. 80; ed. Garin, p. 94.

37. "Nec audebimus illum suis meritis ornare, praesertim cum hic vir studia humanitatis, quae iam extincta erant, repararit et nobis, quemadmodum discere possemus, viam aperuerit?" *Loc. cit.*

38. "Per istum enim poetam resuscitata est mortua poesis. Nam oblivioni iam tradita erat ipsa scientia et summi philosophi qui studuerunt et floruerunt in ea. Et ad hoc demonstrandum dicit ipse auctor in primo cantu primae canticae ubi loquitur de Virgilio: *chi per lungo silenzio parea fioco*. Ipse vero poeticam scientiam suscitavit et antiquos poetas in mentibus nostris reminiscere fecit." Quoted from the unpublished early Dante commentary of the Carmelite friar Guido da Pisa in O. Bacci's *La Critica Letteraria (Dall' Antichità classica al Rinascimento)*, in the series "Storia dei Generi Letterari Italiani," (Milan, 1910), p. 163. Attention has recently been drawn to this passage by P. O. Kristeller in his paper "Humanism and Scholasticism in the Italian Renaissance," *Byzantion*, XVII (1944-45), 347.

39. "E perciò, avendo egli [that is, Giotto] quella arte ritornata in luce che molti secoli sotto gli errori d'alcuni, che più a dilettar gli occhi degli ignoranti che a compiacere allo 'ntelletto de' savj dipignendo, era stata sepulta, meritamente una delle luci della fiorentina gloria dir si puote." Boccaccio, *Decamerone*, Giornata VI, novella V; J. Huizinga first called attention to this passage

in his paper "Das Problem der Renaissance," first published 1920, last in his *Parerga* (1945), p. 93. The passage in Boccaccio's *Trattatello in laude di Dante* runs: "Questi fu quel Dante, il quale primo doveva al ritorno delle Muse, sbandite d'Italia, aprir la via. . . . Per costui la morta poesi meritamente si può dire suscitata." (Ed. Solerti, *op. cit.*, p. 13.)

We may add that an excellent appraisal of Boccaccio's statements on Dante and Giotto, and of the elaboration of those views in Filippo Villani's *De Origine Civitatis Florentiae*, has recently been given in W. K. Ferguson's *The Renaissance in Historical Thought*, p. 19ff. It should be noted, however, that Filippo Villani, by assigning the restoration to Cimabue and Dante, whereas Boccaccio had already thought of Giotto and had given Petrarch a place of his own beside Dante, was less important than the authors whom we shall discuss, in carrying on a debate which increasingly concentrated on Petrarch and the nature of Humanism.

40. ". . . amotis vepribus arbustisque quibus mortalium negligentia obsitum comperit, restauratisque aggere firmo proluviis semesis rupibus, *sibi et post eum ascendere volentibus viam aperuit.*" Boccaccio, *Opere latine minori*, ed. A. F. Massèra (Bari, 1928), p. 195.

41a. Boccaccio, *ibid.*, p. 196.

41b. The fact that in the eyes of the humanists of the Trecento the humanistic movement was almost identical with poetry, or with the reawakening of ancient poetry, has recently been strongly emphasized in two important papers: P. O. Kristeller's "Humanism and Scholasticism in the Italian Renaissance," *Byzantion*, XVII (1944-45), esp. 364ff.; and B. L. Ullman's "Renaissance—the Word and the Underlying Concept," *Studies in Philology*, XLIX (1952), esp. 106-112. (Both will be republished in Kristeller's and Ullman's collected papers in the series "Storia e Letteratura," Rome). But these two authors are not sufficiently aware that this identification was no longer made by the leading humanists of the Quattrocento who, when creating, or reviving, the term "*studia humanitatis*," thought of a correlated system of "humane" disciplines in which poetry was fused into a much wider program of intellectual pursuits. Although Kristeller asserts that "the humanists of the fourteenth *and fifteenth* [italics mine] century chose to call their field of study poetry and . . . were often styled poets even though they composed no works that would qualify them as poets in the modern sense," the facts he cites show on the contrary that by the Quattrocento the field of the humanist, even in his daily routine, was bound to appear too wide to admit of the continuation of the Trecento view. In the universities, Kristeller points out himself (*loc. cit.*, p. 365), humanists began to hold chairs of moral philosophy in addition to, or in combination with, the chairs of poetry and rhetoric, and in the libraries of the Quattrocento the classification of "*studia humanitatis*" included grammar, rhetoric, history, and moral philosophy, besides poetry. Ullman, again, after giving a number of characteristic examples of the Trecento, adds what he calls "one set of examples from the fifteenth century" (*loc. cit.*, p. 111f.); but this fifteenth-century evidence actually discloses the fact that Sicco Polentone, a writer who cannot be counted among the original minds of the century, characterized the movement of the Trecento as a reawakening of the "Muses" and the "cura poetandi" merely in the first draft of his *Scriptorum illustrium Latinae linguae libri XVIII* (about 1425), but in the published edition (between 1433 and 1437) talked of Petrarch as having in his "studia" surpassed all those famed in the "litterae" for a thousand years, and having been the earliest stimulator both of "studii et poetici *et omnis eloquentiae*." (Italics mine.) The actual situation, then, is that after the first quarter of the Quattrocento even average opinion conceived the historic achievement of Petrarch and his followers no longer in terms of Boccaccio's enthusiastic acclamation of the return of the Muses of Roman poetry, but as the restoration of the true "studia," "litterae," and "eloquentia," while at the same time more original minds realized that Petrarch's role had been the rediscovery of the Ciceronian ideal of "studia humanitatis," and worked for a new integrated program of those studies. In the present writer's opinion, the rise of this new conception is one of the distinguishing marks between the Quattrocento view of Humanism and that held in the Trecento; there is urgent need of a much more penetrating study of this distinction than can be devoted to it in the present book. Meanwhile, the importance of such a differentiation for the interpretation of the transition from the Trecento to the Quattrocento will be seen from the examples to which we have referred or shall refer on the pages which follow.

42. For the date of Vergerio's *Vita* of Petrarch see Smith in *Archivio Veneto*, ser. v, vol. IV (1928), 99f.

43. "Poeticam processu temporis neglexit sacris litteris delectatus, . . . poeticis litteris nonnisi ad ornatum reservatis. Incubuit unice . . . ad notitiam vetustatis. . . . Eloquio fuit claro ac potenti, . . . atque (ut vere dixerim) unicus fuit, qui per tot saecula exulantem, et iam pene incognitam dicendi facultatem in nostra tempora revocaret." Ed. Solerti, *op. cit.*, p. 299.

To cite an illuminating Trecento parallel, the gradual abandonment of the identification of Petrarch's work with a revival of ancient poetry can be illustrated also with the history of Salutati's verdicts on Petrarch. Whereas Salutati, as we have just observed (Vol. One, p. 230f.), in all his later utterances did not see the focus of Petrarch's activities in poetry, he had made this identification in an appraisal of Petrarch in one of his earliest letters, written before 1360. (In a letter to Nelli, ed. in Novati's *Epistolario*, vol. IV, p. 244.) Attention has been drawn to this passage by B. L. Ullman in his "Renaissance—The Word and the Underlying Concept," *loc. cit.*, p. 108.

44. "Existimavique omnes, qui his nostris studiis delectantur, ei quamplurimum debere; quippe qui primus suo labore, industria, vigilantia haec studia *pene ad internicionem redacta* nobis *in lucem erexerit* et aliis sequi volentibus *viam patefecerit*." Salutati, *Epistolario*, vol. IV, p. 161. Cf. above note 22.

45. ". . . studia humanitatis, quae *iam extincta* erant, *repararit* et nobis, quemadmodum discere possemus, *viam aperuerit*." *Dialogi*, ed. Klette, p. 80; ed. Garin, p. 94. See note 37 above.

46. Boccaccio had said of Petrarch that by having himself crowned as a poet on the Capitol he had revived traditions forgotten for more than a thousand years, and thus "he opened up a path for himself and those eager to ascend after him" ("sibi et post eum ascendere volentibus viam aperuit"). When we now find Poggio in his characterization of Petrarch employing the phrase that "he opened the path to those others who were eager to follow" ("aliis sequi volentibus viam patefecerit"), we cannot doubt that Boccaccio's words "eager to ascend after him" ("ascendere volentibus") are reflected in Poggio's "eager to follow" ("sequi volentibus"). And since this significant term is not adopted by Bruni in his *Dialogus II*—the only words Bruni literally repeats from Boccaccio are "viam aperuit"—Poggio also must have known Boccaccio's letter.

47. Boccaccio, therefore, does not exactly say, as Bruni and

Poggio were to say, that Petrarch had opened a path for his "followers" or "for us"; but that he had "opened a path for himself as well as for those who wished to ascend after him" (*sibi et post eum ascendere volentibus viam aperuit*). And the expression "viam aperuit" is explained, immediately afterwards, as the rediscovery and restoration of the forgotten ascent to the "summit": "Inde helyconico fonte limo iuncoque palustri purgato, . . . in extremos usque vertices Parnasi conscendit. . . . Spem fere deperditam in generosos suscitavit animos ostenditque quod minime credebatur a pluribus, pervium scilicet esse Parnasum et eius accessibile culmen: nec dubito quin multos animaverit ad ascensum." (Boccaccio, *loc. cit.*, pp. 195-196.)

48. Poggio, *Ep. II 16*, ed. Tonelli, vol. 1, pp. 129ff. (Also quoted by Bertalot in *Bibliofilia* [1928], pp. 402-403.)

49. ". . . cum primo libro viros praestantissimos doctissimosque Dantem, Franciscum Petrarcham, Johan. Boccacium, eorumque doctrinam, eloquentiam, opera impugnasset; secundo in superioris excusationem ipsorum et virtus laudata est." Poggio, *Oratio Funebris*, ed. Mehus in his introduction to Bruni's *Epistolae*, vol. 1, p. cxxii f.

50. For *Dialogus II* and Poggio, see the quotations, Vol. One, pp. 232 and 237f.

51. "Posto che in lui perfetto non fusse, pur da sè vide e aperse la via a questa perfezione . . . ; e per certo fece assai, solo a dimostrare la via a quelli che dopo lui avevano a seguire."

52. *Bruni, Schriften*, pp. 65-66; but the reader should change the punctuation, there given, "fece assai solo, a dimostrare" (meaning, Petrarch did enough as a sole pioneer [solo, i.e. alone] in opening the way) to the traditional version, found in Solerti's edition, *op.cit.*, p. 290, "fece assai, solo a dimostrare" (meaning, Petrarch did enough by merely pointing the way [solo, i.e. solamente, merely]). Even though many of the Italian scholars the writer has consulted in the matter have been in favor of reinterpreting "solo" as "alone," closer observations of Bruni's style must lead to a change in the choice between the two readings, equally possible as far as meaning is concerned: 1) If "solo" here meant "alone," it would presumably have been connected with the words "da sè" (as used by Bruni two lines earlier), or would have been given a different position in the sentence; 2) the use of a verb plus "assai" is a frequently employed sentence ending in Bruni's

Vite, e.g. p. 57 line 33 on Dante, "s' affaticò assai," and similarly p. 54 line 12, p. 55 line 12, p. 63 line 1; 3) the use of "solo a dimostrare" has a close parallel in "A che proposito si dice questo da me? Solo per dimostrare, che . . . ," p. 65, lines 11-12. Bruni, then, may be thought to have meant that Petrarch "did enough by merely pointing the way for those who were to follow after him" —our rendering of the passage in Volume One.

53. See Vol. One, pp. 223 and 226.

54. Bruni's letter of September 13, 1405, to which Salutati replies, has been found by L. Bertalot in a manuscript volume of the Preussische Staatsbibliothek, Berlin, and published in *Archivum Romanicum*, xv (1931), 321-323. Salutati's answer is his *Ep. XIV 17*, Nov. 6, 1405, *Epistolario*, vol. IV, pp. 113-120; the passage quoted is on p. 118f.

55. "Mihi porro nunquam tantum vel honoris vel utilitatis contingere posset, quin illud tempus longe iucundius ducerem, quo ego una cum ceteris familiaribus sociatus litteras graecas auidissime perdiscebam, *aut cum cetu facto apud te conuenientes* quid dispongere, quid versuram facere, quid boni consulere, quid decoquere, quid alucinari, quid nauare operam, quid celeres, quid nequitia, quid sexcenta eiusmodi significarent addiscebamus. Horum quotiens mihi venit in mentem, dispeream nisi tota mente commoueor meque stultitiae condemno, qui unquam a latere tuo, mi Coluci, demigraui." (*Archivum Romanicum*, xv [1931], 323.) For the interpretation of this letter see also Vol. One, pp. 223 and 268.

56. See Vol. One, pp. 213 and 228.

57. ". . . quanto clarius in patrie laudes versabaris; celebrationi cuius adeo affectus es, quod copiosa et ornatissima oratio, quam stilo luculentissimo non presentibus solum, sed posteris edidisti, te non potuisti satiare, quin etiam, ubicunque se dederit occasio, quasi nihil dixeris, velut ex integro idem propositum ordiaris." Salutati, *Ep. XIV 17*, Nov. 6, 1405, *Epistolario*, vol. IV, p. 119.

58. *Dialogi*, ed. Klette, p. 67f.; ed. Garin, p. 76.

59. See Vol. One, pp. 210f. and 215.

60. The Excursus "Indications that *Dialogus II* Was Written After Bruni Had Left Florence," in *Humanistic and Political Literature*, Chapter VI, section 4, discusses two further pieces of evidence enhancing the probability of composition late in 1405.

Part Four

CHAPTER 13

1. See Vol. One, pp. 67f., 73f.

2. See B. Croce in *La Critica*, XXVII (1927), 426f., on Wesselofsky's place in these historiographical trends; Croce, *Storia della Storiografia Italiana nel Secolo Decimonono*, vol. I (Bari, 1921), pp. 118ff., 217, on "the low esteem for the age of the Renaissance, as the period which marked the national ruin"; and G. Gentile, *G. Capponi e la Cultura in Toscana nel Secolo Decimonono* (Firenze, 1922), chapters V-VIII, on the "nuovi Piagnoni," with the inclusion of P. Villari.

3. ". . . iniziava il decadimento politico, che non va mai disgiunto dal decadimento letterario. . . . A mano a mano che decadeva l'antica libertà e la civiltà nazionale, sorgeva la classica civiltà del principato."

4. "... una continua gradazione di decadimento e di progresso."

5. Wesselofsky, I, pp. 47-49; II, pp. 6f., 20, 49f.

For the long survival of these opinions—identification of Humanism with the culture of the Tyrant courts, and the assertion that in the Quattrocento there existed everywhere a cleavage between the humanistic outlook and the inherited civic traditions—compare such outstanding examples as: G. Voigt, *Die Wiederbelebung*, I³ (1893), pp. 444f. ("The real ideal of the humanists was the honored and generously rewarded court poet. . . . At bottom, therefore, they were all of them monarchists, not excepting even those Florentines who flocked around the Medici.") Francesco de Sanctis, *Storia della Letteratura Italiana*, passim. (See the appraisal of De Sanctis' attitude in H. Friedrich, "Francesco de Sanctis," *Romanische Forschungen*, LI [1937], 187ff., esp. 210f.) G. Gentile, *La Filosofia* (published in the series *Storia dei generi letterarii Italiani*, 1904-15; incomplete, but spanning the early Quattrocento), pp. 213ff., 267ff.; also his paper "Il carattere del Rinascimento," in Gentile's volume *Il Pensiero Italiano del Rinascimento* (Bari, 1940), passim. V. Rossi, "Nazione e Letteratura in Italia" (first 1916), in Rossi's *Scritti di critica letteraria*, vol. III (1930), pp. 361ff.; also his *Il Quattrocento*³ (1933), p. 109. (In contrast to the "communal pre-Humanism and the Volgare art of Dante," there arose in the Quattrocento "the literature of the humanists, expression of that culture as it was turning from the Commune to the Signory.") E. Emerton, *Humanism and Tyranny* (1925), pp. 48ff., 58, 63 (see note 38 to Chap. 7). F. Schevill, "The Society of the Italian Renaissance," in the symposium volume *The Civilization of the Renaissance* (Chicago, 1929), pp. 57ff. (In justice to Schevill it should be noted, however, that in the course of his later studies of Florentine history he became more acutely aware of the dangers of the customary identification of Humanism with the culture of the Renaissance tyranny; see Schevill's *History of Florence* [1936], passim.)

Even more recently, A. Corsano, in his volume *Il Pensiero Religioso Italiano dall' Umanesimo al Giurisdizionalismo* (Bari, 1937), p. 9, has paid Wesselofsky the special compliment to call him "un prudentissimo filologo" because "he recognized the existence of two tendencies in Florentine culture in the late Trecento and earliest Quattrocento," the one which with scholastic traditions combined the "culto delle istituzioni comunali e della grande letteratura volgare trecentesca," and the other, the "classical" tendency, contemptuous of all those traditions and ready for a complete break "in politica come in letteratura come in filosofia."

6. See Wesselofsky, grouping together Giovanni da Prato, Cino Rinuccini, and Domenico da Prato as representatives of the "scuola volgare," vol. II, pp. 48, 52-54. That this triad has been a major factor in shaping the view of the period about 1400 among modern scholars has been stressed by E. Santini. "The *Paradiso degli Alberti*," Santini writes, "and the invectives of Cino Rinuccini and Domenico da Prato are the chief documents on the basis of which critics have formulated their opinions. The authors of these writings have been regarded as the legitimate representatives of the old society, standing in complete opposition to the generation of the humanists whose voice is thought to reach us through Leonardo Bruni's *Dialogi ad P. Histrum*" ("La Produzione Volgare di . . . Bruni," *Giorn. Stor. Lett. Ital.*, LX [1910], 290).

7. Cf. what we have found on Cino's role as a civic prehumanist, in Vol. One, pp. 61f. and 79ff. More details will be added in the next chapter, Vol. One, p. 266ff. Cino's *Invettiva* is published in Wesselofsky, II, pp. 303-316.

8. For this political poem, written in 1424, see Vol. One, p. 336f.

9. See Wesselofsky, II, pp. 322, 326.

10. This invective is published in Wesselofsky, II, pp. 321-330. The basic study on Domenico da Prato, after the pioneering appraisal in Wesselofsky, II, pp. 54-67, is M. Casella's "Ser Domenico del Maestro Andrea da Prato Rimatore del Secolo XV," *Rivista delle Bibliotheche e degli Archivi*, XXVII (1916), 1-40. On the imitative character of Domenico's poetry see Casella, pp. 17, and 26-30. Rossi, *Il Quattrocento*, p. 231f., emphasizes the dry pedantry of Domenico's erudite poetizing. We have no information about the date of Domenico's birth, but from the indications discussed in note 15 below we may conclude that he must have been roughly coeval with Niccoli and Bruni.

11. See Wesselofsky's opinion in note 46 to Chap. 14.

12. He noted on p. 55 that Domenico was "aged" ("vecchio") when writing his preface-invective, and that he lived beyond the year 1425.

13. Della Torre, *Storia dell' Accademia Platonica di Firenze* (1902), p. 221. Casella, in his chronological discussion of Domenico's invective, *loc. cit.*, seems to have overlooked Della Torre's preceding observations.

14. Wesselofsky, II, p. 325.

15. The few facts known of Domenico's life fit excellently with the dating of his invective around 1420. According to notarial protocols signed by Domenico with place and date (a collection has been preserved in the "Archivio Notarile Antecosimiano" in the Florentine Archivio di Stato) he was in the city of Florence during the years 1419-22 (though with interruptions, caused by notary business in the territory); he notarized in the city in April 1419, February 1421, and December 1422—in the last case "in domo habitationis mei [sic] Dominici notarii," a definite indication that he had his domicile in Florence at that time. During 1417-18, on the other hand, he had been constantly in Pisa, whereas during 1423-24 he lived again outside Florence, until he returned at the time of the first great Florentine defeats in the war against Filippo Maria Visconti—events which moved him deeply, as is attested by his long patriotic poem after the defeat of Zagonara (see note 8 above). That first, ill-fated year of the war with all its tension certainly offered no proper occasion for the collection of

his youthful love-lyrics; immediately afterwards (1425) he again left Florence on his professional wanderings and did not return until 1430, when he settled down for a stay that lasted to 1432, the last known date in his life. Our knowledge of these dates, taken from notarial documents, is due to M. Casella's article, quoted above (see esp. Casella, pp. 6-12). Casella's own hypothesis that the collection of the poems and the composition of the preface-invective fell as late as this last (1430-32) Florentine sojourn is refuted by the consideration that Domenico in 1430 could not have stated Bruni had produced no historical, philosophical or poetical works; and equally by the unlikelihood that Domenico should have written of Bruni in the contemptuous fashion of the invective at a time when Bruni was already the chancellor, and one of the best-known personalities of Florence. Although Casella asserts that Domenico's invective "with every probability" belongs to the years 1430-32, his sole basis for choosing this late date is clearly the fact that Domenico, in his preface-invective, remarks of his now distant youth: "and although some of the little pieces which follow and which deal with love, must be ranked in their expressions as youthful inanities rather than as ripe ['senili'] eulogies of authentic workmanship, . . . yet I do not want for that to leave them out or omit them" (". . . e bene che alquante delle infrascritte operette trattanti d'amore, meritino più tosto giovinili vaghezze nelle loro pronunziazioni che laude senili d'autentiche construzioni . . . non per tanto le voglio obmettere nè intralasciarle." See Casella, pp. 2, 31). These words, however, are far from implying that Domenico was already an old man. If he was born not later than the 1370's or 1380's, he could quite well write in these terms as early as about 1420. There is every reason to assume so early a date for the unknown time of his birth, since in all his works his manner of speaking of Florentine acquaintances is that of a man of the generation of Bruni and Niccoli. Not only does Domenico fail to give the least indication in his invective, where such an indication would have been natural, of considering the leaders of the opposite "sect" his elders; in a letter written in 1413 to a younger friend still less advanced in the studies, he refers to Brunelleschi (born 1379) and the future archbishop Antonino (born 1389) in a manner which clearly implies that these two were the elders of the "young" ("giovane") addressee but not of himself. (See the edition of the letter in Wesselofsky, II, p.

336f.) In addition, Domenico exchanged poems with Roberto de' Rossi, who was at least fifteen years older than Bruni, and thirty-five years older than Antonino; and such an exchange would be unlikely if the difference in age between Domenico and Rossi had been still greater. (See the recent publication, by A. Manetti, of the *inedita* of this poetical exchange, in *Rinascimento*, II [1951], 35-44.) Finally, the letter of 1413 just quoted refutes any doubts that Domenico in 1420 may have been too young for the tenor of his invective; for even in 1413 he talked with the voice of a man who has left his youth far behind, and who looks out upon life with the eyes of a philosopher. In sum, all the pertinent facts known of Domenico's life and literary works combine to support the attribution of his invective to the time around 1420.

16. "Per loro falso giudicio dannano Dante, messer Francesco Petrarca, messer Johanni Boccaci, messer Coluccio et altri."

17. Doubts were expressed already by Casella, *op. cit.*, pp. 15-17. But we cannot hope to get beyond conjectures unless we attempt to determine for each of Domenico's arguments separately whether it can have been aimed at Niccoli or at Bruni.

As for the reference, which follows in the text, to Bruni's vindication of Boccaccio, the last chapter of Bruni's *Vite di Dante e di Petrarca* includes a brief appraisal of Boccaccio ("Notizia del Boccaccio"); see *Bruni, Schriften*, p. 67f.

18. "Et tutte queste cose dicono dimostrando, o vero volendo mostrare se essere eccelenziori et più intelligenti di lui." Wesselofsky, II, p. 323.

19. *Ibid.*, p. 322f.

20. *Ibid.*, p. 323.

21. "Or non confondono questi dannosissimi uomini li animi non ancora fermi delli adolescenti e ricenti uditori, quando dicono, . . . non potersi alcuna cosa fare o dire sì bene, che meglio non sia stata detta o fatta per li antichi passati. . . . O depopulatori et usurpatori de quel bene che dare non possono! . . . Et se tutto è stato detto a bastanza secondo che dicono, a che favellano?" *Ibid.*, p. 324.

22. Nothing but a desiderata list for investigators of manuscripts has come down to us from his pen; see note 3 to Chap. 4. To his biographers, Poggio, Manetti, Enea Silvio and Vespasiano da Bisticci, it appeared that he did not write anything because he

had formed an ideal of the perfect classical style that was beyond his own reach. Cf. Voigt, *Die Wiederbelebung*, I, p. 302f.

23. Compare Domenico da Prato (in Wesselofsky, II, p. 324): ". . . quando dicono: Chi si farà Omero o Virgilio in poesia? Chi Solone o Aristotele in filosofia? Chi Demostene o Cicerone in retorica et in orare? Chi Aristarco o Prisciano in gramatica? Chi Parmenide in dialettica? et così di ciascuna arte liberale quanto di qualunque altra virtù manuale . . . ," with Bruni, *Prologus in Vita Quinti Sertorii ex Plutarcho traducta* (*Bruni, Schriften*, p. 124f.): "In hac itaque ingenii et intelligentiae parte, si recte iudicare voluerimus nec nos metipsos caritate nostri decipere, iam videbimus manifeste: nec in re militari nec in gubernatione rerum publicarum nec in eloquentia nec in studiis bonarum artium tempora nostra antiquis respondere. Nisi forte Platoni aut Aristoteli aut Carneadi aut multis aliis veteribus in sapientia et doctrinis, aut Demostheni et Tullio in eloquentia, aut in gubernatione rerum publicarum Pericli, Soloni et Catoni, aut in hac ipsa, de qua contendimus, militari arte Pyrrho aut Hannibali aut Fabio Maximo aut M. Marcello aut C. Iulio Caesari saecula nostra pares aliquos aut comparandos queunt proferre." Bruni's translation of the *Vita Sertorii* had already been current at the time of the Council of Constance, and the period between October 1408 and January 1409 can be inferred as the exact time of origin (see note 24 to Chap. 17). Consequently, Domenico may be expected to have known the work.

24. Books III and IV of the *Historiae Florentini Populi* were written in 1420 and 1421; see note 14 to Chap. 17.

25. *Bruni, Schriften*, p. 176f.

26. Bruni's *Isagogicon Moralis Disciplinae* was written during the summer, 1423; see note 22 to Chap. 17. For the dates of Bruni's poetical works, see note 12 to Chap. 15.

27. Wesselofsky, II, p. 325f.

28. *Bruni, Schriften*, pp. 102f. and 161.

29. Wesselofsky, II, p. 328f.

30. *Bruni, Schriften*, pp. 103f. and 78. For Domenico's familiarity with Bruni's translation of the *Nicomachean Ethics* see Vol. One, p. 255.

31. Wesselofsky, II, p. 328.

32. The *Invective Against Certain Slanderers of Dante and Messer Francesco Petrarca and of Messer Giovanni Boccaccio,*

whose names are passed over in silence for the sake of decency—written by the learned and conscientious Cino di Messer Francesco Rinuccini, Florentine citizen, and rendered from the Latin into the Volgare ("Invettiva contro a cierti caluniatori di Dante e di messer Francesco Petrarca e di messer Giovanni Boccaci, i nomi de' quali per onestà si tacciono, composta pello iscientifico e ciercuspetto uomo Cino di messer Francesco Rinuccini cittadino fiorentino, ridotta di gramatica in vulgare") is published in Wesselofsky, II, pp. 303-316. Since then, the most intensive use of it as a source of historical information has been made by G. Gentile in his *La Filosofia* (see note 5 above). By carefully comparing and integrating the information contained both in the *Invettiva* and in Bruni's *Dialogi*, Gentile (pp. 206-218) already reached some of the conclusions to be drawn presently, though his findings were not yet always based on critically established facts, but rather took the form of questions and conjectures. Starting from the observation that several of Cino's demands are virtually met by Bruni in his second dialogue, Gentile concluded that "it seems to be more reasonable to think (*par più ragionevole pensare*) that Rinuccini's *Invettiva* preceded Bruni's work." V. Rossi, in his paper on Dante (*Scritti di critica letteraria*, I, 296), adopted this argument. (For Rossi's indebtedness to Gentile on this score cf. his reference, *op. cit.*, p. 299, n. 1.) But, for obvious reasons, neither Gentile nor Rossi were able to proceed very far from this auspicious start. Since Gentile did not know that only *Dialogus I* originated in 1401, he regarded the Dante and Petrarch vindication of the second dialogue as Bruni's and Niccoli's common attitude in 1401, and could, therefore, not see the decisive chronological fact: that only *Dialogus II* can be assumed to have followed Cino's *Invettiva*, while *Dialogus I* may have preceded it. This fact virtually deprives Gentile's argument of all its consequences for the interpretation of the relations between Bruni and Niccoli, as well as for the establishment of a *terminus ad quem*. But the conclusion remains valid that Cino's pamphlet, far from being an attack on Bruni, gives us a picture of the situation which existed before some of the key ideas of *Dialogus II* emerged; through a comparison of the *Invettiva* with other early works of Bruni, we shall, indeed, be able to confirm and elaborate in a changed form an hypothesis which, in its general outline, had already suggested itself earlier to two eminent scholars.

33. "E de' libri del coronato poeta messer Francesco Petrarca si beffano, diciendo che quel *De viris illustribus* è un zibaldone da quaresima. Non dicono quanto e' fu gienerale in versificare così in latino come in vulgare. . . . Poi, per mostrarsi litteratissimi, dicono che lo egregio e onore de' poeti Dante Alighieri essere suto poeta da calzolai; non dicono che 'l parlar poetico è quello che sopra agli altri come aquila vola. . . . Lo inlustre ed esimio poeta Dante . . . gli umani fatti dipigne in vulgare più tosto per fare più utile a' suo' cittadini che non farebbe in gramatica. Nè tonando deridano e mali dicienti, però che 'l fonte della eloquenca, Dante, con maravigliosa brevità e legiadria mette due o tre comparazioni in uno rittimo vulgare che Vergilio non mette in venti versi esametri. . . . Il perchè tengo che 'l vulgare rimare sia molto più malagevole e maestrevole che 'l versificare litterale." Wesselofsky, II, pp. 309-311.

34. "Hunc igitur ego virum . . . a litteratorum collegio ideo heri disiunxi, ut non cum illis, sed supra illos sit." *Dialogi*, ed. Klette, p. 75; ed. Garin, p. 86.

35. "Sola enim hec in tota Italia civitas purissimo atque nitidissimo sermone uti existimatur. Itaque omnes qui bene atque emendate loqui volunt ex hac una urbe sumunt exemplum. Habet enim hec civitas homines qui in hoc populari atque communi genere dicendi ceteros omnes infantes ostenderint." *Laudatio*, *L* fol. 155v; ed. Klette, p. 104. For the importance of this praise of the Florentine attainments in the field of the Volgare, see also Vol. One, p. 302.

36. "Delle storie con grande ansietà disputano se dinanzi al tempo di Nino si trovano istorie o no, e quanti libri compuose Tito Livio, e perchè e' non si truovano tutti, e quali sieno gli errori degli storiografi, affermando Valerio Massimo esser troppo brieve, e Tito Livio interrotto, e le cronache troppo prolisse. E tanto tempo in cotali disputazioni vane perdono, che niuna veracie istoria possono aprendere o apresa fissa nella memoria tenerla per recitarla secondo il tempo e 'l luogo utile pella republica." Wesselofsky, II, p. 309. As for the suspicion that the reference to the discussions on the lost books of Livy might have aimed at Bruni, see note 48 to Chap. 14.

37. "Dicono che Platone è maggior filosafo che Aristotile, allegando Sant' Agostino diciente Aristotile principe de' filosofi, eciетto sempre Platone. Non dicono perchè sant' Agostino il

premette: perchè in sua openione dell'anima è più conforme alla fede cattolica . . ." *Ibid.*, p. 313.

38. See Bruni in his "Prologus in Phaedonem Platonis," *Bruni, Schriften*, p. 4. The agreement between Rinuccini and Bruni on this score deserves emphasis because different positions were possible and did exist: Salutati, in his *De Laboribus Herculis*, presumably at the same moment, responded to the same situation not with an avowal of Augustinian Christian Platonism, but rather with a refusal to accept Cicero's, and Augustine's, Platonist reservation "always excepting Plato." In talking, in the introduction to the *Hercules*-treatise, of Aristotle's opinion on the poets, he says he accepts it as the most valuable, "nec Platonem ut Arpinas excipio." (*De Laboribus Herculis*, ed. B. L. Ullman, p. 4.)

CHAPTER 14

1a. This copy is now Cod. Vat. Ottobon. Lat. 1156; it has the colophon "Scriptum ad instanciam Cini domini Francisci de Ranucinis de Florencia. Anno domini MCCCLXXXIII." See V. Branca in *Pensée Humaniste et Tradition Chrétienne aux XVe et XVIe Siècles* (Paris: Le Centre National de la Recherche Scientifique, 1950), p. 82.

1b. ". . . che nel mio tempo la mia città crescendo in essa una brigata di giovani di maravigliosa indole, ex . . . . . (sic!) che sarebbe idonea nella città litter[at]issima d'Atene, e che di sua iscienzia, e mirabilità d'ingegno mi diletta, e alta isperanza nell' animo mi ripone." *Risponsiva*, ed. Moreni, pp. 246-247.

2. See note 4 below.

3. See Vol. One, p. 261f.

4. ". . . le vane e scioche disputazioni d'una brigata di garulli." Wesselofsky, II, p. 306.

5. "Per parere litteratissimi apresso al vulgo gridano a piaza quanti dittonghi avevano gli antichi e perchè oggi non se ne usano se non due; e qual gramatica sia migliore, o quella del tempo del comico Terrenzio o dell' eroico Virgilio ripulita; e quanti piedi usano gli antichi nel versificare, e perchè oggi non s'usa l'anapesto di quatro brievi. E in tali fantasticherie tutto il loro tempo trapassano." *Ibid.*

6. Bruni, in his repeatedly quoted letter to Salutati, September 13, 1405; see notes 54 and 55 to Chap. 12.

7. "Della filosofia divina dicono che Varrone iscrisse molti libri dell' osservazione degli idei de' gientili con istilo alegantissimo, e molto eciessivamente il lodano, prepognendo in segreto ai dottori della nostra cattolica fede; e ardiscono a dire che quegli idei erano più veri che questo, nè si ricordano de' miracoli de' nostri santi." Wesselofsky, II, p. 315.

8. G. Gentile in his *La Filosofia*, p. 208f., with his fine feeling for the problems of the period already took this assertion of Cino's seriously enough to put it at the head of his chapter on classicism and its relation to paganism in the Quattrocento; though Gentile did not yet know the source material that would have supported his conjecture that there was something real behind Cino's remark. Cino's contention, he said, "might appear true if one reflects upon the natural tendencies of humanistic philology . . . ;

and it is not improbable that someone like Niccoli, his head filled with thoughts of Virgil, eventually felt and often expressed a certain paganism. . . ." The actual background of Cino's contention will emerge from the subsequent discussion.

9. ". . . rerum humanarum divinarumque cognitio. . . ." *Dialogi*, ed. Klette, p. 54; ed. Garin, p. 60.

10. In addition to the consequences of militant classicism for the civic attitude and outlook, one of its characteristic by-products is the rise, around 1400, of a sympathetic interest in classical religiosity. This trait of the transition from the Trecento to the Quattrocento is sorely in need of investigation. The writer, many years ago, explored one of the major problems in a short history of the belief in a secretly monotheistic "theology" of the ancient poets—a belief already found in late antiquity and in the Middle Ages, which played a significant part in the thought of Albertino Mussato, Petrarch, and Boccaccio during the Trecento, and reached its climax in the transition period around 1400. Since conditions have not yet permitted the completion and publication of that monograph, the illustrations following in the text are used to enlarge the picture drawn in the present book of the civic and political aspects of the crisis. The comprehensive work by J. Sezner, *La Survivance des Dieux Antiques. Essai sur le Rôle de la Tradition Mythologique dans l'Humanisme et dans l'Art de la Renaissance* (London: Warburg Institute, 1940), is chiefly concerned with iconographical themes and hardly mentions the problem of the "monotheism" of the ancient poets; it does not touch upon the fact that around 1400 there was a new phase of this train of thought.

Of the extant two major sources for the time around 1400, Salutati's unfinished treatise *On the Labors of Hercules* (*De Laboribus Herculis*) has just been edited by B. L. Ullman in a critical edition which will be a mile-stone for all studies in this field (Thesaurus Mundi, Zurich, 1951). The other major source, Francesco da Fiano's polemical pamphlet *Against the Ridiculous Contradictors and Detractors, Steeped in Gall, of the Poets* (*Contra Ridiculos Oblocutores et Fellitos Detractores Poetarum*), has been used in the text established by this writer in the course of his earlier studies, an unpublished edition based on the only manuscript that has come to his attention, Cod. Ottobon. Lat. 1438.

11. That the Hercules treatise was meant to supplement Boc-

caccio's *Genealogiae* is stated by Salutati himself; ed. Ullman, p. 456f. From the wording of the title, *De Laboribus Herculis*, this broad purpose may not be readily divined; but that wording stems from an early stage of Salutati's labors. Presumably, the book became known in Florence under this title through Filippo Villani's *De Origine Civitatis Florentiae et Eiusdem Famosis Civibus*, where this title-form was used as early as 1381/82, and it recurs unaltered in the revision of 1395/96. (See the two versions of the passage in question in *Epistolario di Salutati*, ed. Novati, vol. IV, p. 492.) As late as 1398, Salutati himself referred to his treatise as *De Hercule eiusque laboribus* (cf. Novati, *op. cit.*, vol. III, p. 311). But in the last years of his life, Salutati elaborated and enlarged his work to such an extent that, when summarizing its contents in 1405, he used the earlier name of "Labores Herculis" for only one of the four books of the ultimate version, while giving the title of the entire work now as "De sensibus allegoricis fabularum Herculis." (Salutati, *Ep. XIV 10*, *Epistolario*, vol. IV, pp. 76-77.) The two manuscripts of the treatise that have come down to us reveal knowledge of a concordant form of the title, "Allegoriarum libri IV super fabulis Herculis," in the suprascriptions and subscriptions of the Fourth Book. (See Ullman's edition, pp. 449, 582.) The first chapter of the First Book is suprascribed "De poesi contra detractores compendiosa defensio"; this heading reveals the intellectual kinship of the work with the almost synonymous pamphlet of Francesco da Fiano. Attention was first drawn to the guiding ideas of Salutati's treatise by A. v. Martin in some incisive paragraphs of his *Mittelalterliche Welt- und Lebensanschauung im Spiegel der Schriften Coluccio Salutatis* (Munich, 1913), pp. 142-149, and his *Coluccio Salutati und das humanistische Lebensideal* (Leipzig, 1916), pp. 63-66.

12. Lib. I, cap. I: "Et hac quidem necessitate figuratus iste loquendi modus quem poetica profitetur, . . . habilitate quadam exprimendi conceptum cum fiat de supernaturalibus operibus disputatio, fuit repertus. Nam cum et Moyses ipse scripsit, 'Et dixit deus, *Fiat lux*', et infra, 'Et vidit deus quod esset bonum, et ait, *Faciamus hominem ad imaginem et similitudinem nostram*', sub quodam velamine dicta sunt. . . . Nec habet deus, cum incorporeus sit, linguam, pulmonem, dentes, labia, vel palatum quibus conceptum mentis formatis vocibus soleat enarrare. Similiter . . . quod 'penituit eum quod hominem fecisset in terra', et . . . '*Delebo*',

inquit, 'hominem.' . . . Nam cum nec penitere deo conveniat nec angi dolore, nec cor intrinsecus habeat, oportet hec omnia non secundum litteram intelligi sed alterius sensus ministerio declarari, ut apertum sit divinam scripturam totam plenam esse locutionibus quas ipsos poetas cernimus usurpasse". (Ed. Ullman, pp. 8-9). Lib. I, cap. II: "Fuit autem hoc loquendi genus a paganis adhibitum cultui deorum suorum. . . . Quanquam et ipsos sapientes . . . impossibile foret aliis verbis quam creature convenientibus id quod de deo perceperint enarrare. Nam . . . non possumus illum exprimere, prout etiam nec videre, donec in hac carne vivimus, sicut est, nec ultra conceptus nostros vocabula reperire. . . . Et hac necessitate factum est ut sublimius perfectiusque poema non sit quam divina scriptura, licet apud nos metrica deficiat melodia." (*Ibid.*, pp. 15-16). Lib. II, cap. V: "Sed forte movebitur aliquis et inconvenienter arbitrabitur fictas apud poetas deorum collocutiones. . . . Et si Iuno, ut proxime sumpta est, intelligitur Iovis dispositio seu voluntas, que nichil sunt aliud quam ipse Iupiter volens seu disponens, . . . incongruentissime finxerunt poete quod Iupiter Iunoni quasi cuidam alteri loquatur." But then we ought to make the same objection to divine scripture in view of passages like " 'Dixit dominus domino meo, *sede a dextris meis*', et cetera que sequuntur. Que verba constat esse patris ad filium; qui siquidem unum sunt, audebimusne talem loquendi formulam de patre et filio qui non iidem sunt, quam usurpant divine littere, in poeticis sermonibus condemnare?" (*Ibid.*, pp. 102-103).

13. See esp. Lib. I cap. I and II. Here the secret monotheism of the ancient poets is described with all the pertinent quotations from Virgil, Augustinus' *Civ. Dei* VII, 9, and the Mythographus Vaticanus, and defined in passages like these: "Denique de deo quantum in se est, licet videantur poete multitudinem affirmare deorum, unum tamen proculdubio reputabant." (Ed. Ullman, p. 84). "Ut facile sit videre poetas illa deorum multitudine non plures sed unum deum tantummodo designasse. . . . Et tunc, ni fallor, nullatenus arbitrabitur poetas aliud quam unum deum illa sua deorum turba sensisse. Nam sicut unum et idem numen in celo Lunam, Dyanam in silvis vocant, et Proserpinam in inferno, sic omnem illam deorum numerositatem unam omnium presupponentes essentiam iuxta potentiarum varietatem et actuum diversis nominibus vocaverunt, ut nomina, que quidem aliud sunt a rebus, non res plures sed multiformes eiusdem rei potentias, actus, et

effectus significarent. Que quidem latius in sequentibus apparebunt." (*Ibid.*, pp. 85-86).

14. For Salutati's tendency to contrast the monotheism of the poets with the erroneous notions of divinity among the ancient philosophers, see esp. Lib. II cap. I: "Nec latuit commenticiorum deorum falsitas eruditissimos hominum poetas, . . . longe magis amici et publici veritatis testes quam ipsi philosophi, qui se ipsius veritatis professores gloriabantur" (ed. Ullman, p. 78f.); also Lib. IV chapters I and II, where the philosophers' ideas of the nether world and of the soul are shown to be inferior to those of the poets who may have been divinely inspired (pp. 459-461, 469-470). For Salutati's use of Varro, and of Varro's references to Valerius Soranus, see the index to Ullman's edition, p. 657, and the last section of note 16 below.

15. For Petrarch, see in particular the third of his four invectives written in 1355 against an anonymous physician (*Invectivae Contra Medicum Quendam*). The pamphlet elaborates the two key-ideas that ancient poetry in its earliest phase was a pious "theology," and that this "theology of the poets" ("theologia poetarum") was based on the knowledge that the various deities merely denoted personifications of the one God. For Boccaccio, see his *Genealogiae Deorum* (1371), where many specific myths are explained with the help of the theory that the deities in question signified different manifestations of the one God. This manner of justifying ancient mythology is continually counteracted, however, by Boccaccio's apprehensiveness of polytheism, until in the later portions of his work the initially acknowledged theory of the secret monotheism of the poets is drowned in an increasing tide of hostility.

16. The novelty of the comparative aggressiveness of Salutati's *De Hercule* is a matter of significance for the historical appraisal of the intellectual crisis about 1400. The following sketch of the development of Salutati's attitude towards the religion of the ancient poets will illustrate the assertion that at that time something new was being added which had not existed in Salutati's earlier years.

(1) There had been an earlier phase of Salutati's reflections on the ancient poets—during the years 1378-79. At that time he had exchanged letters with Ser Giuliano Zonarini, chancellor of Bologna (*Ep. IV 15*, and *IV 18*, *Epistolario*, vol. I, pp. 298-

307, 321-329; an English translation in E. Emerton, *Humanism and Tyranny*, pp. 290-308), polemical pamphlets in which he proves to be familiar merely with the standard medieval arguments: enjoyment of ancient poetry is legitimate *despite* the pagan mythology of the poets, because that mythology, after the victory of Christianity, is no longer dangerous; and some of the ancient poets, especially Virgil, in the midst of their errors, have presentiments of Christian doctrines (including the dogma of Trinity) that are special gifts of divine revelation. Salutati's active interest in the theme of the *Hercules* treatise began in precisely the same years: between 1378 and 1380, he wrote a short explanation of the myths surrounding the figure of Hercules; this work, which was as yet no more than a commentary on Seneca's tragedy *Hercules Furiens*, has been published by B. L. Ullman in the appendix to his edition of *De Laboribus Herculis* as "Prima Editio" of the treatise. (*Op. cit.*, pp. 585-635. Ullman, *ibid.*, p. vii, dates this first version "inter annos 1378 et 1383"; but Filippo Villani was acquainted with Salutati's work as early as 1381/82, when he was engaged in writing the first version of his *De Origine Civitatis Florentiae*; see above note 11). A reading of the 1378/80 version of the *Hercules* shows that Salutati at that time did not as yet ascribe monotheistic beliefs to the poets, nor evaluate their religion as sympathetically as he would in later years. The *poetae* were not yet supposed to have been free of the errors of the *philosophi* about the nature of the soul, but were said to have erred themselves by following the erroneous teachings of the various schools of philosophy. (Ed. Ullman, p. 623, lines 16f., 25f.) In consequence, Salutati was still writing an apology in the medieval manner to defend his reading of the pagan poets in spite of their errors, instead of advancing the later justification of the poets as early seekers after genuine piety and divine truth.

(2) This later justification does not seem to appear in Salutati's works until the end of the 1390's, and it is highly probable that an important stimulus to the development of Salutati's thought came from the well-known episode (or rumor?) of the year 1398 that the *condottiere* Carlo Malatesta of Rimini had plunged the famous ancient statue of Virgil in Mantua into the Mincio river, with imprecations against the poets and with the challenging assertion that statues were owed only to Saints. In his endeavors to make out a safe case for the poets, Salutati be-

gan to develop the idea of the equal need of both poetry and religion to employ figurative speech. (Cf. *Ep. X 16*, April 23, 1398, to Pellegrino Zambeccari, *Epistolario*, vol. III, esp. p. 292f.). From these still cautious beginnings, he developed after 1400 the idea that any human notion of the divine, in any religion, was bound to be anthropomorphic; and by the time of his death in 1406, this idea had grown into a kind of religious philosophy used as a key for the proper approach to classical mythology. Simultaneously, he had revived Petrarch's and Boccaccio's theory on the secret monotheism of the ancient poets. Through the combination of this theory with the thesis that human notions of the divine were inevitably anthropomorphic, the explanation of the polytheistic stories of the poets as shells concealing the kernel of a purer insight appeared more convincing than ever, and produced a spirit of aggressiveness formerly unknown. Simultaneously with the exposition of his theory in the final version of the *Hercules* treatise in 1405-06, Salutati presented the new interpretations in various polemical letters almost of book length, especially letters addressed to, and directed against, the two monks Giovanni da Samminiato and Giovanni Dominici. (*Epistolario*, vol. IV, pp. 170ff.; partial English translations in Emerton's *Humanism and Tyranny*, pp. 309-341, 346-377; a survey of the chief ideas of the letters in question, in J. Cinquino, "Coluccio Salutati, Defender of Poetry," *Italica*, XXVI [1949], 131-135.) In these letters as in the treatise, we find not only the argument that theology and poetry are akin through their common use of figurative speech, but also the reference to the teachings of Varro, and the opinion that the poets had attained nearer to religious truth than the philosophers had done. (Cf. *Epistolario*, vol. IV, p. 197ff.). The fact itself did not escape v. Martin, who (in *Salutati und hum. Lebensideal*, p. 240, n. 1) noted that all earlier opinions of Salutati "had been reserved when compared with what is said in *De Hercule*. . . . He, who with advancing age grew constantly more Christian-minded, grew more and more extreme in his defense of antiquity." That Salutati went beyond Boccaccio with his insistence on the inadequacy of human speech to express the nature of the Divine, is stressed in v. Martin's *Mittelalterliche Welt- und Lebensanschauung im Spiegel . . . Salutatis*, p. 147f.

17. Cf. the quotations collected in A. v. Martin, *Salutati und hum. Lebensideal*, pp. 64-65.

18. Even the poets, Salutati stated, were not innocent of the misuse of allegory for the purposes of false polytheistic teachings: "Fuit autem hoc loquendi genus a paganis adhibitum cultui deorum suorum . . . , ut per hec rudium populorum animos facilius suis religionibus alligarent, et ipsorum deorum humanitatem atque turpitudinem figmentis . . . occultarent." Ed. Ullman, p. 15. For an example, from another field, of the cautiousness and the reservations which remained characteristic of Salutati even in his last years, cf. some of the arguments Salutati advanced in the course of his controversy with Poggio 1405-06; see the interesting analysis by v. Martin, *Salutati und hum. Lebensideal*, pp. 54-61.

19. For Boccaccio cf. his *Genealogiae Deorum*, XV 7, and passim, and his letter to Jacopo Pizzinga (1372)—see Vol. One, pp. 234f.—esp. ed. Massèra pp. 192, 194.

20. Compare the speeches of Petrarch (for "The Coronation of Petrarch" see E. H. Wilkins, *The Making of the "Canzoniere" and other Petrarchean Studies* [Rome, 1951], p. 9ff.) and of Zanobi da Strada (see the extract in H. Friedjung's *Kaiser Karl IV. und sein Anteil am geistigen Leben seiner Zeit* [Vienna, 1876], p. 308f.) on the occasions of their coronations with the laurel as poets, in 1341 and 1355. (An English translation of "Petrarch's Coronation Oration" by E. H. Wilkins, which fully identifies the ancient sources on which the oration draws, has just become available in *Publications of the Mod. Lang. Assoc. of America*, LXVIII [1953], 1241-1250).

21. "Quippe sive ipse deus, sive natura, ipsius qui cunta potest docilis et erudita ministra, causa sit, non sine quadam cupiditate laudis humane nascimur omnes. . . . Homines quidem sumus, et non marmorei, nec etiam adamantinum cor habemus. . . . Siquidem Ieronimus, Augustinus, Ambrosius et Gregorius et, ut reliquos sileam, Orizenes, licet sancti fuerint, homines tamen fuerunt; et, . . . quia omnes in cupiditatem glorie quodam, ut sic dixerim, humanitatis unco pertrahimur, credo quandoque ardenti laudis et humani preconii desiderio caluisse. Illos, preter uberem fructum vere credulitatis nostre ex devotissimarum scripturarum suarum sacris manantem eloquiis, nisi sperate et optate fame compositorum voluminum ignitus mulxisset amor, profecto non tanta in eis floridi et culti sermonis cura, non tante in eis studiorum et scribendi vigilie crebruissent." *Contra Detractores*, fol. 144r-144v.

22. *Ibid.*, fol. 135r f. That Francesco da Fiano's opinions on

biblical allegory were potentially dangerous and more extreme than the known ideas of other early humanists was already surmised by v. Martin. Cf. his *Salutati und hum. Lebensideal*, p. 232, n. 3.

23. *Contra Detractores, loc. cit.*

24. "Non solum apud cuntos populos, quos sacre religio Christianitatis includit, sed apud quoscumque alios certum est deum omnia creavisse (MS: creãsse) rerumque cuntarum opificem extitisse. . . ." *Ibid.*, fol. 137v.

25. *Ibid.*, fol. 138v.

26. *Ibid.*, fol. 140v.

27. *Ibid.*, fol. 139v.

28. ". . . antiquorum poetarum libros non esse legendos eo quod illorum anime, a fide nostra dannate quia illi unda sacri baptismatis non purgati Christianeque fuerint perfectionis immunes, apud inferos variis suppliciis crucientur." *Ibid.*, fol. 139v.

29. ". . . nedum Christum venturum cognoscere, sed illum somniare ab alto negatum est. Sed in hoc velim mihi respondeat Augustinus, respondeat etiam Orizenes. Si Homerus, Hesyodus, Pindarus, Menander, si Cecilius, Plautus, Terentius et Lucillius compluresque alii poete eloquio utriusque lingue preclari fuerunt ante adventum Christi per tam longa tempora, quomodo in eo credere potuerunt, cum postea per annos innumerabiles natus est? Quomodo in eorum mentibus ante tantam futurorum temporum longitudinem lux illa veritatis que illuminat omnem hominem potuit illuxisse, siquidem futura prescire non humanum sed divinum est? . . . Igitur, si precedens tantorum futurorum temporum longitudo Christi cognitionem abstulit poetis antiquis, an sit equitas, cum apud leges et canones nulla statuatur de futuro delicto punitio, an iniquitas, illos propter futurum peccatum in profundum baratrum opinione sua mersisse, Augustini et Orizenis aliorumque catholicorum exquisitiori judicio et maturiori equitati relinquo." *Ibid.*, fol. 139v.

30. See the first passage of the preceding note.

31. Francesco, after exculpating the poets of pre-Christian times in the manner cited above in note 29, makes this difference still clearer by continuing as follows: In an entirely different position were those poets "who shone in the time of Christ or later, and whom either the report of the marvelous works of the Son of God, . . . or the evidence they had seen with their own eyes,

could and should have turned into professing Christians" ("qui vel Christi temporibus vel postea claruerunt, quorum animos aut vera fama admirabilium gestorum filii dei . . . aut experientia manifesti visus eorum potuit et debuit Christiane religionis professores efficere"). Those among them who failed to accept the truth nonetheless were deserving of the most severe punishment, in contrast to the pre-Christian poets. At least Virgil, however, foresaw and foretold Christ; and Statius and Claudianus became Christians. *Ibid.*, fol. 139v-140r.

32. "Profanum dici non debet quicquid pium est. . . . Et fortasse latius se fundit spiritus Christi quam nos interpretamur. Et multi sunt in consortio sanctorum qui non sunt apud nos in catalogo." Erasmus, *Convivium Religiosum; Opera Omnia*, ed. Clericus, vol. I (1703), p. 681f.

33. For these early sixteenth-century developments, and for the general perspective from which the attitude of Quattrocento humanists to the doctrine of damnation of the pagans must be appraised, see the writer's article "Erasmus-Probleme. II. Der Humanismus und die thomistische Lehre von den 'gentiles salvati,'" *Archiv für Reformationsgeschichte*, XLIII (1952), 256-263.

34. "Ubi nunc agat anima Ciceronis, fortasse non est humani iudicii pronuntiare." Erasmus in the preface to his edition of Cicero's *Tusculanae Disputationes; Opus Epistolarum*, ed. P. S. Allen, vol. V (1924), p. 339.

35. *Contra Detractores*, fol. 137v-138v.

36. "Cur isti antiquos accusant poetas deos quanplurimos in eorum poematibus nominantes? Equidem si rem ac vim effectumque rei et non exteriorem verborum sonitum velimus inspicere, fides nostra suos etiam habet deos. Nam illi deos, nos vero sanctos vocamus; quos non solum, sed quoscumque divinas atque humanas res excellentibus contemplantes ingeniis theologi nostri non negant esse deos participatione divine bonitatis. Quod autem divine participatio bonitatis homines mortales efficiat deos, illud Boetii Severini vulgatum est [cf. Migne, LXIII, 767]. Sed illud Augustini, cuntorum noticie non ita publicum, super psalmo centesimo decimo octavo inquit ita: 'Non enim existencia sunt homines dei, sed fiunt dei, participando illius qui verus est deus.' [Cf. Migne, XXXVII, 1545, and, similar in meaning, 1906]." *Ibid.*, fol. 139r-139v.

37. "Credo ego Augustinum, si illum nostra haberet etas, non

minori risus ludibrio persequi quosdam, quos non probata miracula, non ipsa mater ecclesia, sed inanitas ridicularum opinionum quorundam . . . sanctos fecerunt. . . . Que huiusmodi ficte sanctitatis inanis aviditas! Que ista ex[e]crabilis superstitio! quam nedum nos, qui sumus luce Christianitatis illustres, sed Quintus Lucillius Balbus huius expers lucis in secundo libro *De natura deorum* apud Ciceronem de superstitione disputans execratur. . . ." *Ibid.*, fol. 139r.

38. "Validius enim et firmius robur laudis est, si invictam Hannibalis virtutem laudet Scipio hostis, quam pater Amilcar seu germanus Hasdrubal aut Hanno vel Mago. . . . Itaque theologorum nostrorum argumenta non minus validioris rationis viribus firmarentur, si ita gentilium autorum Christi sacerdotium innuentium sicut sanctorum scripta catholice probationis producentur in medium. Ipsi enim . . . non adverterunt . . . illud Pomponii jurisconsulti inter digesta veterum: nullum testem in re sua debere intelligi ydoneum. Profecto [MS: prefecto] mea et aliorum quorumcumque sententia: domesticis pugnare testimoniis nichil est aliud quam causam sui in ridiculam ruinam impellere." *Ibid.*, fol. 142r.

39. See Vol. One, pp. 99ff. and 121ff.

40. According to a local Roman legend, Peter was leaving Rome when, near the spot on the *Via Appia* where now stands the church called *Domine Quo Vadis*, he encountered the figure of his Master. To his question: "Domine quo vadis?" Peter received the answer "Venio iterum crucifigi." Thereupon the apostle, filled with shame at his weakness, returned to Rome to die the death of a martyr.—The passage in *De Fato et Fortuna*, lib. II cap. IX, to which we have referred, runs: "O virum dignissimum, qui in Christi tempora pervenisset, ut non fame gloriam ex suis illis virtutibus procedentem admiratus, sed veram beatitudinem agnoscens, pro certa germanaque iustitia proque veritate moriens, princeps nostrorum martyrorum haberetur." Then, on Socrates' thoughts in prison: "Hec secum similiaque versantem in illa gentilitatis cecitate maximoque errore doctrine et ignorantia summi boni Socratem, si sibi vere iustitie lumen et gratia christiani dogmatis illuxisset, sique Christum predicantem audisset, pendentem aspexisset in cruce, tandemque trihumphata morte iuxta sue prenuntiationis monita resurrexisse vidisset, putasne, si tamen astitisset divina gratia, metu mortis ab urbę Roma fugiturum fuisse, Christi confessionem et eterne ac incommutabilis veritatis causam desertu-

rum?" Quoted by v. Martin, *Salutati und hum. Lebensideal*, p. 64f.

41. For Francesco's relations with Salutati compare the references in Novati's *La giovinezza di Coluccio Salutati*, passim, and Novati's designation of Francesco as Salutati's "vecchio amico" in *Epistolario di Salutati*, vol. IV, p. 171.

42. See Appendix 4, p. 403f.

43. "Credo eos [the Bishops of Rome] secutos nebulonis cuiusdam sententiam, qui cum diffideret virtute sibi nomen comparare posse, Ephesi Diane templum cremavit. Ita hi nostre religionis antistites, cum urbis excellentiam pulchritudinemque parum admirari, consequi nullo modo possent, huiusmodi ruinam atque perniciem moliti sunt. Itaque tam inhumanam tamque efferam stultitiam maledictis insectemur." Ed. L. Bertalot, in "Cincius Romanus und seine Briefe," *Quellen und Forschungen aus italienischen Archiven*, XXI (1929-30), 224f.

To realize the harbinger position as well as the utter recklessness of these expressions of the mind of early Quattrocento classicism, one must compare them with the references to the same subject in the famous letter which, under the inspiration of Raffael, then papal overseer of the antiquities of Rome, was phrased by Baldassare Castiglione and addressed to Pope Leo X in 1518 or 1519: "How many Popes, Holy Father, possessing the same dignity as Your Holiness, but not the same knowledge, ability, and highmindedness, . . . have demolished the ancient temples, statues, triumphal arches, and other magnificent buildings! . . . How many have reduced ancient pillars and marble ornaments to lime! The new Rome, which we now see standing in all its beauty and grandeur, adorned with palaces, churches, and other buildings, is built throughout with the lime obtained in this way from ancient marbles." (According to the English translation in L. Pastor's *History of the Popes*, vol. VIII [2nd edn.: St. Louis, Mo., 1923], p. 245f., where also full information on the problems of authorship, date, and the program then propounded by Raffael is given.)

44. The document is preserved in Cod. Ottobon. Lat. 2992, fol. 27v-29r (not in other manuscripts; the several references given in *Bruni, Schriften*, p. 179, refer to one manuscript whose identification mark has been changed repeatedly, as has been established by L. Bertalot, in *Historische Vierteljahrsschrift*, XXIX

[1934], 393, on the basis of information from the Administration of the Vatican Library), under the title of a *Responsio* Francesco's to an "*Interrogatio ad peritissimum virum dominum Franciscum de Fiano per elegantissimum Leonardum Aretinum transmissa*, videlicet quo tempore fuerit Ovidius, causam propter quam Ovidius fuerit in exilium relegatus, et si revocatus ab exilio fuerit ad patriam remissus, scire cupientem."

45. "Ut honestati clericalis mee professionis deserviam, cui ne victu vestituque caream asscriptus sum, cogor omelias et Bede, Orizenis [*sic*; as n. 21, 29 above], Johannis Crisostomi Gregoriique in matutinis non sine insupportabili algore seculi et tremula voce legere et quandoque cantare; que, si cum lucidissima felicitate admirabilis eloquencie priscorum (MS: pistorum) vatum et oratorum in comparationem ponantur, licet earum omeliarum autores sancti fuerunt (MS: fuernt), ut Dantis Alditherij poete Florentini verbis utar, tibi carbones extincti viderentur." (From a photostat of the MS.) The data on p. 404 prove 1412/25 the time of composition.

46. Wesselofsky (II, p. 50), after referring to Cino's accusations (quoted in the next paragraph), adds this comment: "During the last years of the Trecento, the elements of the future Medicean civilization are in a state of ferment among those men who, in their desire to shake off the yoke of the medieval tradition, are seen to bow their heads openly under the yoke of the principate which promised to free them of that tradition. It is precisely for this reason why the Medici and the men of learning appear joined in a common cause."

47. "Della familiare iconomica nulla sentono, ma isprezato il santo matrimonio vivono mattamente sanza ordine, sanza curare che sia l'onor paterno, il beneficio de' figliuoli, che sarebono degni del giudicio di Cammillo e di Postumio ciensori di Roma, i quali l'avere di due uomini, ch'erano casti insino alla vecchiaia vivuti, comandarono che fusse confiscato in comune; ancora affermandogli degni di punizione, se in niuno modo di sì giusto ordine fussino arditi di ramaricarsi. Della politica non sanno qual regimento si sia migliore, o quello d'uno o quel di più, o quel di molti o quello di pochi eletti; fugono la fatica affermando che chi serve a comune serve a niuno, nè colla guarnaca consigliano la repubblica nè con l'armi la difendono. Nè si ricordano che quanto il bene è più comune, tanto à più del divino." Wesselofsky, II, pp. 314-315.

48. As the discovery of any reference to Bruni in the *Invettiva*

would arouse suspicion of the above conclusions, it should be noted that the two minor cases in which E. Santini, in his often cited paper on "La produzione volgare di Bruni," *Giornale Stor. della Lett. Ital.*, LX (1912), 291f., has believed to be able to identify Bruni as the accused, are far from convincing. This is true of Santini's inference that Bruni is the real target of Rinuccini's reproaches against those who "most anxiously discuss (*con grande ansietà disputano*) whether before the time of Ninus there existed any historical accounts or not, and how many books were composed by Livy." As Santini points out, Bruni poses and answers the question about Livy in his *Ep. X 22*. But this letter, if we accept the date proposed by Luiso, may probably be assumed to have been written more than thirty years later (cf. *Bruni, Schriften*, p. 220); it does not mention Ninus; and no Bruni was needed for hypotheses regarding the fortunes of the books missing in the Livy manuscripts since, early in the fourteenth century, Giovanni Colonna in his *De viris illustribus* had already discussed this question, had even inspected Livy manuscripts, and had recounted the legend that the last books had been burnt by the emperor Caligula (cf. Sabbadini, *Le Scoperte*, vol. II, p. 56). No more convincing is Santini's reference to an assertion made by Bruni in his *Vite di Dante e di Petrarca* in 1436. Santini makes the point that, while Cino quotes one of the classicists he censors as saying "that the stories of the poets are inventions for women and children, and that the . . . teller of such tales, messer Giovanni Boccaccio, did not know Latin" (". . . le storie poetiche essere favole da femmine e da fanciugli e che il . . . recitatore di dette storie, cioè M. G. Boccaci, non seppe grammatica"), Bruni, in his *Vite*, reproaches Boccaccio for having told Dante's life in the fashion of a love story with little emphasis on the more serious aspects, and asserts that Boccaccio never possessed a perfect command of Latin because he learnt it when he was already an adult. (*Bruni, Schriften*, pp. 50f., 67.) Quite obviously, these objective statements of Bruni are something very different from the contemptuous attack on Boccaccio that incensed Rinuccini; if the comparison of these two statements proves anything, it is rather that their profound difference in tone makes it improbable for them to have come from one and the same author.

49. For this aspect of Florentine Humanism in the Trecento, see this writer's observations in "The Historical Background of

the Florentine Renaissance," *History*, n.s., XXII (1938), 323f. (in an Italian translation in *La Rinascita*, I [1938], 64f.), and in "Franciscan Poverty and Civic Wealth as Factors in the Rise of Humanistic Thought," *Speculum*, XIII (1938), 15ff.

50. In a letter written in his old age; cf. Wesselofsky II, pp. 104, 382.

51. The following two paragraphs from Filippo's works will illustrate this effect of the growing classicistic extremism better than any comment could do. In the "Prologus" to his continuation of the chronicles of Giovanni and Matteo Villani, Filippo remarks on his father, Matteo: "We can say that he is rightly to be praised to the extent to which he, in the style accessible to him, kept from becoming lost the memorable things that happened in the world at the time when he wrote, thus preparing the material for more delicate and superior talents who would transform his memoirs into a happier and more exalted style." ("Il quale in tanto possiamo dire meritevolmente essere da laudare, in quanto esso con lo stile che a lui fu possibile non sofferse che perissero le cose occorse nel mondo per lo tempo che scrive degne di memoria, quindi apparecchiando materia a' più delicati e alti ingegni di riducere sue ricordanze in più felice e rilevato stile.") In his *De Origine Civitatis Florentiae*, Filippo comments upon Giovanni and Matteo: "Giovanni, my uncle, and Matteo, my father, tried to entrust to Volgare literature what memorable events the times brought with them. To be sure, they did not accomplish anything very beautiful; they did it, I think, so that the events would not be lost to those who with better minds promised to do better, and in order to prepare the material for a more polished presentation. The reason for their recapitulation was perhaps that they, as far as it was up to them, did not want to allow the deeds worthy of record in the public annals which the centuries had performed, to be lost by the negligence of the pen." ("Ioannes mihi patruus, Matthaeus pater conati sunt quae tempora secum attulerunt memoratu digna vulgaribus litteris demandare. Rem sane non confecere bellissimam: id fecere, ut reor, ne gesta perirent iis qui ingenio meliori meliora portenderent, et ut scribendi politius materiam praepararent. Ea fortasse gratia recolendi, quod, quantum in eis fuerit, perpessi non fuerint quae secula relationibus publicis inserenda confecerint, calami negligentia deperire." Ed. Galletti [Florence, 1847], p. 40.)

52. ". . . quod soleant recessus remotissimi bona alere studia." *Ibid.*, p. 3.

53. ". . . utilem ad detestationem negotiosae vitae, qua bonis temporalibus implicamur." *Ibid.*, p. 19. On the impression made by *De Saeculo* upon Filippo Villani, see also Vol. One, p. 90.

54. On Filippo Villani's personality cf. G. Calò, *Filippo Villani e il "Liber de origine civitatis Florentiae et eiusdem famosis civibus"* (1904), in particular p. 52ff.; for the traits stressed above, see the fine sketch of Filippo's personality in G. Lisio, *La Storiografia* (in *Storia dei Generi Letterarii Italiani*), pp. 477-479. Filippo's own program of "vita contemplativa," already referred to in the last few notes, is found in his introduction to his *De Origine* (ed. Galletti, p. 3), and passim in that work, especially in the biography of Salutati (*ibid.*, p. 19), and in Filippo's concluding note (*ibid.*, p. 41f.).

55. See Vespasiano da Bisticci, *Vite di Uomini Illustri del Secolo XV*, ed. Frati, vol. III, p. 37. Manetti's appraisal of Rossi is from his unpublished *Adversus Judaeos et Gentes*, written between 1453 and 1459, and preserved in Cod. Vat. Urbin. Lat. 154. The sketch on Rossi, fol. 120v, runs: "Robertus Russus, civis Florentinus de generosa et clara Russorum familia oriundus, ceteris omnibus cum civitatis magistratibus tum uxor[e] et liberis tum denique seculo et pompis suis posthabitis, assiduam quandam et admirabilem <operam> diversarum litterarum, et poeticę et oratorię, historiarum et mathematicarum (MS: mathematicorum) et philosophie naturalis ac moralis ac demum metaphysice, grece ac latine lingue cognitioni navavit. Quocirca in omnibus predictorum studiorum generibus usque adeo profecisse creditur, ut magnus orator ingensque illius temporis philosophus haberetur. Atque ob hanc singularem et precipuam doctrinę et eruditionis sue excellentiam factum est ut eius domus magna quadam generosorum ac nobilium discipulorum caterva quotidie frequentaretur. Inter cetera rerum suarum monumenta omnes Aristotelis libri ab eo e greco in latinum traducti comperiuntur." (From a photostat.)

As to the date of the *Adversus Judaeos et Gentes ad Alfonsum clarissimum Aragonum regem*, Vespasiano da Bisticci tells us in his *Vite* that Manetti during his last years at Naples (1455-59) "corrected and polished that part of *Contra Judaeos et gentes* which he had already finished, and to it he added some books, so that there were ten books altogether" ("corresse ed emendò quella parte ch'egli aveva finita *Contra Judoeos et gentes*, e aggiunsevi alcuni libri, che in tutto furono libri dieci"). But in a larger, separate biography of Manetti, his *Commentario della Vita di Messer Giannozzo Manetti*, Vespasiano says that Manetti during his Neapolitan years "polished the work he had composed *contra Judaeos*, and to it he added two books, until there were twelve books" ("emendò l'opera che aveva fatta *contra Judoeos*, et arrosevi libri dua insino in libri dodici"); in harmony with this latter assertion, the list of Manetti's works attached to the *Commentario* calls the work as preserved in ten books "incomplete" ("*Contra Judeos*. Lib. x. Opus imperfectum. Lib. x"). (See Vespasiano da Bisticci, ed. Frati, vol. II, pp. 79, 178, 199.) Manetti had been forced to leave Florence in 1453, and had spent the years 1453-55 in Rome, aided by Pope Nicholas V at whose request he translated some portions of the Bible. Evidently, then, the first version of *Adversus Judaeos* I-X was also a product of Manetti's Roman years, and the work was continued between 1455 and 1459 at Naples. The only moot question is whether at Naples the work was revised only, or whether it was revised and extended to twelve books. In the latter case, the version in cod. Vat. Urbin. Lat. 154, which comprises ten books, may represent the stand of the work before Manetti's departure from Rome, and the revision of the period 1455-59 may not have survived.

56. Vespasiano da Bisticci, *Vite di uomini illustri del secolo XV*, ed. L. Frati, vol. II (Bologna, 1892), p. 230.

57. This emerges from the letter in which Guarino in 1418 thought it necessary to justify his marriage before Corbinelli and refute Corbinelli's assertion, "mulieres magno philosophantibus impedimento esse." See Guarino, *Ep. 125*, *Epistolario di Guarino*, ed. R. Sabbadini, vol. I (Venice, 1915), pp. 213-215.

58. See R. Blum, *La Biblioteca della Badia Fiorentina e i Codici di Antonio Corbinelli* ("Studi e Testi," vol. 155 [Città del Vaticano, 1951]), p. 42. Corbinelli's natural son may be presumed to have been born before Rinuccini's writing, because in 1410 he was named to be Corbinelli's sole heir, and it is improbable that Corbinelli would have made this important decision unless the bastard had reached the age where his character and personality were recognizable.

59. R. Blum, *op. cit.*, p. 41.

60. "Neque postea ullo unquam tempore . . . aut aucupandis

honoribus . . . aut rei uxorie procreande prolis gratia indulsit, sed potius egenus et inglorius et celebs omni seculari cura liber et vacuus in summa quiete et tranquillitate una cum libris suis feliciter vivebat. Per hunc itaque modum publicis simul atque privatis pene occupationibus carens, otio . . . litterato et generoso fruebatur." "In huiusmodi igitur bonarum artium studiis sine uxore et liberis, nullo fere privato nec publico negotio impeditus . . . felicem profecto ac beatam vitam ita probe instituerat. . ." "Unius ancille ministerio exemplis Socratis summi philosophi atque Ennii veteris poete multorumque aliorum eruditissimorum virorum contentus, cum libris suis diu ac multum commorabatur. . ." From the biography of Niccoli in Manetti's *De Illustribus Longaevis* (see note 22 to Chap. 15); according to a photostat of Cod. Vat. Urbin. Lat. 387, foll. 156r-v, 157r, 157v, corrected by collation with Cod. Vat. Palat. Lat. 1605, which seems to have been revised by Manetti himself. The text of Manetti's biography of Niccoli is reproduced in Mehus' *Vita Ambrosii Traversarii*, pp. lxxvi-lxxviii.

The portrait of Niccoli in the obituary written on his death by Poggio confirms the characterization given by Manetti, at all relevant points. Although Niccoli's flight from the burdens of public office may not have been quite as strongly stressed by Poggio as we find it done by so civic-minded a humanist as Manetti, Poggio, too, is emphatic about the fact that Niccoli had lived only for his studies, books, and friends, while any "honorum cupiditas" or political "ambitio" had remained foreign to him. Contemptuous of material wealth, "he led a bachelor's life without wife and children" ("vitam coelibem duxit absque uxore et liberis"). Poggio, *Opera* (Basel, 1538), pp. 271, 275.

61. Niccoli's quarrels with his five brothers, at any rate, which cast a cloud upon his life, and in the 1420's caused a public scandal when the brothers insulted his concubine on the street (see Voigt, *Die Wiederbelebung*, I, p. 304), had according to Manetti's account already started by 1400. For Manetti blames these troubles for the well-known fact that Niccoli did not advance very far in his Greek studies under Chrysoloras: "Si hoc ergo singularissimo magistro et optimo preceptore in perdiscendis litteris Grecis ob familiares et pernitiosas germanorum suorum discordias, que non modo externa sed domestica etiam studia perverterunt, Nicolao nostro uti licuisset, quantum in illis profecisset ex eo facile iudicari

potest quod ingenio et diligentia plurimum valebat." (*De Illustribus Longaevis*, fol. 156v.) It is, therefore, very well possible—although it cannot be proven by direct documentary evidence—that Niccoli's conduct, out of harmony with the citizen's way of life, was resented and criticized at that early time, just as citizen-humanists like Bruni criticized Niccoli and sided against him after the incident with the concubine in the 1420's.

62. See Vol. One, p. 90f.

63. See Vol. One, pp. 123ff. and 135f.

64. The fragments of Rossi's work that have been preserved have just been collected and published by A. Manetti in *Rinascimento*, II (1951), 33-55. On Rossi as a translator from the Greek see now E. Garin, *Le Traduzioni Umanistiche di Aristotele nel Secolo XV* (Florence, 1951, reprinted from the "Atti dell' Accademia Fiorentina di Scienze Morali 'La Colombaria,' " 1950), pp. 5-8. Here we should also note a biographical fact. It is hardly without significance that Niccoli's and Rossi's intellectual interests were first shaped in the school of Luigi Marsili, Augustinian friar of the convent of Santo Spirito; both are classed among his closest disciples in Poggio's obituary on Niccoli. (Poggio, *Opera* [Basel, 1538], p. 271). "Our Niccoli," says Poggio, "never left Marsili's company, spent most of his time with him, and was instructed by him in the best precepts for life. . . . For it is often found that we imitate the conduct of those in whose company we are educated. Steeped as he was in this way of life, Niccoli plainly scorned two things: wealth and the zeal for public office." ("Hic noster Nicolaus, nunquam a latere Ludovici discedens, et optimis vivendi praeceptis institutus est, et plurimum temporis impertiit. . . . Accidit enim, ut imitemur mores quibuscum ab adolescentia educamur. Hac ratione vitae imbutus, duas res . . . aperte contempsit, divitias videlicet et honorum cupiditatem.") He thus embraced as "the best rule for life . . . that one should be free for literary leisure and not burdened by either wealth or ambition" (". . . normam vivendi optimam, . . . quo ocio literarum vacaret, neque opibus inserviret, neque ambitioni"). Giannozzo Manetti, in his *De Illustribus Longaevis*, also emphasizes Marsili's influence on the formation of Niccoli's mind. (Fol. 156r.)

65. "Si nihil esset aliud . . . quod ad scribendum nos et transferendum merito alliceret, id satis esset, quod multos insanos motus turbationesque plurimas interea fugimus. . . . Cum videas . . .

extolli quidem malos bonosque opprimi, despici rerum peritos atque abici, . . . ut ille inter fortissimos sit numerandus, qui e loco non cesserit, diutius inter illecebras atque molestias seculi obversatus. Quot vitamus interea vanitates, quot pericula magni que plures existimant, dum litteris operam damus! Quot presentis preteriteque etatis nugas atque inanes auras obliviscimur, dum legimus, dum scribimus, dum sapientum monimenta pervolvimus! Atque ob hec tantum mihi videor, si statim cuncta etiam que tra[n]stulerim in profluentem aliquem deiecerim, iam bonam mei ocii rationem cuivis sapientum reddidisse. . . . Sed arbitror haud . . . inutilis esse civibus meis, si forte planius talem tantumque virum e peregrina lingua in domesticam illis transtulero." Ed. Manetti, p. 52f.

66. ". . . huius posteriorum analeticorum . . . divinum opus. . . . Quod . . . non solum nobilissima hominum ingenia, sed nec superi legere dedignentur. . . . Nostra cum angelis hic humanitas gaudet dumtaxat enim terminos intellexerimus ritu quidem celestium potestatum, nullo percurrente discursu, dignitates percipimus. . . ." *Ibid.*, p. 55.

67. This would appear to be a balanced paraphrase of the following, not quite easily understood poem:

> "Hec ego dum conor nostris aperire Latinis
> carmina que superum, que argenti digna papiro
> aurea queve notis signent elementa decoris,
> interea nostri reparabant turribus arcem
> Pisanam, murisque novis atque aggere cives.
> vim alias etiam curabant condere: cuncta
> fervebant opere assiduo strepituque virorum
> atque he reliquie quas nulla ex urbe fugarat
> suspicio: in celum communique ere videbat
> turrigeras extolli arces, miserisque minari
> servitium, solito dum current sidera motu."
>
> (*Ibid.*, p. 47.)

68. Lorenzo di Marco de' Benvenuti, *Oratio in Niccolaum Nicholum*, ed. G. Zippel, *Giornale Storico della Letteratura Italiana*, XXIV (1894), 168-179.

69. "Meministine igitur, cum mediolanensium ducis potentia premeremur, quibus verbis acerbissimis lacerares senatum atque omnes huius florentissime urbis magistratus ac rempublicam universam, partem civium ignavos ac dementes, partem ob nimiam

potentiam tyrannos ac predones appellans, tantam ex hoc patrie maximo periculo letitiam pre te ferens, quantam bonus civis in victoria percepisset?" *Oratio, loc. cit.*, p. 177.

70. Vol. One, p. 352.

71. "... nonne ... hoc esse dicebas a primoribus nostre civitatis inventum, ut assiduis tributis bella ex bellis ferendo exausta pecunia ex attritis viribus compotes illius dominationis evaderent?" *Oratio, loc. cit.*, p. 178.

72. "Pisas vero cum adepti sumus ..., exitialem nobis coronam impositam audientibus nobis exclamasti. Prefecturam vero aretinam, cortonensem, volterranam, pistoriensem, ... puerorum deliramenta esse dicebas, posteris nostris fatale futurum." *Ibid.*, p. 178.

73. "... teque omni dignitate privatum malle dicebas imperium tyranni quam paucorum potentiam ac dominationem sufferre." *Ibid.*, p. 177.

74. "... quamquam tu nichil sapias, quid civi conveniat, nedum optimo, tamen mediocri quidem ac tolerabili." *Ibid.*

75. This is the way in which the words "qui omnes artifices tam insolenter contemnis" must be understood, for "artifex" is the usual term to denote the manufacturers in the Lana guild.

76. "... in taberna lanaria educatus inter vilissimos mercenarios, ut tu ipse appellas, atque ultime fecis homines. .." *Ibid.*, p. 169.

77. See Vol. One, p. 114.

78. See Vol. One, p. 80.

79. Bruni's poem, with the superscription *Spreta iuventutis hec carmina sunt Leonardi*, has been preserved in a manuscript of Reichenau Abbey, today Cod. Augiensis CXXXI of the Badische Landesbibliothek in Karlsruhe. The scribe has noted at the end: "This poem was composed by Leonardus Aretinus in the time of his youth, to deal with the approach of the Emperor. (*Hec carmina sue iuventutis tempore de adventu Imperatoris composuit Leonardus Aretinus.*) Bruni himself later scorned it as a childish thing. Yet it is nothing to be despised; for it betrays a better than mediocre mind, as will be evident to those who read it." See A. Holder, *Die Reichenauer Handschriften*, vol. 1 (Leipzig, 1906), pp. 323-325. The scribe of this manuscript, then, must have been in personal touch with Bruni; and there need be no doubt about the reliability of his ascription for other reasons as well. The manuscript contains other rare texts by the humanists around Salutati, including Poggio's letter to Niccoli written on the

death of Salutati, which has been preserved in its original form only here and in one other manuscript, in the Biblioteca Laurenziana in Florence. See *Epistolario di Salutati*, ed. Novati, vol. II, p. 394; vol. IV, p. 471. Obviously, the volume came from a member of Bruni's and Poggio's early circle at the Curia, and made its journey to the north in the baggage of a curial official who attended the Council of Constance. The first among Bruni scholars to draw attention to the existence of the poem was L. Bertalot in *Archivum Romanicum*, XV (1931), p. 300. The poem must have been composed in 1397 or 1398 because there was no other span of time in Bruni's youth when a German King was planning an expedition to Rome, in order to acquire the imperial crown, while being in conflict with Florence so that he could be classed with Hannibal and Pyrrhus among the invaders of Italy, as is done in the poem. It is true that King Wenceslaus as early as the autumn of 1394 and the first months of 1395 had made diplomatic moves to assure the help of Italian states on his planned Roman expedition. (See Vol. One, p. 23.) But at that time he had sought the cooperation of Venice and Florence, and had offered the two republics his aid against Milan—an episode which was closed by Florence's definitive decision, in March 1395, not to enter into an alliance with an Emperor in contradiction to all Guelph traditions, and by Wenceslaus' reconciliation with Giangaleazzo who, in May 1395, was made Duke and a Prince of the Empire. The situation presupposed by the poem did not develop until 1397-98 when Wenceslaus, now as the ally of Giangaleazzo, resumed his Italian plans in earnest, and Florence was using every diplomatic means to obviate Wenceslaus' expedition. See De Mesquita, *Giangaleazzo*, pp. 172f. and 213ff., for these political conditions. The writer could consult a microfilm kindly sent him by the administration of the Badische Landesbibliothek in Karlsruhe.

80. "Roma tuas iterum valido fulcire cohortes / milite festina! Veniunt iam bella, quirites. / Tollite victricis fulgentia signa volucris / et patrie prestate (MS: prestare) manus! Summittite colla / ad magne virtutis honus! Non terreat hostis / rumor, et invictum celus (MS: tilus) qui possidet orbem / inveniat qui iura tenent, qui sanguine cunctos / non nisi diffuso discant servire per artus." Cod. Augiensis CXXXI, fol. 93v.

81. A systematic analysis of the civic-humanistic elements in Palmieri's *Della Vita Civile* is still wanting. But the above high

estimate follows from varied observations by V. Rossi, *Il Quattrocento* (1934), pp. 135ff.; H. Baron, "La Rinascita dell'Etica Statale Romana nell' Umanesimo Fiorentino del Quattrocento," *Civiltà Moderna*, VII (1935), 11ff.; H. Baron, "Franciscan Poverty and Civic Wealth," *Speculum*, XIII (1938), 23f.; F. Battaglia, in the introduction to his edition of *Della Vita Civile* in the series "Scrittori Politici Italiani," vol. XIV (Bologna, 1944); E. Garin, *La Filosofia*, in "Storia dei Generi Letterari Italiani," vol. I (1947), p. 257ff.; and E. Garin, *Der Italienische Humanismus* (1947), p. 71ff. For the time of the composition of *Della Vita Civile* see note 16 to Chap. 15.

82. Bruni's estimate of Dante as a citizen who discharged his obligations toward his community by serving in public office and as *paterfamilias*, is contained in Bruni's *Vita di Dante*. (In *Le Vite di Dante, Petrarca e Boccaccio*, ed. Solerti, p. 99ff.; in *Bruni, Schriften*, p. 53ff.) This estimate is a feature of Bruni's vindication of Dante which emerged in the years of maturity of his Humanism, and must be added to the vindication of Dante the poet and historical thinker that had occupied Bruni since he had begun to emancipate himself from Niccoli's contempt of the *tre corone fiorentine*. For this civic aspect of Bruni's final appraisal of Dante see H. Baron, "The Historical Background of the Florentine Renaissance," *History*, n.s., XXII (1938), 324ff. (Italian translation in *La Rinascita* I [1938], 69ff.); H. Baron, "Cicero and the Roman Civic Spirit in the Middle Ages and the Early Renaissance," *Bulletin of the John Rylands Library*, XXII (1938), 95ff.; and E. Garin, "Noterelle di Filosofia del Rinascimento," *La Rinascita*, IV (1941), 409ff. That Bruni's opinion, in this as in other respects, may be considered typical of that of Florentine civic humanists, is proven by the adoption of his views on the role of office and family in Dante's life by the later Florentine biographers of Dante, in particular by Giannozzo Manetti and Cristoforo Landino. An interesting by-way in the history of this influence is the almost literal insertion of a substantial part of Bruni's *Vita di Dante*, obviously as a gem of civic sentiment, in the memoirs of Cino Rinuccini's son, Filippo di Cino Rinuccini (see in Aiazzi's edition of Filippo Rinuccini's *Ricordi* [Florence, 1840], p. xi ff.), presumably about 1450. In the eighteenth century, this latter adaptation of Bruni's life of Dante was published as a separate work in the *Delizie degli Eruditi Toscani* (vol. XII

[1779], p. 245ff.); it was reprinted as late as 1848 (in Fossombrone; a copy is in the Harvard College Library) as "Filippi Rinuccini Vita di Dante scritta nel sec. XIV (*sic*)"—apt to mislead the reader with regard to the decisive fact: that the civic appraisal of Dante which Filippo Rinuccini makes his own reflects the views that had emerged from the crisis of the early Quattrocento.

CHAPTER 15

1. V. Rossi, *Il Quattrocento* (3rd edn., 1933), p. 228. For Giovanni da Prato's relations to Cino Rinuccini cf. also *Humanistic and Political Literature*, Chapter I, last pages of section 1.

2. Cf. the concluding pages of the section "The *Paradiso* as Anachronistic Fifteenth-Century Fiction," in *Humanistic and Political Literature*, Chapter I.

3. See the Excursus "The Date of the *Paradiso*," in *Humanistic and Political Literature*, Chapter I, section 2.

4. End of 1428, or early in 1429. See note 4 to Chap. 18.

5. This *Canzona morale di patria e di libertate* is published by Wesselofsky, II, pp. 435-440. According to F. Flamini, *La lirica toscana del Rinascimento* (1891), p. 58ff., the date of its composition falls probably into the end-phase of the war with Giangaleazzo, i.e. 1402; according to A. Medin, *Archivio Storico Lombardo*, XVIII (1891), 784f., certainly "after 1399" ("dopo il 1399").

6. ". . . di quelli dico che . . . alle cose della nostra santa republica con somma diligenza tutto il lor tempo tengono iustissimamente quella nella dolcissima libertade governare e salvare." *Paradiso*, I, p. 2.

7. *Ibid.*, pp. 47f., 52-54.

8. Cf. the survey of the paragraphs of the *Paradiso* dealing with political and historical themes, in *Humanistic and Political Literature*, Chapter I, beginning of section 1.

9. "Scusimi ancora l'ardentissima voglia che continuamente mi sprona il . . . edioma materno con ogni possa sapere esaltare e quello nobilitare, come che da tre corone fiorentine principalmente già nobilitato et esaltato si sia." *Paradiso*, I, p. 2.

10. ". . . che l'edioma fiorentino è si rilimato e copioso che ogni astratta e profonda mater[i]a si puote chiarissimamente con esso dire, ragionarne e disputarne." *Paradiso*, II, p. 84. These words are attributed in the novel to the Paduan philosopher, Marsilio di Santa Sofia, and not to Luigi Marsili as E. Santini asserted in his "La Produzione Volgare di Bruni," *Giornale Stor. Lett. Ital.*, LX (1912), 290f. The passage is an acknowledgment of the national Florentine attainment, put into the mouth of a distinguished scholastic scholar from abroad who is forced to admit of not having

been sufficiently familiar with the Volgare in the past, but promises to do better in the future. (He says "E per certo . . . e' conviene che io l'abbia per l'avenire dimestico e familiare, dogliendomi forte che per lo arietro fatto non l'abbia." *Ibid.*, p. 84f.). This scene in the conversations of the novel undoubtedly reflects the patriotic hue of Giovanni's own love of the Florentine Volgare. In its general form and motivation, to be sure, the judgment attributed to Marsilio di Santa Sofia is indebted to the well known paragraph of Boccaccio's *Vita di Dante* (cap. XIV) where Dante's role for the "poesia volgare" is likened to what Homer had done for poetry among the Greeks and Virgil among the Latins (". . . con le sue dimostrazioni fece piú scolari in poesia e massimamente nella volgare; la quale, secondo il mio giudicio, egli primo non altramenti fra noi italici esaltò e recò in pregio, che la sua Omero tra' greci o Virgilio tra' latini"), and where the conclusion is reached that Dante made the Volgare, which before him had served for frivolous love poems alone, into an instrument of high art, thus "demonstrating by his performance that volgare poetry can deal with any lofty matter" ("mostrò con effetto con essa [i.e. la poesia volgare] ogni alta materia potersi trattare. . ." Ed. D. Guerri in Boccaccio's *Comento alla Divina Commedia e gli Altri Scritti intorno a Dante*, vol. I [Bari, 1918], p. 24f.). But in the hands of Giovanni da Prato, writer of the Quattrocento, Boccaccio's recognition that the Volgare was adequate to the highest tasks of poetry has been transformed into the assertion that the Volgare even was a suitable medium for the cultured intercourse and the subtle ways of scholarly reasoning that had always been believed to be necessarily confined to Latin.

11. See note 35 to Chap. 13.

12. To be specific, Bruni's *Canzone Morale* may have been written as early as the later part of the 1420's; see *Bruni, Schriften*, pp. 150, 169. His *Canzone a Laude di Venere* (not yet dated in *Bruni, Schriften*, p. 180), on the other hand, must have been written on the eve of the 1430's, in October 1429 or not much later. This can be inferred from the close likeness between the subject of the poem, and that of Bruni's *Ep. VI 1* which contains a famous explanation of the Platonic "furor divinus." The letter was written on October 7, 1429; in the three years preceding that date, Bruni's literary production had shown no signs of interest in philosophical matters since all his energies were ab-

sorbed by political activity and historiographical work. For the list of Bruni's writings from 1426 to 1428, see Vol. One, p. 357f., note 4 to Chap. 18, and Appendix 8, Vol. Two, p. 433ff.

The date of the *Novella: Storia di Seleuco, d'Antioco e di Stratonica, Raccontata da un Nostro Cittadino* is neither 1438, as the traditional assumption (still repeated in *Bruni, Schriften*, p. 176) has been, nor "mid-January 1436," as L. Bertalot, relying on the indications in a number of manuscripts, proposed in 1931 (*Archivum Romanicum*, xv, 298), but rather mid-January 1437, i.e., January 15, 1436 *stilo florentino*. The need for this interpretation of the date found in manuscripts will be shown in the revised chronology of Bruni's works, referred to in note 4 to Chap. 10. An excellent appraisal of the language and the literary value of the *Novella* is given in E. Santini's "La Produzione Volgare di Bruni," *loc.cit.*, 316-320.

13. "Ciascuna lingua ha sua perfezione e suo suono e suo parlare limato e scientifico." *Bruni, Schriften*, p. 61.

14. Until recently there has been little protest against the inveterate opinion (for which, as we have seen, Wesselofsky was greatly responsible) that during the larger part of the Quattrocento the effect of Humanism on Volgare literature was mainly of a negative nature: obliteration of Trecento Volgare to the benefit of humanistic Latin; and opposition, not help, to the Volgare when it again came to the fore in the second half of the Quattrocento. One of the props of this thesis, it is true, has long been tacitly abandoned; students realized the active part of some Florentine humanists in the vindication of the Volgare from the second third of the century onward, and especially the significant role played in this vindication by L. B. Alberti and Cristoforo Landino. But these observations did not bring about a reexamination of the opinion that Humanism—not merely in some groups and schools, but by its very nature—was the mortal enemy of the Volgare and did for a time succeed in deflecting the growth of Florentine and Italian literature. Even today, writers like Alberti and Landino are looked upon as exceptions—as liberators from a prejudice that is thought to have dominated Florentine Humanism previously. This is the tenor of the basic monographic study in the field, not yet in any way replaced, V. Cian's "Contro il Volgare" (*Studi Letterari e Linguistici dedicati a Pio Rajna* [Milan, 1911], pp. 251-297)—a presentation of the subject which, in spite of the

increased attention it paid to Alberti and Landino, has helped to perpetuate the old view by its very title and by the repeated reference to the alleged common "pregiudizio umanistico" in matters of the Volgare. The situation is about the same in the most generally used introduction to the subject, the chapter "L'Umanesimo e il Volgare" in V. Rossi's *Il Quattrocento* (3rd edn.: 1933, pp. 104-115), which, side by side with an excellent analysis of many data that should be a warning against rash generalizations, presents a genuine diatribe against the supposed shortsightedness of the early Renaissance humanists and their alleged obnoxious influence on everything affecting the vernacular. A good survey of the language controversies in Renaissance Italy, "The Fight for the Vernacular [in] Italy," in Vernon Hall Jr.'s *Renaissance Literary Criticism* (New York, 1945, esp. pp. 19-26), by and large follows this view of the early Quattrocento, giving fresh currency to the old estimate within the framework of a comparative study of the Italian, French, and English theories. Strangely enough, some of the basic facts that should cause us to reconsider the accustomed perspective even for the early Renaissance have been known since E. Santini's study "La produzione volgare di Bruni" (*Giorn. Stor. Lett. Ital.*, LX [1912], 289-332). But the implications of Santini's view of Bruni could evidently not be fully understood as long as it had not been incorporated in a comprehensive and coherent interpretation of the phenomenon of Florentine civic Humanism. In the absence of such an interpretation, even Santini's attempts to reconcile some apparently contradictory facets of Bruni's own attitude to the Volgare remained unsuccessful. It is only quite recently that a revision has been convincingly tackled in P. O. Kristeller's fundamental paper on "The Origin and Development of the Language of Italian Prose" (*Word*, II [1946], 50-65)—a revision from a different vantage-point. Kristeller points out that, although the first half of the Quattrocento cannot, to be sure, boast of any great Italian poet, "the development of literary Italian seems to have been quite different as far as prose is concerned." "More important than the theory is the actual practice of the humanists and their contemporaries, which presents an entirely different picture [from the accepted opinion]. The fifteenth century, including its earlier phases, shows no interruption or decline in the development of vernacular prose literature, but rather an advance and expansion, and the humanists took an active part in this literature" (pp. 53, 58). The following observations will prove that the growth of the Florentine ideas of the nature and value of the Volgare is in perfect agreement with Kristeller's findings about the actual development of prose-writing in the vernacular. Although the thumb-nail sketch which we shall draw will leave room for qualifications and supplements, it will show conclusively that a coherent evolution of the linguistic and literary views of the Florentine citizen-humanists had long been underway when Alberti and Landino produced their more conspicuous Volgare writings and language-theories.

15. "Con tutto che queste sono cose, che mal si possono dire in vulgare idioma, pur m'ingegnerò di darle ad intendere. . ." *Bruni, Schriften*, p. 60. To see in this definite and revealing statement merely the expression of a "pregiudizio umanistico," as Cian does in his study (p. 260), is an anachronism which obscures the actual problem encountered by early Quattrocento humanists.

16. ". . . m'amonirono, non però dannando la inventione et opera ordinata da noi, ma me più tosto riprehendendo che così publicamente m'era dato a comporre libri volgari." In the introduction to the Fourth Book of the *Della Vita Civile*, where Palmieri recounts that he had submitted the first three books to friends for their opinion. Florence, Bibl. Naz. Ms. II, IV, 81 (autograph), fol. 73v; in F. Battaglia's reedition of the text printed in Florence, Giunta, 1529—in "Scrittori Politici Italiani," vol. XIV (1944)—p. 125f. As to the date of the *Vita Civile*, there seem to be good reasons to place it between 1432 and 1436, though proof of this date would require a lengthy argument. In any case, the suggestion (first made by V. Rossi in his *Quattrocento* and adopted by others [cf. A. della Torre, *Storia dell'Accademia Platonica di Firenze*, Firenze 1902, p. 306]) that the date of composition was as early as 1431/32 since Palmieri in book IV talks of himself as being still young and little experienced in the "vita civile," is easily refuted by the observation that Palmieri excused himself on the same score in a *Protesto* recited as late as 1437. (See on this oration, available only in a rare print of 1850, A. Messeri's statement in *Archivio Stor. Ital.*, ser. v, vol. XIII [1894], 276: Palmieri, in his speech, "fa allusione alla sua molto giovanile età.") The Fourth Book may not be much earlier than 1437, for it originated later than the first three books as is at-

tested, in addition to the indication in the Fourth Book itself, by the fact that Leonardo Dati, Palmieri's contemporary, in his commentary on Palmieri's *Città di Vita* speaks of "libros *tres* in prima adolescentia sua patrio sermone conscriptos, quos *Civilem Vitam* vocavit." As for the growing appreciation in recent scholarship of the significance of Palmieri's work, see note 81 to Chap. 14.

17. Biondo, in the crucial paragraph of his *De Verbis Romanae Locutionis* (in his *Scritti Inediti e Rari*, ed. B. Nogara in "Studi e Testi," vol. 48 [Rome, 1927], p. 129), had begun by asserting that even before the Germanic invasions any deviation, both inside and outside Rome, from the norm of the literary language was nothing but deterioration and barbaric infection: "Temporibus vides quae Ciceronis aetatem praecesserant illos qui aut extra Romam vixerant, aut Romae domesticam habuerant aliquam barbariem, a nitore locutionis Romanae aliqualiter recessisse et barbarie illa infuscatos fuisse." After this disparaging introduction he proceeds to his denunciation of the effects of the barbarian migrations: "Postea vero quam urbs a Gothis et Vandalis capta inhabitarique coepta est, . . . omnes sermone barbaro inquinati ac penitus sordidati fuerunt; sensimque factum est, ut pro Romana latinitate adulterinam hanc barbarica mixtam loquelam habeamus vulgarem." How essential this negative and critical note for Biondo's interpretation was, is documented by the fact that, when twenty years later, in preparing his *Italia Illustrata*, he discovered that among the German tribes it was the nation of the Lombards which more than others contributed to the changes of Roman culture, including the transformation of the Latin into the Volgare, he stated with bitter words "that the madness of precisely this nation went as far as this." The interesting passage which illuminates Biondo's feelings toward the Volgare runs: "Nam Longobardi omnium qui Italiam invaserint externorum superbissimi romani imperii et Italiae dignitatem evertere ac omnino delere conati, leges novas . . . condidere, mores ritus gentium et rerum vocabula immutavere, ut affirmare audeamus locutionis romanae latinis verbis quae nedum Italia sed romano quoque imperio subiecti plerique populi utebantur mutationem factam in vulgarem italicam nunc appellatam per Longobardorum tempora inchoasse. Idque incognitum nobis quando opus de locutione romana ad Leonardum Aretinum dedimus. . . . Quin etiam publicae administrationis et privatim vivendi instituta accuratissime ab eisdem

sunt mutata et eo usque ipsius gentis processit insania ut romanorum caractere litterarum penitus postposito novas ipsi et sua ineptia gentis barbariem indicantes cifras pro litteris adinvenirent. [*Print* adinvenerunt]. E contra vero Ostrogothi aeque ac cives romani latinis delectati litteris nullam in illis barbariem effuderunt." *Italia Illustrata*, at the beginning of the section "Nona Regio: Marchia Tarvisina." (Ed. Verona, 1482, fol. H IIIv-H IIIIr).

18. "Atque latina lingua a vulgari in multis differt, plurimum tamen terminatione, inflexione, significatione, constructione, et accentu." "Haec ne quaeso mulierculae et nutrices et vulgus illitteratum dicent, quae nos litterati vix dicere valemus? Quid si probo per ea tempora vulgarem sermonem distinctum a literato fuisse?" Bruni, *Ep. VI 10*, ed. Mehus, vol. II, p. 66f.

19. "Denique etiam hodie mulieres Romanae judicio meo elegantissime loquuntur, et purius certe quam viri. Et quanquam non litteratus sit earum sermo, potest tamen figura ipsa dicendi nitorque verborum eloquentiam adjuvare." Bruni had listened to a certain Roman matron. "Haec illa puro nativoque Romano proferebat sermone, ita ut admodum sim equidem delectatus, cum et verba nitorem gravitatemque sententiae et pronunciatio ipsa vernaculam quandam habere[n]t suavitatem. Hoc ego modo filiis matres, et nutrices alumnis profuisse ad elegantiam puto. Non quod casus inflecterent aut verba variarent ac terminarent litterate, sed quod purum et nitidum ac minime barbarum sermonem infunderent. Nam et habet vulgaris sermo commendationem suam, ut apud Dantem poetam et alios quosdam emendate loquentes apparet." *Ibid.*, p. 68.

20. "Lo scrivere in istile litterato o vulgare non ha a fare al fatto, nè altra differenza è, se non come scrivere in greco od in latino. Ciascuna lingua ha sua perfezione e suo suono e suo parlare limato scientifico." In *Le Vite di Dante, Petrarca e Boccaccio*, ed. Solerti, p. 106; in *Bruni, Schriften*, p. 61.

21. "Uno strano sapore di modernità." V. Rossi in "Dante nel Trecento e nel Quattrocento," in Rossi's *Scritti di critica letteraria*, vol. I (1930), p. 328.

22. It is true that (as far as this writer is aware) the rather inexact approximation: between 1436 and 1459, set forth by L. Mehus in 1747 (reprinted in the edition of Filippo Villani's *De Origine Civitatis Florentiae* by Galletti, p. 60), is so far the only date suggested for Manetti's biography of Dante. But in

Manetti's *Praefatio* one reads that the composition was made in a period of relaxation after completion of work on his *De Illustribus Longaevis*, and this treatise in turn, was, according to its introduction, composed not long after Manetti's *Apologia Nunnii*, a pamphlet undoubtedly written in the second half of 1439 or immediately afterwards. (Nunnius was in Florence at the time of the Church Council, and on that occasion was in personal contact with Manetti).

23. This sums up the contents of Manetti's preface, ed. in Solerti, *Vite di Dante, Petrarca e Boccaccio*, pp. 109-112.

24. "Hanc suam materni sermonis poeticam hic noster poeta primus apud Italos perpaucis ante annis adinventam . . . non secus nobilitavit, quam aut Homerus graece apud Graecos aut Virgilius latine apud Latinos quondam suam quisque apud suos illustraverit"; *ibid.*, p. 138. The same idea had been already expressed in Boccaccio's *Vita di Dante* (see the quotation in note 10 above); and, no doubt, Manetti was drawing from this source. In spite of his plagiarism, however, the fact that he was ready to follow Boccaccio's opinion remains remarkable. Two generations of humanistic classicists between Boccaccio and Manetti had refused to place the work of a Volgare poet on one level with its Greek and Latin counterparts, as several examples on the pages which follow will illustrate. On the other hand, during the generation subsequent to Bruni and Manetti the reference to the equality of the life-works of Homer, Virgil, and Dante became a veritable household phrase for Florentine writers.

25. Benedetto Accolti, *Dialogus De Praestantia Virorum Sui Aevi*; published in the edition of Filippo Villani and other *De Florentinorum litteratura principes fere synchroni scriptores* by Galletti, pp. 101-128 (see above note 33 to Chap. 3). Composed between 1459 and 1464; cf. A. Gaspary, *Geschichte der italienischen Literatur*, II (1888), 179.

26. ". . . a multis dubitatum scio, duplexne an unus loquendi modus esset." Accolti, *op. cit.*, p. 122.

27. For Salutati see Rossi, *Il Quattrocento*, p. 109, p. 119, n. 53, and v. Martin, *Salutati und hum. Lebensideal*, p. 220, n. 3. In Bruni's *Dialogus I*, Salutati is made to express precisely the same idea. ("Dantem vero, si alio genere scribendi usus esset, non eo contentus forem, ut illum cum antiquis nostris compararem, sed et ipsis et Graecis etiam anteponerem." Ed. Klette, p. 60; ed.

Garin, p. 68). For Poggio see Rossi, *Il Quattrocento*, p. 110, p. 119, n. 55. The same reserve is apparent in Palmieri's praise that Dante, "fuori della lingua, poco si truova drieto a' sommi poeti latini." (*Della Vita Civile*, Ms. Bibl. Naz. II, IV, 81, fol. lv; ed. Battaglia, p. 4). These utterances suggest the only half-sympathetic attitude which must have been the starting-point for Bruni in his youth. By comparing that earlier estimate with the recognition of the Volgare as a language in its own right in Bruni's *Vita di Dante*, we can grasp the extent of the transformation which had occurred in his outlook during his life.

28. "Nec multifacio qua quisque lingua, materna scilicet, an Latina proloquatur; modo graviter, ornate, copioseque pronuntiet." Accolti, *op. cit.*, pp. 121-122.

29. In the "Proemio" of Alberti's *Teogenio*, written about the same time, or even a few years earlier, but not published until about 1442, we also read "che molti m'ascrivono a biasimo, e dicono ch'io offesi la maestà letteraria non scrivendo materia sì eloquente in lingua piuttosto latina."

30. "Fu Italia piú volte occupata et posseduta da varie nationi: Gallici, Gothi, Vandali, Longobardi, et altre simili barbare et molto asprissime genti. Et, come o necessità o volontà inducea, e popoli, parte per bene essere intesi, parte per piú ragionando piacere a chi essi obediano, cosí appreendevano quella o quell' altra lingua forestiera, et quelli strani et adventitii uomini el simile se consuefaceano alla nostra, credo con molti barbarismi et corruptela del proferire. Onde per questa mistura di dí in dí insalvatichí et vitiossi la nostra prima cultissima et emendatissima lingua." *Della Famiglia*, in the introduction to the Third Book; ed. G. Mancini (Florence, 1908), p. 144.

31. "Ben confesso quella antiqua latina lingua essere copiosa molto et ornatissima: ma non però vegho in che sia la nostra oggi toscana tanto da averla in odio. . . . Et sento io questo: chi fusse piú di me docto o tale quale molti vogliono essere riputati, costui in questa oggi comune troverrebbe non meno ornamenti che in quella. . . . Et sia quanto dicono quella antica apresso di tutte le genti piena d'auctorità, solo perché in essa molti docti scrissero, simile certo sarà la nostra, s' e' docti la vorranno molto con suo studio et vigilie essere elimata et polita." *Della Famiglia*, *loc. cit.* p. 145.

As for the right, and necessity, in the context of our present discussion to consider Alberti a "Florentine humanist," we shall remember that, although he had been born and bred in exile, he had visited Florence since 1434 and had been deeply impressed by the civic life in the Republic; the ideas and problems of the *Della Famiglia* were the direct outcome of these contacts.

32. For the *Regole della Lingua Fiorentina*, also called *Grammatichetta Vaticana*, see C. Trabalza, *Storia della grammatica italiana* (Milan, 1908), pp. 15ff. and 532ff. (where it is published), and the bibliographical note on its authorship in V. Rossi's *Il Quattrocento*, p. 120. On Bembo and Florence, cf. V. Cian, "Per Bernardo Bembo. Le sue relazioni coi Medici," *Giornale storico della letteratura italiana*, XXVIII (1896), 348-364; "Per Bernardo Bembo. Le relazioni letterarie, i codici e gli scritti," *ibid.*, XXXI (1898), 49-81; "*Le Regole della lingua fiorentina* e le prose bembiane," *ibid.*, LIV (1909), 120-130 (where, p. 124, note 2, the brief preface is reprinted).

33. Lorenzo de' Medici, *Comento sopra alcuni de' suoi Sonetti* (in *Opere*, ed. Simioni, vol. I [1913], pp. 18-22).

34. "E questo si può più presto chiamare felicità e prosperità che vera laude della lingua [latina] . . .; perchè la propagazione dell' imperio romano non l'ha fatto solamente comune per tutto il mondo, ma quasi necessaria." *Op. cit.*, pp. 19-20.

35. Which is the most adequate rendering of "lingue materni e naturali."

36. *Op. cit.*, pp. 21-22.

37. Landino (in his "Vita e Costumi di Dante" introducing his commentary upon the *Divina Commedia*, quoted in the following note): Dante "primo dimostrò quanto fosse idoneo il Fiorentino idioma, non solo ad exprimere, ma ad amplificare ed exornare tutte le cose che caggiono in disputazione." Dante "fu el primo che la lingua nostra patria . . . molto nobilitò e fecela culta et ornata. Trovò Omero la lingua greca molto già abondante e exculta da Orfeo e da Museo e da altri poeti più vetusti di lui. Trovò la latina Virgilio già elimata et exornata e da Ennio e da Lucrezio, da Plauto e da Terenzio et altri poeti vetusti amplificata. Ma innanzi a Dante in lingua toscana nessuno avea trovato alcuna leggiadria. . ." (p. 191f.).

38. See Landino's *Orazione quando cominciò a leggere in Studio i sonetti di M. Francesco Petrarca* (1460), edited in Fr. Corazzini's volume *Miscellanea di Cose Inedite o Rare* (Florence,

1853), pp. 125-134; and Landino's introduction ("Vita e Costumi di Dante") to his commentary upon the *Divina Commedia*, first published 1481, reprinted in Solerti, *op. cit.*, esp. pp. 191-193.

39. The place in this galaxy ascribed by Landino to Bruni has been modified, but not basically changed, by G. Mancini's correction of the text of Landino's speech. Landino, after first listing "Leonardo Aretino" next to Boccaccio as the pioneer in the "fiorentina eloquenzia," later returns to "Lionardo detto" to pay the highest respect to his Volgare poetry, if we believe the customary version of the speech. As Mancini has shown (in his *Vita di L. B. Alberti*, 2nd edn. [Florence, 1911], p. 441), the correct reading is "Lionardo Dati," a younger humanist and poet, born in 1408. In spite of this correction the fact remains that Landino in 1460 placed Bruni side by side with Palmieri, Alberti and other kindred minds in the group of men who in the early Quattrocento broke the ground for the final rise of Florentine Volgare literature—an appraisal which would be incomprehensible without the reinterpretation of Bruni's attitude to the Volgare at which we have arrived.

40. *Vita e Costumi*, ed. in Solerti's *Vite di Dante, di Petrarca e di Boccaccio*, pp. 191-193.

41. "Ma non sia alcuno che creda non solamente essere eloquente ma pure tollerabile dicitore, se prima non harà vera et perfecta cognizione delle latine lettere." *Ibid.*, p. 192.

42. ". . . è necessario essere Latino chi vuole essere buono Toscano." Corazzini, *loc. cit.*, p. 131. For an estimate of Dante, and comparison with Homer and Virgil, by Landino's contemporary, Ugolino Verino, see below note 16 to Chap. 18.

43. For an appraisal of this result in the light of recent scholarship it may be noted that Vernon Hall, in his cited discussion of the history of Renaissance literary criticism in Italy, France, and England (see note 14 above), concludes on the basis of a wider-than-Italian approach that the Italian ideas that are comparable to those subsequently found outside Italy are encountered specifically in Florence, but, he thinks, not until the sixteenth century. At that time, he observes, "the fight for the vernacular" was different in Florence from that in the rest of Italy; "it was in Florence . . . that there was a love for the native soil transferred to the native tongue that finds an echo in French and English writings. . . . Characterized as they were by a strong feeling of

local pride, the writings of the Florentines offer the closest parallels to the English and French writings on the subject of the vernacular" (p. 35f.). What we believe to have proved in our study is that the roots of all these characteristics lay actually as far back as the first decades of the Quattrocento.

After the manuscript of the present book had been sent to the publisher, a picture of the relations between fifteenth century Italian Humanism and Volgare literature that closely resembles the account just given appeared in August Buck's *Italienische Dichtungslehren vom Mittelalter bis zum Ausgang der Renaissance* (Tübingen, 1952)—a work which refuses to submit to the prevailing prejudices about the part played by the humanistic element. In the chapter "Humanismus und volkssprachliche Dichtung" (cf. esp. pp. 97-112), Buck arrives at the same rejection as here proposed of the opinion that the growth of Italian literature and the interest in the Volgare were merely injured by the Latin humanists. When in the second half of the Quattrocento the point is reached, says Buck, where a great school of Italian poetry reemerged, "the reemergence does not occur . . . in opposition to Humanism, but as an evolution from the humanistic standpoint. The opposition which had originally divided the humanistic and vernacular traditions is now replaced by a synthesis of both traditions. Humanism becomes integrated in the course of the intellectual history of the Italian nation. Such an integration, however, could take place only because Humanism, as far as it is a living movement, is by its nature not simply a revival of a past culture, but involves a reaction of the modern mind to ancient culture" (". . . weil der Humanismus—soweit er wirklich fruchtbar ist—eben stets eine Auseinandersetzung des modernen Geistes mit der Antike und nicht eine Restauration einer vergangenen Kultur darstellt." P. 100f.). This is an excellent definition of the complexity and fruitfulness of the humanistic challenge to the Volgare that we have tried to make better understood by emphasizing the kinship of the Florentine Quattrocento attitude to familiar features of later classicism in France. But in order to reveal the full value of Buck's results, we must needs integrate them with the three basic facts established in the present investigations: First, our restatement of the meaning of Bruni's *Dialogi* and of the meaning of his theory of a simultaneous use of Latin and Volgare in ancient Rome—a reinterpretation which solves the riddle why (as Buck,

p. 103, puts it) "the same Bruni who [in his *Dialogi*], through the mouth of Niccoli, had made himself the speaker of the purely negative humanistic criticism of Dante," in 1436 could take the positive stand characteristic of his *Vite di Dante e di Petrarca*, although as late as 1435 he had fought the view of the origin of the vernacular language that was adhered to subsequently by most defenders of the Volgare (Buck, p. 101). Secondly, our discovery that, when Bruni's actual opinion on the Volgare is considered together with the other known expressions of the mind of the Florentine civic humanists, the Florentine group is seen from the first decade of the Quattrocento onward to become a more and more clearly marked exception from the "purely negative" attitude toward the Volgare typical of practically all other humanistic writers in early Quattrocento Italy. Finally, our observation that the exceptional course of the Florentine development was largely caused by the political experiences of the Florentine citizenry in the era of the Florentine-Milanese struggle.

Part Five

CHAPTER 16

1. For this role of Pisa in the time of Giangaleazzo see Vol. One, pp. 20, 23, 26. For other details illustrating Florence's vital dependence, during the Giangaleazzo wars, on free passage through the Pisan ports, see *Humanistic and Political Literature*, Chapter II, Excursus "Pitfalls in the Dating of Loschi's *Invectiva*."

2. The most satisfactory picture of the period of Ladislaus of Naples is still that contained in the sixth volume of F. Gregorovius' *Geschichte der Stadt Rom im Mittelalter* (5th edn. 1908), pp. 577-616. A. Cutolo, *Re Ladislao d'Angiò-Durazzo* (2 volumes, Milan, 1936), is now the best guide to the diplomatic events and archival documents, but hardly speaks the last word on the historical significance of Ladislaus' conquest of Italy. See below note 8.

3. On the conclusion of this league, June 27, 1409, see the information in Scipione Ammirato, *Istorie Fiorentine*, end of lib. XVII (in the edition Florence, 1647, vol. II, p. 949f.). Cf. also C. Cipolla, *Storia delle Signorie Italiane 1343-1530* (Milan, 1881), p. 298; and Cutolo, *op. cit.*, vol. I, p. 340f., vol. II, pp. 171-174, for documentary details on the final establishment of the league, especially with Siena, during the months of June and July.

4. See Vol. One, p. 16f.

5. The fact that the nearly hundred fifty years between the rapprochement of the year 1409 and the end of Siena's independence saw periods of conflict, and even moments of armed clashes, between Siena and Florence, does not detract from the correctness of this general statement. In the first half of the Quattrocento the reestablished friendship of the two Tuscan republics was disturbed only during Florence's attack on Lucca in the early 1430's, when Siena became fearful of the stronger neighbor and aided Lucca; but from 1433 to 1447 Siena was again in alliance with Florence against Filippo Maria Visconti. After 1447, during the sweeping shifts of the alliances of the early Quattrocento

out of which sprang the equilibrium system of the late Renaissance, Siena stood for a while with Venice and Alfonso of Naples against Florence; but when the peace of Lodi in 1454 made reconciliation possible, she joined the 'Santissima Lega' so quickly that Alfonso was full of indignation about his short-time Sienese ally. Between 1478 and 1480, when after the conspiracy of the Pazzi Florence's Italian position and Lorenzo de' Medici's authority were in jeopardy, there was another outburst of Sienese-Florentine local rivalries, and Siena became once more a diplomatic and military ally of Naples. But from 1480 on, both in the periods when Siena enjoyed republican freedom, and during the decades when she was under the signory of Pandolfo Petrucci, the relationship between the two major states of Northern and Southern Tuscany was continually one of friendship and mutual cooperation, even though the formal and normal amity was now and then disturbed by dissensions, misunderstandings, and even by secret deals with other Italian states, made with the purpose of exerting pressure. In the 1550's, when the hour had come in which the Medici, who had been made Dukes of Florence with the help of Spain, decided also to include the southern state in the new Duchy of Tuscany, the last Florentine republicans, like Donato Giannotti and Bartolommeo Cavalcanti, looked on the defense of Siena's liberty as their own cause and aided Siena's last fight by their advice and active cooperation. It is in the frame of this long but rarely remembered historical development that we must read Machiavelli's well known opinions (in his *Discorsi*, I 17 and 55, and similarly in others of his works) that, while there was no room for freedom and republican life in Lombardy and Naples, regions accustomed to obedience to a ruling lord, Tuscany was made for a free life, because, "in the territory of Tuscany, small as it is, one finds that there have long been three republics, Florence, Siena, and Lucca; and that the other cities of this province, though in a way servile, yet are of such a mind and have such a constitution that either they maintain their freedom, or would like to do so." (Trans. by L. J. Walker, in his English edition of *The Discourses*, London, 1950.)

6. ". . . cum magna pars civium iam tunc ad illum inclinaret." Leonardo Bruni, *Rerum Suo Temp. Gest. Comm.*, pp. 441, 443. Domenico Buoninsegni, *Storia della Città di Firenze dall' anno 1410 al 1460* (Florence, 1637), p. 7, speaks of "gran differenza

e discordie fra' cittadini" over the question of accepting or not accepting the King's conciliatory gestures. On the indignation of such old leaders of the Giangaleazzo period as Gino Capponi (he imputed "treachery" to those ready to come to terms with Ladislaus) we have documentary evidence from the year 1414; see Vol. One, p. 322.

7. See Vol. One, pp. 292, 352, and Appendix 5, Vol. Two, p. 412f.

8. Especially by A. Cutolo, who (*op. cit.*, passim, and in particular p. 433f.) vigorously denied any "imperialismo napoletano" with the somewhat astounding comment that Ladislaus "went to the offensive, occupied entire regions, and threatened the Papacy, Florence, and eventually the German King, only to defend himself." (". . . e, per difendersi, offese ed occupò regioni interi, e minacciò il papato, Firenze e financhè il Re dei Romani.")

9. "In tutto avea diretto l'animo a occupare la nostra libertà." "Desiderava lo Imperio . . ." Buoninsegni, *op. cit.*, p. 7; Giovanni di Paolo Morelli, *Cronica*, edn., in the appendix to Ricordano Malespini, *Istoria Fiorentina* (Florence, 1718), p. 355.

10. Ladislaus "libertati totius Italie inimicus semper extiterat"; "quem nichil aliud quam totius Italie servitutem machinantem vidimus." *Laurentii Marci de Benvenutis in Niccolaum Nicholum Oratio*, ed. Zippel, *Giorn. Stor. Lett. Ital.*, XXIV (1894), 178 and 177. On Lorenzo de' Benvenuti see Appendix 5, Vol. Two, p. 413ff.

11. On Loschi's hope that Ladislaus, as a monarch, would unite Italy, see G. da Schio, *Sulla vita e sugli scritti di A. Loschi vicentino* (Padua, 1858), p. 171f. On Saviozzo's praise for Ladislaus on the same score, see N. Sapegno, *Il Trecento* (Milan, 1934), p. 473. If Cutolo had considered these facts from the history of contemporaneous publicism, he might have modified his verdict.

12. Uzzano's opinion, in a meeting of June 4, 1414, is reproduced by A. Dainelli in *Archivio Stor. Ital.*, ser. VII, vol. 17 (1932), 82. The speeches of the members of the peace party and the rejoinders by Corsini and Capponi, all in a meeting on May 17, are published in *Commissioni di Rinaldo degli Albizzi*, vol. I, pp. 235-237. S. Gutkind, in his recent biography of *Cosimo de' Medici* (Oxford, 1938) p. 52, ascribes Capponi's exclamation "melius esset sub Ciompis esse . . ." to an alleged deathbed speech

of Capponi on party affairs rather than to the debates about the defense against Ladislaus. This ascription, however, springs from the author's fancy, one suspects.

13. *Commissioni*, vol. I, p. 235f.

14. These facts are assured by a simultaneous entry in the trustworthy *Diario Fiorentino di Bartolommeo di Michele del Corazza, 1405-1438*, published in *Archivio Storico Italiano*, 1894, ser. V, tom. 14, p. 253.

15. *Commissioni*, vol. I, p. 239 (*Consulta* of June 26th): "Gino di Neri Capponi counselled: The mission was sent to observe, and not to act on its own. And if steps were taken against them, such as are taken in Venice, this would not happen. . . . And if the emissaries have acted against their mandate, let them give satisfaction, even by taking punishment." ("Ginus Nerii Capponi . . . consuluit: . . . Mandatum fuit ut observaretur, et non ut agerent modo suo. Et si contra eos fieret, ut fit Venetiis, non sic ageretur. . . . Et si oratores egerunt contra mandata, ipsi satisfaciant, etiam de pena. . . .")

Since the most likely place where a present-day student may become familiar with these events is the biography of Agnolo Pandolfini in Vespasiano da Bisticci's *Vite di Uomini Illustri del Secolo XV*, and since Vespasiano attributes to Pandolfini as one of his undying merits that he was courageous enough to win for Florence a safe and lucrative peace which had been senselessly obstructed by the bellicose oligarchy of Pandolfini's day, it should be said that Vespasiano's story, written about 1490, is a fantastic novel in this as in other respects. How thoroughly the real historical situation is distorted can be gathered from the fact that Vespasiano sees the lasting attainment of Pandolfini's diplomacy in the acquisition of Cortona for Florence by the pact. (Ed. Frati, vol. III, p. 120f.). But by that time Cortona had actually been Florentine for several years, as Guasti already noted in *Commissioni*, vol. I, p. 235. Also, Capponi's just mentioned grave fears and opposition to the pact have, in Vespasiano's description, turned into the naive and sentimental story that the ruling optimates had been planning to execute Pandolfini after his return—a plan secretly communicated to Pandolfini by a peasant; only the general rejoicing, and the gratitude of large groups of the citizenry to the man who had done so much to promote peace, forced the optimates to abandon their evil design. (Vespasiano da Bisticci, *op. cit.*, p. 123f.). Examples like this fable are a reminder of the extent to which the political face of early Renaissance Florence is bound to be distorted as long as we continue to see it, as it has been for centuries, through the eyes of the artistically alluring authors of the late Renaissance, who wrote in a changed political atmosphere, a hundred years after the events.

16. ". . . qui cum terribilis ac praepotens esset lateque per Italiam dominaretur nec ulla resistendi cerneretur spes." "Eius mors Florentinos ceterasque liberas civitates magnis suspicionibus et manifestissimo certissimoque periculo liberavit. Nullum enim diffugium erat eo vivente, quin colla tandem submittenda fuissent." Bruni, *Rerum Suo Temp. Gest. Comm.*, pp. 441, 443.

17. ". . . nostra aetate potentia immodice adauctus, et cum potentissimo Mediolanensium duce et cum Ladislao bellicosissimo rege ita contendit, ut ab Alpibus in Apuliam, quantum Italiae longitudo protenditur, cuncta armorum strepitu quateret, ac transalpinos insuper reges magnosque exercitus ex Gallia et Germania commoveret. Accedunt ad haec Pisae captae; quam ego urbem . . . alteram Carthaginem . . . appellarim. . . . Haec mihi perdigna litteris et memoria videbantur." Bruni, *Historiae*, p. 3.

18. See the text of the *Capitula Pacis cum Duce Mediolani* in *Commissioni*, vol. II (Florence, 1869), p. 232ff., and the supplementary material referred to by F. T. Perrens, *Histoire de Florence jusqu'à la domination des Médicis*, vol. VI (Paris, 1883), p. 272, n. 5.

19. "Seems to have foretold," because these arguments are attributed to Capponi by Scipione Ammirato, *Istorie Fiorentine* (lib. XVIII, ao. 1420), who, as is well known, still had access to archival documents since lost, but may have reshaped Capponi's speech in the light of the subsequent events. The official minutes of the meetings held in 1420 have not been preserved.

20. We know no more than this bare fact. N. Dainelli's attempt (*La Cultura*, x [1931], 478-482) to reconstruct the gist of Uzzano's speech from the version which Guicciardini, a hundred years later, put in Uzzano's mouth (in the draft of an oration found among Guicciardini's preparations for his *Storie Fiorentine*) fails on the ground that Guicciardini's version is a text couched throughout in the typical language of Guicciardinian reasoning; this version shows no trace of the ideas characteristic of Uzzano

and his time, i.e., that concessions to the Visconti had in the past merely encouraged stronger Milanese aggressions, and that the question of a peace of compromise had to be judged in the light of the fact that Florence had been repeatedly forced to fight against the Visconti for her existence and liberty. Instead of these natural arguments, Guicciardini's Uzzano sets forth the general maxim that the only peace a state must ever accept is one "which does not increase the power of the enemies, and which does not open the way for a more dangerous war" ("che non accresce la potenza degli inimici, quella che non apre la via a più pericolosa guerra"). This is the language of sixteenth-century diplomacy, and there is no reason to believe that Guicciardini did anything but use an historical event to present a freely invented oration, in order to drive home a point of his own political philosophy.

21. As for the events connected with the annexation of Genoa, the Introductory Note (p. 20ff.) to the important *Diario di Palla di Noferi Strozzi*, in *Archivio Storico Italiano*, 1883 (see note 39 below), is still a useful survey of the facts as well as of the information given by humanistic historians.

22. Pandolfini in the *Pratica* of October 5, 1423; see *Commissioni*, vol. I, p. 518. ("Et si Forlivium occupavit, non nobis abstulit. . . .")

23. See the resolutions made "con somma unità," Vol. One, p. 329.

24. Machiavelli, *Discorsi*, II. 25.

25. Rinaldo degli Albizzi, May 28, 1423; see *Commissioni*, vol. I, p. 442.

26. "Vidimus quod pater et maiores istius fecerunt: Ante quam contra nos se moveret, pater dominium Lombardie voluit acquirere. . . ." "Vita pro salvanda libertate est exponenda. . . . Populus hic congregatus, libere consulens, salutem dabit nostre libertati, viriliter agendo. . . . Semper profuit providere ad tempus." Niccolò da Uzzano, May 19, 1423; *ibid.*, p. 413.

27. These are the words used in the message of the Florentine *Signoria* to Rinaldo degli Albizzi published in *Archivio Storico Italiano*, ser. IV, vol. XI (1883), p. 23.

28. ". . . simulatas et venenosas operationes dolis et machinationibus plenas." ". . . prout semper fuit voluntatis quorumcumque maiorum eius contrariis et fictis verbis infectam mentem et inten-

tionem simulantis." *Provvisione* of appointment of the *Dieci*, May 25, 1423, in *Arch. Stor. Ital., loc. cit.*, p. 24.

29. ". . . quod . . . iniuste oppressiones perfidi tiranni . . . de Mediolano, qui sua tirannide non solum florentinam libertatem sed italicam occupare conatur, adeo creverunt. . . ." *Provvisione* of appointment of *Dieci*, Oct. 22, 1423, *loc. cit.*, p. 300.

30. "Però che naturale appetito sempre è suto del popolo e della città nostra desiderare et abbracciare la vera e buona pace, e a fine di quella sostenuto lunghe guerre e gravissimi spendii, e al tempo . . . del suo illustre padre. . .; tutto a fine di poter vivere in pace sicura e quieta, e per mantenere quella libertà, la quale ci ànno lasciata e nostri padri." Instruction for envoys to Milan, August 4, 1423, in *Archivio Stor. Ital., loc. cit.*, p. 47. "E benchè cognoscessimo con questa nostra pace lui facilmente doversi fare signore di Lombardia, perchè togliavamo a ciascuno ogni nostra speranza, che cognosceva[n]o noi severi osservatori delle nostre promesse, condiscendemmo, e conchiudemmo la pace." "E per conservare la nostra libertà, la quale, come i suoi passati, cercare voleva occupare. . . ." "Però che, come le esperienzie passate evidentissimamente possono dimostrare, in tale proposito in eterno persisteremo, per conservare la nostra libertà; la quale più che la vita c'è cara. E per tale effetto non recuseremo le sustanzie, i figliuoli e fratelli, la vita, e similmente l'anima mettere, sanza alcuno riservo. . . ." Instruction for envoys to Pope Martin V, July 11, 1425, in *Commissioni*, vol. II, pp. 330, 332.

31. Rinaldo degli Albizzi to Viero di Guadagni, October 12, 1423, in *Commissioni*, vol. I, p. 523.

32. "Quod non fit facinus magnum et memorabile sine periculo." *Commissioni*, vol. II, p. 6.

33. *Riformagione* (resembling a declaration of war) of March 6, 1424, in *Commissioni*, vol. II, pp. 47-49.

34. "Dulce pacis elogium preferens . . ."; "a Florentino populo, suapte natura pacifico et tranquillo."

35. "Nolentes pacis assertorem sub pacis velamine, umbra pacis premissa, gravissima bella parare, sed suum mentis habitum qualis sit toti Italie demonstrare volentes; . . . iudicantesque non umbratilem, sed veram pacem suo populo . . . procurare. . .; quoniam sub pacis verbo servitutis iugum querit."

36. Matteo Villani, *Cronica*, esp. in the "Prologo" to Lib. XI: Peace "è certo fermo e indubitato fondamento e grado delle

mondane ricchezze, e della mondana felicità secondo il mondo. Ella è madre di unità e cittadinesca concordia; . . . i popoli liberi, intenti a loro arti e mercatanzie, moltiplicano in ricchezze, . . . e per li sicuri matrimonii cresce e moltiplica il numero de' cittadini. . . . E non solo i popoli che vivono in libertà, ma quelli che sottoposti sono al crudelissimo giogo della tirannia, la quale . . . senza niuna pietà o discrezione li [i.e. their own subjects] disfanno e scacciano . . . , affermando meglio essere terra guasta, che terra perduta. Nè contenta loro perversa iniquità alle occupazioni delle loro cittadi, per cupidigia d'ampliare signoria le nazioni vicine tormentano, e massimamente i popoli che vivono in libertà, con continove guerre, tradimenti e trattati." Salutati, *Invectiva*, ed. Moreni, p. 182: ". . . cumque nihil inimicitius esse possit mercatoribus, quodque mercimoniis ac artibus plus afferat detrimenti, quam strepitus turbatioque bellorum, certum omnibus esse debet mercatores et artifices, in quorum manibus nostrae reipublicae gubernacula sunt, pacem diligere, vastitatemque bellicam abhorrere." F. Gilbert, in his article "Machiavelli: The Renaissance of the Art of War," in *Makers of Modern Strategy*, ed. E. M. Earle (Princeton, 1943), p. 21, also draws attention to Salutati's assertion.

37. ". . . perocchè i Fiorentini vivono della pace e fannone frutto come l'ape del mêle de' fiori e mai non presono guerra se non per avere pace." "A Firenze non è mai il caso della guerra tanto giusto e necessario che quando al popolo è ragionato di pace non vi si corra; pare che la natura loro sia tutta di pace e la guerra è cosa forzata." Gregorio Dati, *Istoria*, ed. Pratesi, pp. 41, 55.

38. "E giammai non fu loro pensiero di volere in Lombardia nè di là dalle Alpi acquistare terre, perchè contenti stanno ai loro termini con più sicuro stato e riposo che possedere più di lungi, e tutta la guerra che hanno sostenuta e menata è suto per difendersi e per offendere il nemico che voleva occupare la loro libertà, insino a tanto che da lui sieno sicuri non potere più essere offesi, nè avere a temere; e come viddono questo essere advenuto, rivolsono la loro gente in Toscana e lasciarono lavorare per se medesimo il fuoco acceso in Lombardia. . ." *Ibid.*, p. 96.

39. As is noted in the *Diario di Palla (di Noferi) Strozzi*, in *Archivio Storico Italiano*, ser. IV, tom. XI (1883), which has been the basis of many of the preceding observations on the Florentine conduct in the summer of 1423. "Nanni di Carlo degli

Strozzi . . . mostrò, la grandezza del Duca procedere da cagion nostra, sì per avere fatte rivocare le genti da Milano, al tempo era morto il Duca vecchio, e non prendere Milano etc.; sì per la pace fatta con lui, quando il signor Pandolfo era in Brescia etc." (P. 32f.). Palla Strozzi was on the board of the *Dieci* and, consequently, a first-hand witness. On Nanni degli Strozzi's personality see our last chapter, especially p. 358.

40. ". . . che sempre e nostri Signori e questo popolo era ben disposto alla pace, e così era sempre stato. Et in dimostratione di ciò era, che dopo la morte . . . del suo illustre padre, avendo il nostro Commune ridotta la casa de Visconti a termine, . . . si ritrasse. Dipoi più volte crescendo la potentia di questo illustre signore, essendo richiesti dovere etc., perchè desideravano vivere in pace; già mai si prestò gli orecchi, non a Cremona, non a Crema, non a Brescia, non a Parma nè a chi queste possedeano; a' quali se pur avessimo dimostrato voler dar favore, non sarebbono venute dove venute sono. . . . Nondimanco, perchè nostra natura s'inchina alla pace, fumo contentissimi. . ." From Niccolò da Uzzano's answer to the Milanese envoys, Nov. 9, 1423, in Palla degli Strozzi's *Diario*, *loc. cit.*, p. 306f. The conformity of this answer with Nanni degli Strozzi's propositions does not seem to have been noted by any student; but it is obvious and helps to explain Bruni's appreciation of Strozzi as one of the leading spirits in the struggle with Milan—the backbone of Bruni's Funeral Speech on Strozzi, as will be seen in our last chapter.

41. See the instruction for Florentine envoys to Pope Martin V, July 11, 1425, in *Commissioni*, vol. II, pp. 328-333.

42. See Chap. 18 and Appendix 8.

43. Giovanni Cavalcanti, *Istorie Fiorentine*, lib. II cap. XXI. (Ed. G. di Pino [Milan, 1945], p. 39f.).

44. See Machiavelli, *Storie Fiorentine*, IV 7, a chapter which recapitulates the scene from Cavalcanti, *Istorie Fiorentine*, II 21, and Machiavelli's general judgment on the period in IV 1 and IV 14. Cf. also the description of the crisis following Zagonara in Perrens, *Histoire de Florence*, vol. VI, pp. 282-288.

45. "Rimolatino per lo quale conforta Firenze dopo la rotta di Zagonara" by messer Antonio di Matteo di Meglio (called Antonio di Palagio), published in Guasti's *Commissioni di Rinaldo degli Albizzi*, vol. II, pp. 75-80, and the "Risposta" by "Ser Domenico al prefato Messer Antonio, in vice della Città di Firenze," published *ibid.*, pp. 80-85.

46. "Madre mia cara, . ./ . . . dimmi, onde procede/ Che 'l tirannico pede/ Scalpiti i membri tuoi con tal baldanza?/ Fermando i tuoi malivoli speranza/ Della submersione/ Di tua reputazione,/ Che Italia triumfar solea già tutta./ È la gran providenzia sì distrutta,/ Che esser ne' tuoi car figli/ Solea, con tai consigli,/ Che a più potente assai mise già il freno?/ . . . Fatti avarizia o invidia il tuo tesoro/ Ascondere al bisogno?" *Loc. cit.*, p. 75f.

47. "Volete ora esser capi/ Del governo d'Italia e guidatori?/ Usurier, sogdomiti e traditori,/ Saria il parlar più onesto." P. 76.

48. "Noi siam pur Fiorentini,/ Liber Toscani,/ in Tàlia specchio e lume./ Resurga il giusto sdegno per costume/ Avuto sempre a tempo,/ Nè più s'aspetti tempo;/ Perchè nel più tardar tutto è il periglio/ . . . Perchè nulla varrebbe il penter tardo." Pp. 78, 80.

49. "Facciam danar, che bene aremo onori." P. 81.

50. "Ov' è Orazio/ Che pel tagliar del ponte si fe' eterno?/ Nullo tanto constante in me dicerno,/ Che per picciol spavento/ Non gli pai' ogn' or cento/ Ch' al suo nimico dia le bianche carti." P. 82.

51. According to the figures of a statistical document preserved in Sanudo the younger's *Vite dei Dogi*, the revenues of Florence and Bologna were halved and that of Venice diminished by one third during the thirty years from the early 1420's to the early 1450's. See the reedition of the document in *Bilanci Generali della Repubblica di Venezia*, vol. I, tom. I (Venice, 1912; ed. L. Luzzatti for the "Commissione per la Pubblicazione dei Documenti Finanzari della Repubblica di Venezia"), p. 98f., and the comments by Luzzatti, *ibid.*, and by C. Barbagallo in his *Storia Universale*, vol. III 2 (Turino, 1935), p. 1103f.

52. In the form of the *Pratica*, an advisory meeting of *richiesti*—a type to which some of the other gatherings discussed in this chapter belonged—debating had a somewhat larger scope. But even the *Pratica* did not admit voting of any kind and is essentially characterized by what has been said about the *Consulta*. An excellent technical analysis of the proceedings in both types of advisory councils—basic agencies of Florentine constitutional life—has been given by F. C. Pellegrini in the article "Intorno ad alcune istituzioni della Repubblica Fiorentina," *Rassegna Nazionale*, IL (1889), 405-411.

53. See the extracts from the minutes of the *Consulta* on August 3, 1424, in *Commissioni*, vol. II, pp. 145-149.

54. "Libertas utilior ceteris est; et omnia, pro ea servanda, exponenda sunt." "Vicecomites nobis semper inimici fuerunt, et nos subicere quesiverunt." "Terreri non debemus per infeliciter gesta, sed vitam exponere pro nostra salute." These are reliable passages from the minutes. The fuller and rhetorically more impressive text as given by Cavalcanti, *Istorie Fiorentine*, lib. II cap. XXIII, must not be used since Cavalcanti evidently phrased the speech as he thought fit to serve *in maiorem gloriam* of Gianfigliazzi.

55. "Virili animo intendendum est ad libertatem nostram, et non se deserere; . . . in adversis virtus consistit et cognoscitur." "In adversis homines, qui liberi vivere volunt, demonstrari debentur, quoniam in prosperis unusquisque se gerit." "Virtus in adversitate perficitur; pro auro omni libertas non venditur."

56. "In adversis virtus cognoscitur; in prosperis omnes sciunt incedere. . . . Quantum maius est periculum, tanto provisio maior. Et extimanda libertas ultra vitam est . . . Animus vinci non potest, nisi voluntarie."

57. "Libertatem habere magnificat civitates et cives, ut notum est: et que sub thirannide sunt, civium sunt deserte, cum thiranni virtutes bonorum timent et omnino eos exterminant." ". . . cives apti requirendi sunt . . . pro castellanis."

58. "Quod inter cetera magna et laudabilia, que de Populo Romano scribuntur, duo memorantur: quod de adversis animum non minuerunt, et ex prosperis non sunt elati; et magnanimes fuerunt magis in adversis, quam prosperis. Lignum habere spem; et si incisus fuit, rursus frondescit et facit comam."

59. "Tu ne cede malis sed contra audentior ito, quam tua te Fortuna sinet." *Aen.* VI, 95f.

60. "Animus reassumendus est, et viriliter incedere: et nos a Romanis originem habemus. Et sic tempore patris huius Ducis actum est, dum Bononiam occupavit. . . . Et tunc Bononiam, Cremonam, Brisiam et alias multas civitates amisit."

61. The second and third of the three speeches attributed to Tommaso Mocenigo in Sanudo's *Vite dei Dogi* (in Muratori, *Rerum Italicarum Scriptores*, tom. XXII, col. 949-958 and 958-960). Mocenigo's alleged three speeches are usually assumed to have been delivered in January 1421, July 1421, and early in 1423. But the first speech is a forgery in its entirety (probably

produced between September 1433 and August 1434), the second in its genuine parts can safely be placed in the second half of 1422, and the third falls into March/April 1423 since it was made by Mocenigo on his deathbed. These are the results reached in *Humanistic and Political Literature*, Chapter IX, "The Anti-Florentine Discourses of the Doge Tommaso Mocenigo. (1422-23)." The passages to which we shall refer are from authentic sections of the second and third speech.

62. Mocenigo, *loc. cit.*, col. 952-955 and 959.

63. J. Burckhardt, *Die Kultur der Renaissance in Italien*, Neudruck der Urausgabe, ed. W. Goetz (Stuttgart, 1922), p. 53f.

64. Cf. Vol. One, p. 125ff. and the further references there given.

65. Mocenigo, *loc. cit.*, col. 952.

66. "Ser Francesco Foscari . . . ha detto . . . ch'egli è buono lo soccorrere a' Fiorentini, a cagione che il loro bene è il nostro, e per conseguente il loro male è il nostro." Mocenigo, *loc. cit.*

Another much more passionate speech of Foscari, supposedly made when he was Doge, and delivered on the eve of the alliance with Florence before the Venetian Senate and in the presence of Florentine and Milanese ambassadors, is found in the so-called *Cronica Savina* (preserved in a manuscript of the Biblioteca Marciana)—a work which, as Kretschmayr (*Geschichte von Venedig*, vol. III, p. 557) notes, must be ascribed to the middle of the seventeenth century. In this speech, Foscari is made to refer to Filippo Maria as "that raving tyrant" ("questo furibondo tiranno"), and to announce the resolve of Venice to crush "this common enemy of all" ("sto inimigo comun di tutti"). It may be that the Venetian Volgare in which the *Savina* is written has inspired the modern readers with particular confidence; at any rate, down to the most recent studies Foscari's political program has as a rule and without qualms been interpreted according to the version of the speech in the *Savina*, and illustrated with the strong language used there. (So S. Romanin, *Storia Documentata di Venezia*, vol. IV [Venice, 1855], pp. 108-110; A. Medin, *La storia della Repubblica di Venezia nella poesia* [1904], p. 106; Picotti in *Rivista Storica Italiana*, XLIII [1926], 29; L. Simeoni, *Le Signorie* [1950], vol. I, p. 463; and N. Valeri, *L'Italia nell' Età dei Principati* [1950], p. 438.) Only Kretschmayr, *op. cit.*, vol. II, p. 547, has expressed doubts of the trustworthiness of this late source, and has quietly ignored Foscari's alleged speech. We do in fact possess no proof whatever that Foscari made any public speech at all at the time when the alliance with Florence was concluded; but even if he did, we may rule out the possibility that a Doge, in a speech before the Senate and in the presence of foreign emissaries, could have used the unbridled language we have just quoted. The only safe and solid way to reconstruct Foscari's views is to establish the genuine part of the speeches of Mocenigo in which Foscari's program is cited and defined for the purpose of refutation.

67. The fact that the coming of Foscari and his generation signifies the last and decisive event in the genesis of the Italian equilibrium and the political program of *libertas Italiae* has been widely recognized in recent years. It is of particular interest that R. Cessi, in the first volume of his *Storia della Repubblica di Venezia* published in 1944, reached conclusions (still unknown to this writer when the present chapter was written) which, even though Cessi's focus of attention is Venice and not Florence, are in full harmony with our own analysis. Mocenigo's words, Cessi explains, were the "ultimate melancholy thought" of a period drawing to its close, when Venice, in spite of the establishment of her *terra-ferma* state, "had not given up the traditional prejudice of the policy of isolation" ("non aveva rinunciato al tradizionale pregiudizio della politica di isolamento"). (p. 363). The younger generation, on the other hand, "embraced the principle of the liberty and the peace of Italy, which emerged . . . from the fundamental problem of the political equilibrium. . . . In 1397, the equilibrium could be maintained, for Venetian ends, by preserving the territorial integrity of the existing *signories* in the Venetian region; in 1425, . . . the tensions among small *signories* had been replaced by the conflict among three great states: Florence, Milan, and Venice. . . . The stimulus of expansion . . . filled the Viscontean spirit with arrogance, . . . and this spirit, making defense an imperative necessity, called into life the coalition of the two great republics. . . . The liberty of Italy, which was invoked by both parties, prompted the establishment of the so-called equilibrium which was endangered by the expansion of the Visconti. . . . A higher necessity for equilibrium, and not a preconceived thirst for adventure, as Mocenigo had insinuated, drove

the Venetian government into the Italian conflicts" ("Una superiore necessità di equilibrio, non preconcetta volontà di aventura, come aveva insinuato il Mocenigo, sospinse il governo veneziano nel turbine dei conflitti italiani"). (p. 370f.). For consonant evaluations of Venice's intervention see an excellent chapter in N. Valeri's *L'Italia nell' Età dei Principati* (1950), p. 425f. and 436ff., and this writer's "A Struggle for Liberty," p. 559ff.

68. ". . . hanno et aranno quello pensiero alla conservazione del vostro stato . . . , che al loro proprio."

69. ". . . alla conservazion di vostra libertà e del resto d'Italia." See Ridolfi's letters of August 14, and September 19, 1425, in *Commissioni*, vol. II, pp. 375f. and 402f. In fact, the Venetian government wrote to Filippo Maria that they looked upon the Florentines as their "cari frategli," and that the intention of the new alliance with Florence was "di mantenere queste due Comunità in dolcezza di libertà" (*Commissioni*, vol. II, p. 524f.); in a communication to the Emperor, the league with Florence was said to have been concluded "pro defensione et conservatione statuum nostrorum ac libertatis et pacificis [sic] status totius Italiae." (1426, Febr. 19; quoted by Raulich in *Rivista Storica Italiana*, V [1888], 460).

70. See the text of the pact in *Commissioni*, vol. II, pp. 541-551.

71. Andrea Biglia, *Historia Mediolanensis*, in Muratori, tom. XIX, col. 78-85. To be precise, it should be said that Biglia added a further (fourth) speech by the *condottiere* Carmagnola (col. 82-83), to have one speaker characterize the military aspects of the presumable campaign if Venice joined the struggle; but this speech has no bearing on our subject. Biglia lived through the war and died in 1435 (not 1432 as the recent biography of *Cosimo de' Medici* by K. S. Gutkind [Oxford, 1938], p. 69f. contends, with disastrous consequences for the appraisal of Biglia's work as a historical source); see F. Novati's note on Biglia's death in *Archivio Storico Lombardo*, ser. IV, vol. VII (1907), p. 221f., and the documents referring to Biglia's last years, including 1435, in *Rinascita*, V (1942), 524-526.

72. Sabellico, *Rerum Venetarum Decades*, Dec. II lib. 9 (in the edition in the series "Degl' Istorici delle Cose Veneziane," tom. I, 1718, p. 474ff.). While in Sabellico's account the situa-

tion is still precisely the same—a discussion among the same four speakers—political reasoning from concrete facts has somewhat restrained the oratory in praise of freedom. But the reasoning ascribed to the speakers shows that the essential experience of the early Quattrocento has not been lost. Sabellico is aware that Florence's war with Filippo Maria was merely one phase in a contest with Milan which had been waged since the mid-Trecento—a "quasi haereditarium bellum." He makes Ridolfi emphasize sharply that the fortunes of the two republics, Venice and Florence, were interdependent: Let Florence be destroyed now, and your turn will come next! "Vestram nostramque libertatem, rempublicam, patriam," save them by the alliance! Whereas Sabellico's narrative is interesting because it provides an opportunity to observe the lasting effects of the early Quattrocento situation on later Renaissance historiography, his account must, of course, not be used as a source for the reconstruction of the political ideas of the 1420's.

73. The concept of *libertas Italiae* as the gist of Barbaro's thought and politics is aptly described in N. Carotti's paper "Un politico umanista del Quattrocento: Francesco Barbaro" (*Rivista Storica Italiana*, ser. v, vol. 2 [1937], esp. p. 20ff.), a refutation of earlier attempts (in particular in P. Gothein's biography of Barbaro) to find modern ideals of national unification in Barbaro's writings.

74. The league had been concluded "libertatis Italiae et salutis populi Florentini, et dignitatis nostrae causa"; "iacta videntur fundamenta libertatis defendendae." The consequences will compel "hunc hominem, qui nimia principandi cupiditate subigere Italiam imperio suo conatur, pacem accipere." Wherefore the common aim now is "ut Italia cum Patria tua salva sit." *Francisci Barbari et aliorum ad ipsum epistolae 1425-1453*, ed. A. M. Quirini (Brescia, 1743), letter no. 2, p. 8f.; for the date, 1426, Febr. 12, see R. Sabbadini, *Centotrenta lettere inedite di Francesco Barbaro precedute dall' ordinamento critico cronologico dell' intero suo epistolario* (Salerno, 1884), p. 17. On a much later occasion Barbaro once said: "Quia in Galliae [i.e. northern Italy's] libertate Etruriae . . . et universae Italiae quoque libertas est constituta." Ed. Quirini, *op. cit.*, no. 37, p. 52; for the date, 1437, Nov. 1, see Sabbadini, *op.cit.*, p. 27.

75. ". . . non quidem libenter sed tamquam coacti pro con-

servatione status nostri ac libertatis prefate Comunitatis Florentie ac nostra et totius Italie, non potuimus aliter facere quod [*correctly* quam?] venire ad guerram cum prefato duce Mediolani." From a memorandum of Giuliano's on diplomatic transactions in northern Italy, in the *Secreta Senatus*, April 1426, in the Venetian Archives, quoted by S. Troilo, *Andrea Giuliano, Politico e letterato veneziano del Quattrocento* (Firenze, 1932), p. 50, n. 1.

76. Card. A. M. Quirini, *Diatriba praeliminaris . . . ad Francisci Barbari et aliorum ad ipsum epistolas* (Brescia, 1741), p. CCCCXLIV; for the date, 1441, January 4, see Sabbadini, *op. cit.*, p. 35. The letter is addressed to Flavio Biondo, who was going to commemorate Barbaro's defense of Brescia in an historical narrative. He was hoping, Barbaro said, that, together with his *patria*, the "*liberi populi*" of Italy and the "*Romana Ecclesia*" would be grateful to him, "sicut pro communi libertate tam diu constantissime pugnavimus."

77. ". . . nos cum liberis populis aequo iure foederatis. . ." Barbaro, *Epistolae*, ed. Quirini, no. 20, p. 33. For the date, 1437, Dec. 13, see Sabbadini, *op. cit.*, p. 27. For Pietro del Monte's statement, and for Barbaro's, Giuliano's, and del Monte's connection with the republican approach of the Florentine humanists to history, see Vol. Two, p. 393f.

78. In 1436, Manetti's *Laudatio Ianuensium ad clarissimos Ianue legatos Florentie commorantes*—an historical sketch of the growth of Genoa, trying to underline the role of liberty in Genoa's past—was dedicated by him to Genoese envoys who, after the successful Genoese revolt against Filippo Maria, came to Florence to negotiate an alliance. In the following year, when Manetti was sent to Genoa as a Florentine envoy, he transformed his sketch with the help of Genoese chronicles which he could then consult, into a larger composition approaching a concise history of Genoa, the *Laudatio Ianuensium ad illustrissimum principem dominum Thomam de Campo Fregoso Ianue ducem*. This history culminates in the political request that the supreme task of the Genoese Doge should be "defensio libertatis" in the widest sense; it could best be achieved "if you never abandon the alliance with Venice and Florence, concluded under happy auspices at the beginning of your reign." The two works are unpublished and little known. The most authoritative manuscript is Vaticanus Palat. Lat. 1605, with corrections presumably from Manetti's hand. (". . . si

societatem cum Venetis et Florentinis ab initio tui principatus faustis ominibus initam . . . nunquam dimiseris." Fol. 29v.)

79. Benedetto Accolti, *Dialogus de Praestantia Virorum Sui Aevi*, ed. Galletti (see above Note 25 to Chap. 15), pp. 116-120. It is interesting to note that Accolti, in appraising the political attainments of the Moderns, lists Francesco Foscari as the statesman of the recent past who most closely approached the greatness of ancient statesmen. Another testimony to the feeling of political community among Florentine and Venetian humanists around 1440 may be found in the opinions of Poggio and Pietro del Monte in the controversy on Caesar and the *Respublica Romana*, discussed in Appendix 2, Vol. Two, p. 391ff.

80. Romanin, *Storia Documentata di Venezia*, vol. IV, p. 213f.

81. For the more profound causes and wider consequences of this transformation of the political trends of the early Renaissance in the mid-Quattrocento see this writer's "A Struggle for Liberty," pp. 564-570.

82. For this role of Cosimo, attested by the day-by-day reports of the Milanese envoy, Nicodemo da Pontremoli, see Perrens, *Histoire de Florence depuis la domination des Médicis*, vol. I (1888), pp. 120ff., 130ff.

83. We know this fact from Naldo Naldi's *Vita Jannotii Manetti* (in Muratori, tom. XX, col. 519-608), which, even more than Vespasiano da Bisticci's *Commentario della Vita di Messer Giannozzo Manetti*, points out Manetti's republican opposition to Cosimo de' Medici and the fact that this opposition and Manetti's eventual fate had much to do with his disagreement from Cosimo's policy of cooperation with Francesco Sforza against Venice. See esp. col. 568-569, 576-579, 604-605.

84. The quoted passage is from Benedetto Accolti (*Dialogus*, ed. Galletti, p. 119), who as an eye-witness judges that "solus Cosma" was the architect of the alliance with Francesco Sforza against Venice, whereas "magna pars Florentini populi" opposed it.

85. The first quotations are from the *Lettera mandata a Vinitiani* by Benedetto Dei, published in G. F. Pagnini's *Della Decima e delle altre gravezze . . . de' Fiorentini*, vol. II (Lisbona e Lucca, 1765), pp. 235-245. See esp. the passages on pp. 236-238: Cosimo had been "chagione . . . che la bella . . . Italia non sia venuta a mano e di Catelani e d'Alamanni e di Franzesi,

dallanno 1400 in quà. . . . Non vi richordegli de Vischonti di Milano, avevano tutta Toschana e Gienova, e Siena, e Pisa, e Bologna, e Lucha, e la Romagna, e 3/4 di Lombardia, come pel mezzo e senno e tesoro Chosimo de Medici sostenne tal furia, che cierto el Duca si facea Re de Taliani." Also to remember "che fè lo Re Lanzalao . . . pigliando Roma, e sottomisela sotto di se, e prese la Città di Chortona, e come Chosimo de Medici fu . . . chagione . . . della sua rovina. . . . Cierto . . . se i Fiorentini non s'opponevano a tanto empito, lo Re Lanzalao si facea Re ditalia . . . , perchè sendo Sig. di Roma, e avendo gran parte in Toschana, gliera una facilissima . . . cosa." Again, "affermiano che se la Signoria di Vinegia pigliava la Città del Duchato di Milano, ella si faceva Regina ditalia." On Dei's personality and political career, cf. M. Pisani, *Un Avventuriero del Quattrocento: La Vita e le Opere di Benedetto Dei* (Genoa, 1923); a brief survey of the *Letter to the Venetians* is given on p. 52f. Francesco Guicciardini's statements are in his *Storie Fiorentine*, ed. R. Palmarocchi (Bari, 1931), p. 6, and in his *Dialogo del Reggimento di Firenze*, ed. R. Palmarocchi (Bari, 1932), p. 62.

CHAPTER 17

1. See Vol. One, p. 339f.
2. See Vol. One, p. 335ff.
3. See Vol. One, pp. 67f. and 301.
4. In Ms. Laur. 54 c. 30: "Antonius Marii filius Florentinus transcripsit Florentiae Kal. Octobris MCCCCXXV, quo tempore nostra Resp. pro tuenda libertate ardens atque acre bellum cum Duce Mediolanensi patiebatur." According to A. M. Bandini, *Catal. codd. Lat. Bibliothecae Mediceae Laurentianae*, tom. II (Florence, 1775), col. 681f.
5. See Vol. One, p. 292f.
6. "Preterea Ladislaum . . . in celum cotidie extollebas; et si quando in levis armature preliis victor evaderet, tu sibi palmam militarem deferendam censebas, et de celo delapsum Cesarem affirmabas, teque omni dignitate privatum malle dicebas imperium tyranni quam paucorum potentiam ac dominationem sufferre." *Laurentii de Benvenutis Oratio*, ed. Zippel, p. 177. ". . . cum Ladislai regis nuntiata mors esset, . . . nonne tu adeo pre mestitia et dolore affectus es, ut domo te contineres et horridiore habitu postridie sordidatus prodires in publicum, extortam tibi ac prereptam spem omnem obtinende dignitatis affirmans." *Ibid.*, p. 178. Whether or not Benvenuti's interpretation of Niccoli's motives is correct, the fact that Niccoli did withdraw during the general rejoicing suggests that he had greatly exposed himself. Concerning Benvenuti's reliability cf. Appendix 5, esp. Vol. Two, p. 411ff.
7. See the letters of 1425 quoted by Walser, *Poggius Florentinus*, p. 136, n. 2.
8. "Solemus exsecrari tyrannos nos, qui nati sumus in liberis civitatibus, et profitemur nos hoc bellum suscepisse pro tuenda Italiae libertate"; *Epistolae*, ed. T. Tonelli, vol. I (1832), p. 205f.
9. See Vol. One, p. 54f.
10. "Non enim unus aut alter imperat, non optimatum aut nobilium fastus regnat, sed populus aequo iure accitus ad munia civitatis. Quo fit, ut summi, infimi, nobiles, ignobiles, divites, egeni communi studio conspirent in causam libertatis."
11. "Haec omnia accepta referimus a sola libertate, cuius diutina possessio ingenia nostra ad virtutis cultum erexit atque excitavit." Poggio, *Opera*, Basel, 1538, p. 337. For the situation in which the letter was written, see Walser, *loc. cit.*, p. 184f.

12. On the position of Poggio as a middleman between the particular outlook of the Florentine humanists and the more general tendencies of Quattrocento Humanism see the writer's observations in *Speculum*, XIII (1938), 31ff.

13. The following outline of Bruni's literary production from his return to Florence in 1415 to the end of the 1420's rests on the author's researches in preparation of a new chronology of Bruni's works; see note 4 to Chap. 10. It is not always possible to give every reason for the newly established dates without including a revision of the dates of other, roughly simultaneous, products of Bruni's pen that go beyond our present interest. In such cases, full exposition must wait for the planned monograph on Bruni, but the nature of the required chronological corrections is briefly indicated here.

14. Book I was finished in 1415, according to Bruni's reference in *Ep. IV 4*; book II presumably during the second half of the year 1419, in any case later than Bruni's work on the *Commentaria Tria De Primo Bello Punico* in the course of which he was criticized for not having brought his History of Florence down into modern times (see note 16 below); book III in 1420, according to Bruni's own statement (p. 67 of Santini's edition) that the institution of the "Priori Artium," created in 1282, had existed for 138 years (1282 + 138 = 1420); book IV in 1421, according to Bruni's statement (*ibid.*, p. 81) that 130 years had passed since Giano della Bella's reform in 1291 (1291 + 130 = 1421). For the dates of books V and VI see note 4 to Chap. 18.

15. *Ep. X 25*; May 27, 1418. See Vol. One, p. 257.

16. Composed in 1418, or possibly in the first half of 1419. The earlier dating of *De Primo Bello Punico* "late in 1421," as accepted by Mehus (*Epistolario di Bruni*, vol. I, p. lvi), Sabbadini (*Giornale Stor. della Lett. Ital.*, XX [1892], 54), Santini (*Bruni e i "Hist. Flor. Pop.,"* p. 22), and repeated in *Bruni, Schriften*, p. 167, was based on a date-line found in cod. Laur. 65 c. 14; but this date-line actually refers to the copy of another work, as L. Bertalot notes in *Archivum Romanicum*, XV (1931), 298. The dating of the *De Primo Bello Punico* must, therefore, be placed on another basis, and a reliable one may be found in Bruni's remark in his preface that he was censured for being absorbed in ancient history while there were "recent" things worthy of commemoration; he felt, however, that the

older an historical event, the nearer it was to oblivion, and consequently the more badly it stood in need of the historian's care. This controversy between Bruni and his critics implies that his work on the *Historiae Florentini Populi*, interrupted in 1415, after a survey of ancient Roman times and the early Middle Ages, had not yet been resumed. Bruni began to work on book II of his *Historiae* in the second half of 1419, or somewhat earlier. (See above note 14.) The date of 1418 or the first half of 1419 which thereby follows for *De Primo Bello Punico*, is confirmed by the fact that a letter of Ambrogio Traversari (*Epistolae*, ed. Canneto, *Ep. VI 14*, col. 292), which according to Luiso's *Riordinamento dell' Epistolario di A. Traversari* (*Rivista delle Biblioteche e degli Archivi*, IX [1898], 108) belongs precisely into the years 1418-19, states that Bruni then was working on *De Primo Bello Punico*.

17. December 1421. *Bruni, Schriften*, p. 166f.

18. A new Statute of the *Parte Guelfa* was approved on March 26-28, 1420; it had been prepared by a commission whose members "in this preparation could rely on the work and aid of Leonardo Aretino, who had been selected by the commission for this purpose" ("freti, in his conficiendis, opere et auxilio Leonardi Aretini ad hoc ipsum per eos delecti"). Different from the *Prologo* of the preceding Statute of 1335, the *Prooemium* of the Statute of 1420 gives a definition of "Guelfi" that conforms to the new politico-historical ideas of Florentine Humanism. This redefinition of the historical role of Guelphism, and probably the entire *Prooemium*, may therefore be considered as Bruni's intellectual property. (As such they have been used Vol. One, p. 15.) The *Prooemium* is edited in *Commissioni*, vol. III, p. 621f.

19. 1416-17. See *Bruni, Schriften*, p. 164, but add that the *Praefatio* to Pope Martin V and the *Praemissio* explaining Bruni's translation method were not prefixed until in March 1419 or little later.

20. Between February 1420 and March 1421. The information given in *Bruni, Schriften*, p. 164f., must be implemented and corrected according to the conclusions reached in *Humanistic and Political Literature*, Chapter VII, "The Genesis of Bruni's Annotated Latin Version of the (Pseudo-) Aristotelian *Economics* (1420-21)."

21. The dating of the *Oratio in Hypocritas* depends on our success in fitting together the date of Bruni's *Ep. IV 14*, in which the oration is referred to as recently written, and the subscription in the oldest known copy of the *Oratio*, a manuscript in Brescia, "Explicit Leonardi Aretini in hipocritas oratio quarto idus septembris M.CCCC° septimo decimo." Since the letter, which is dated April 1 but with no indication of the year, is placed by Luiso and others in 1418 on the ground that this year would best fit in with the dates of the preceding and subsequent dated letters, the chronology at first sight appears to be that *In Hypocritas* was composed shortly before September 1417, was copied September 10, 1417, and referred to by Bruni in April 1418. This, indeed, was the sequence proposed in *Bruni, Schriften*, p. 164f., but the conclusion is rash in view of the fact that *Ep. IV 14* calls *In Hypocritas* a work written "these days" ("his diebus"). It is impossible that Bruni could thus have alluded in April 1418 to a composition made in the summer or autumn 1417. Now there is no guarantee that the accepted dating of *Ep. IV 14* in 1418 is definitive; irregularities in the chronological order of the letters in that part of Bruni's epistolary are frequent, and *Ep. IV 14* may easily have been written in April 1417. Under these circumstances the only satisfactory assumption seems to be that the *Oratio in Hypocritas* originated in March 1417, was said on April 1 (in *Ep. IV 14*) to have been composed "his diebus," and was in circulation in the summer and autumn as is testified by the Brescia manuscript of September 10th.

22. Summer 1423. The dating "1421/1424" in *Bruni, Schriften*, p. 168, can be made more exact in the following way: Galeotto da Ricasoli, ambassador of the Count of Urbino, to whom the *Isagogicon* is dedicated, was in Florence in June and (or, to) September 1423. (See the *Diario di Palla degli Strozzi*, in *Archivio Stor. Ital.*, ser. IV, vol. XI [1883], pp. 32, 151). This visit probably was the occasion for the dedication. By other, more intricate considerations it is possible to determine that the beginning of 1422 is *term. a quo*, and the summer of 1423 *term. ad quem*. The two sets of arguments together lead to the summer of 1423.

23. Between the middle of 1423, and April 1426. Comparison with Bruni's other literary occupations during the same period

allows the dating of *De Studiis et Litteris* in "1422/1429" (*Bruni, Schriften*, p. 169ff.) to be reduced to this briefer span of time.

24. We may be sure that Bruni's translations of Plutarch's *Vita Sertorii* and *Vita Pyrrhi*, made according to *Bruni, Schriften*, p. 167f., "before 1423 (?)," do not fall into the period under review. We can establish the year 1414 as a *term. ad quem* for both translations, on the ground that they are found in the manuscript Reims 1338, written 1416 for Cardinal Fillastre during the Council at Constance. (Cf. *Catalogue Générale des Mss. des Bibliothèques Publ. de France, Départements*, tom. 39 II [1904], pp. 483-484.) The availability of these works for transcription in the Constance circles (indicating that the master-manuscripts must have travelled to Constance in the luggage of one of the Italian secretaries at the Council) implies that the translations must have been done some time before 1414, the year at whose end the Council assembled. An exact chronological reconstruction of Bruni's itinerary and literary production during his preceding curial years would allow further to reduce the periods in which *Sertorius* and *Pyrrhus* originated to the brief spans of time between October 1408, and January 1409, and between autumn 1408, and March 1412, respectively.

Neither need we place during the 1420's Bruni's translation of Plato's *Epistolae*. To be sure, this work, dedicated to Cosimo de' Medici, would belong in the year 1427 if Ms. Laur. 76 c. 57, copied by Antonio di Mario for Cosimo and finished June 25, 1427 (cf. Mehus, in his preface to Bruni's *Epistolarum Libri VIII*, vol. I, p. lxxv, and *Bruni, Schriften*, p. 234), were really the dedication copy, as still assumed in *Bruni, Schriften*, p. 174. But that this is a hasty assumption is shown by Bruni's remark in his dedication letter to Cosimo that the translation had been made "inter clamosos strepitus negotiorumque procellas, quibus Florentina palatia quasi euripus quidam sursum deorsumque assidue aestuant, cum singula modo non dicta, sed verba etiam interrumperentur," that is, at a time when Bruni worked in the Florentine town hall as chancellor. (*Bruni, Schriften*, p. 135). Since in the year 1427 Bruni did not take up his duties until the beginning of December, the translation must fall into the first brief period of Bruni's services as chancellor that stretched from December 29, 1410, to April 4, 1411; and Ms. Laur. 76 c. 57 cannot be the dedication copy. These inferences are confirmed by the fact that the description of Bruni's experience in the chancellor's office, found in the dedication to Cosimo, is almost literally duplicated in one of Bruni's letters from the time of his tenure in 1410-1411, where we read: my fortune has taken me "ad hos aestus procellasque occupationum" (dedication to Cosimo: "negotiorumque procellas . . . aestuant"), whose "fluctuatio nimia me submergit." (*Ep. V 3*, ed. Mehus, vol. II, p. 16; January 27, 1411 according to *Bruni, Schriften*, p. 208).

25. Written between the middle of 1424 and the middle of 1426. The defense of his methods of translation, which Bruni undertakes in *De Interpretatione*, cannot yet have existed, nor even have been planned, in January-May 1424, the time when, in the preface to his *Phaedrus* translation (*Bruni, Schriften*, p. 127; for the date *ibid.*, p. 172), he declared that he felt only contempt for the various criticisms of his translating methods that had come to his notice and would ignore them. As to the *term. ad quem* available for *De Interpretatione*, we have the following data. Berto di Antonio di Berto, chancellor of Siena, to whom *De Interpretatione* is dedicated (cf. L. Bertalot, in *Archivum Romanicum*, XV [1931], 286f., who proves the authenticity of this dedication against unfounded doubts in *Schriften*, p. 166), was of little significance as a humanist, and it is very probable that Bruni's dedication was prompted by a casual personal meeting—just as the dedication of the *Isagogicon* to an ambassador from Urbino seems to have come about casually at the occasion of the ambassador's stay in Florence. (See note 22 above). An opportunity for a meeting with Berto of Siena existed at the end of May 1426 when Bruni, then a Florentine ambassador to the Pope in Rome, was commissioned to stop in Siena and make a report to the Sienese *signori.* (See the instruction, issued to Bruni, in *Archivio Stor. Ital.*, ser. II, tom. V, parte 2, 1857, p. 29.) According to information given by Bruni himself, he did stay in Siena for some time. (*Ibid.*, p. 32). By the middle of 1426, therefore, *De Interpretatione* may be thought to have reached the stage in which its draft was dedicated, or its dedication could at least be promised. The work was not continued after Bruni's return to Florence; it has come down to us unfinished. (See note 4 to Chap. 18.) These several observations must supplement and modify the discussion of the background of *De Interpretatione* in

Bruni, Schriften, p. 165f., where the date was still given inaccurately as "about 1420(?)."

26. 1402 to the spring of 1406. See the section "Florentine Sentiment in Bruni's Pre-Curial Period," Vol. One, p. 220ff.

27. 1415 to about 1421. See Vol. One, pp. 324 and 355.

28. On Bruni as a chancellor, and on the nature of his public activities, we have the competent analysis in D. Marzi, *La Cancelleria Fiorentina* (Rome, 1910), pp. 188-198.

CHAPTER 18

1. See Vol. One, pp. 332 and 334.

2. The parallelism of the two works is emphasized by their titles, since the oration on the Strozzi, in most early manuscripts and in Bruni's obituaries by Manetti and the Anonymous (see note 49 to Chapter 3), is also called a "Laudatio"—*Laudatio Johannis Strozzae Equitis Florentini.* In spite of the conformity of this usage of contemporaries with Bruni's own usage in the Strozzi oration ("Laudationem vero illius merito congruentem . . . parare . . . conemur"), it is, however, for practical purposes preferable not to duplicate the essential word for reference, but to distinguish Bruni's *Laudatio* from his *Funeral Speech* (*Oratio Funebris*) on Nanni degli Strozzi. This, indeed, has at all times been done by users of the work. For not only does the title *Oratio in Funere* sometimes appear in manuscripts (see the codices 1616, 6179, and 6315 listed in *Catalogus codicum manuscriptorum Bibliothecae Regiae* [Paris, 1744], vol. III, p. 159; vol. IV, pp. 211, 228 [for cod. 1616 cf. also *Catalogue général des manuscrits latins*, ed. Ph. Lauer, vol. II, Paris, 1940, pp. 90-92], and the Ms. Vatican. Lat. 5108 which, fol. 31r, shows the title *Oratio . . . in funere Clarissimi Equestris Ordinis Nanni Strocia Florentini*); but already our earliest information on the effect of the speech on the adversaries in Milan in 1429 (see note 3 below) speaks of the "funebris oratio pro Johanne Stroza equite florentino"; and the title in the Paris cod. 5834 (olim Colbertianus) reads in a similar manner *Oratio funebris Nannis Strozae equitis Florentini* (see *Cat. codd. mss. Bibl. Regiae, op. cit.*, vol. IV, p. 165). Toward the end of the century, Vespasiano da Bisticci, in composing in Volgare his list of Bruni's works for his biography of Bruni, gave the title as *Orazione nella morte di messer Giovanni Strozzi* (ed. Frati, vol. II, p. 32). The editors of the only printed edition of the speech—E. Baluze, in his *Miscellaneorum . . . Hoc est, collectio veterum monumentorum*, vol. III (Paris, 1681), p. 226ff., and G. D. Mansi, in the reprint of Baluze's edition in his *Stephani Baluzii Tutelensis Miscellanea novo ordine digesta et . . . aucta*, vol. IV (Lucca, 1764), p. 2ff.—by fusing the title versions of the two manuscripts they followed (apparently the Paris codices 1616 and 5834 just quoted), adopted the form *Oratio in funere Nannis Strozae Equitis Florentini.* It seems desirable that Bruni's

work should continue to be cited in this familiar fashion because the speech is, and is meant to be, a Florentine counterpart to Thucydides' *Funeral Speech* of Pericles, and will be most adequately appraised when known under the same historic title as Bruni's *Funeral Speech.*

A comparison of the edition in *Baluzii Tutelensis Miscellanea,* tom. IV, with Ms. Vat. Lat. 5108, just quoted, and with Ms. Bibl. Laur. Lat. 52 c. 3 and Ms. Vatican. Ottobon. Lat. 1901, two mid-Quattrocento collections of the works of Bruni which have proved to be based on good traditions (cf. *Bruni, Schriften,* p. 5f.), shows that Baluze's text is excellent. In contrast to most other pre-nineteenth-century editions of Bruni's works, it can be used with confidence. (Only in note 43 below, Baluze's "subsistere" has been replaced by "existere" found in the mss.).

3. This letter (already mentioned in notes 46 and 48 to Chap. 6), written by Bartolomeo della Capra, Archbishop of Milan, from Genoa which was then a Milanese dependency, was published by R. Sabbadini in *Archivio Storico Lombardo,* XLIII (1916), 26-28, and rediscussed in Sabbadini's *Il Metodo degli Umanisti* (Florence, 1920), p. 83f. See also Appendix 8, Vol. Two, p. 432.

4. The completion of lib. V and VI, and the publication of lib. I-VI of the *Historiae Florentini Populi* must both fall between autumn, 1426, when Bruni returned from his diplomatic mission to Pope Martin V, and the first weeks of the year 1429. For until Bruni's trip to Rome in June 1426, the schedule of his literary activities had been crowded so much by major and minor scholarly works, last of them *De Recta Interpretatione* (which has come down to us unfinished, presumably because Bruni, after his return from Rome, no longer found the time to complete it), that we may exclude the possibility that Bruni, in addition to all his other labors, could also resume work on his *Historiae.* Quite differently from that period, not a single product from Bruni's pen seems to be known from the years 1427 and 1428, except the oration on Strozzi. Publication of books V and VI of the *Historiae* cannot have occurred later than very early in 1429, since the letter in which the Archbishop of Milan shows a knowledge of the oration and of books I-VI of the *Historiae* was written on April 9, 1429. Consequently, the absence of any known literary products (except the Strozzi oration) between the autumn of 1426 and the end of 1428—a period which included approxi-

mately one year before Bruni, from the end of 1427 onward, became engaged in public activities—presumably must be explained as indicating that Bruni then undertook the extensive reading and archival research necessary for the continuation of the *Historiae*. That these preparations took much time, and that the completion of books V and VI, and the publication of books I to VI, did not occur before the end of 1428, is indicated by the following observations: (1) The lacuna in Bruni's literary production includes the entire year 1428. (2) The letter of the Milanese Archbishop, if read with care, seems to say (see the Latin text in note 5 below): Of books I-VI of Bruni's *Historiae* the Archbishop has just heard, or seen a copy; of Venetian counterparts, still in progress, he has heard; but of Bruni's Strozzi oration it is known that it has already been read by the public and has caused offense: the implication is that *Historiae I-VI* had come to Milan later than the oration. (3) The two oldest dated manuscripts of *Historiae I-VI* are one of June 1429 (written by Antonio di Mario in Florence, Ms. Bibl. Univers. di Bologna, c. 358; see Santini in the preface to his edition of the *Historiae*, p. xvii), and another of December 1429 (coming from, and possibly written in, the Cistercian Abbey San Salvatore on Monte Amiata, near Siena, Ms. Florence Bibl. Laur. Cisterc. Amiat. c. 4; see *ibid.*, p. xv). This means that, in addition to the excitement roused in Milan, knowledge of and interest in lib. I-VI existed in and outside of Florence during the very year 1429—a fact which would well fit in with publication not long previously, and point to the completion of the last part, books V and VI, toward the end of 1428.

5. "Florentini nuper in scriptis sua gesta redigi fecerunt sex libris distincta; Veneti etiam sua scripta componunt . . . , qui quidem quanto sua facta extollent, tanto et veteres et novas actiones nostras obscurare conabuntur. Leonardus Aretinus habuit pridem funebrem orationem pro Johanne Stroza equite florentino, quo quantum Principi quantumque patrie nostre detrahat non ignorant qui legerunt." Edited in Sabbadini's paper referred to in note 3 above.

6. Thucydides, *The History of the Peloponnesian War*, II, 37 and 41. "The school of Greek culture" for τῆς Ἑλλάδος παίδευσις is G. Highet's rendering in his English translation of W. Jaeger's *Paideia*, vol. 1 (New York, 1939), p. 408.

7. For the contemporary objections against Bruni's *Laudatio* see Pier Candido Decembrio in his *De Laudibus Mediolanensis Urbis Panegyricus*, in *Archivio Storico Lombardo*, XXXIV (1907), 38f. For the growth of Bruni's historical thought from the *Laudatio* to the *Historiae* see the first part of our study, Vol. One, pp. 47ff., 52f., 58f.

8. "Romanorum colonia, veteribus Tuscorum habitatoribus permixta." Ed. Baluzius, p. 3.

9. ". . . ut exemplo caeteris gentibus bene vivendi essent, ab aliis vero exemplum ipsi non peterent. . ." *Ibid.*

10. Vol. One, p. 113ff.

11. "In omni principe populo." *Laudatio*, *L* fol. 155v; ed. Klette, p. 104.

12. "Litterae politiorque disciplina," it is true, were thriving elsewhere as well, but their roots had been in Florence. "Iam vero litterarum Graecarum cognitio, quae septingentis amplius annis per Italiam obsoleverat, a civitate nostra revocata est atque reducta, ut et summos philosophos et admirabiles oratores caeterosque praestantissimos disciplina homines, non per aenigmata interpretationum ineptarum sed de facie ad faciem, intueri valeremus. Denique studia ipsa humanitatis, praestantissima quidem atque optima, generis humani maxime propria, privatim et publice ad vitam necessaria, ornata litterarum eruditione ingenua, a civitate nostra profecta per Italiam coaluerunt." Ed. Baluzius, p. 4.

13. The originality of Bruni's interpretation of Florence's cultural mission emerges from comparisons with the ancient city eulogies which Bruni may have remembered. A list of the Greek praises of "Athens the schoolmaster of Greece" has been given in Th. E. Burgess' cited study of *Epideictic Literature* (see note 5 to Chap. 9), p. 152.

14. As such it should be added to the sources collected with great completeness in the chapter "Humanist Views of the History of Literature and Art" of W. K. Ferguson's *The Renaissance in Historical Thought* (1948).

15. "E puossi dire che le lettere e gli studi della lingua latina andassero parimente con lo stato della repubblica di Roma; perocchè insino all' età di Tullio ebbe accrescimento, di poi, perduta la libertà del popolo romano per la signoria degl' imperadori . . . , insieme col buono stato della città di Roma perì la buona disposizione degli studi e delle lettere. . . . A che pro-

posito si dice questo da me? Solo per dimostrare, che, come la città di Roma fu annichilata dagl' imperadori perversi tiranni, così gli studi e le lettere latine riceverono simile ruina e diminuzione, intanto che all' estremo quasi non si trovava chi lettere latine con alcuna gentilezza sapesse. E sopravvennero in Italia i Goti e i Longobardi, nazioni barbare e strane, i quali affatto quasi spensero ogni cognizione di lettere. . . . Ricuperata di poi la libertà de' popoli italici per la cacciata de' Longobardi . . . , le città di Toscana e altre cominciarono a riaversi ed a dare opera agli studi ed alquanto limare il grosso stile. E così a poco a poco vennero ripigliando vigore," until Petrarch "rivocò in luce l'antica leggiadria dello stile perduto e spento." *Bruni, Schriften*, p. 64f.; ed. Solerti, *op. cit.*, p. 289f.

16. From the second half of the Quattrocento on, it is true, few men would contend without qualifications that the rise of medieval and Renaissance culture in Italy was bound up with the reemergence of liberty in the Italian city-states, and under the political conditions of the later Renaissance this is easily understandable. But the idea was still clearly expressed during the 1460's in Benedetto Accolti's *Dialogus De Praestantia Virorum Sui Aevi*, especially in the chapters describing the ruin of ancient culture at the time when liberty under the empire decayed, and the subsequent reemergence of free city-states in medieval Italy as basis of a new culture in Florence, Venice, Pisa, Genoa, and Siena (p. 116ff.; see Vol. One, p. 346f.). As late as the 1480's, we read in Ugolino Verino's *De Illustratione Urbis Florentiae* the following verses, which are also significant because of their vindication of Dante as climax of the reemergence of culture when "liberty had been restored": "Tandem ubi saeva lues bellorum, et barbara proles / depulsa est Latiis cervicibus, et sua priscis / reddita libertas tranquilla pace Latinis, / paulatim rediere artes. . . . / Romanaeque nitor linguae, quia perditus omnis / tunc fuit: erudiit Thusco pede docta Thalia / Pegaseos vates rhythmis, modulisque canoris: / Aequarunt veteres patrio sermone poetas: / Quos Florentinus longe supereminet omnes / gloria Musarum, Dantes; nec cedit Homero; / par quoque Virgilio: doctrina vincit utrunque" (ed. Paris, 1583, pp. 11v-12r).

As to the interpretation of ancient culture, Bruni's view, that the flowering and decay of Roman literature were intimately connected with the rise and fall of civic freedom, became the Florentine consensus even outside the humanistic circles, as we can see from its inclusion in Vespasiano da Bisticci's *Vite*: "To the Roman Empire, in consequence of the civil wars, an immense number of those eminent men were lacking who had been available for the Republic, and [, in addition, Rome] had fallen into the hands of the most wicked emperors; and in a similar manner the writers, and every *virtù*, had spent themselves; for when the *virtù* decline, the states decline also and can no longer exist: and, consequently, because there is no place for men of letters there, literature perishes." ("Erano mancati all' imperio romano, per le guerre civili, infinitissimi, prestantissimi uomini che aveva avuto quella repubblica, ed era venuta nelle mani di scelleratissimi imperadori; e il simile erano spenti gli scrittori e ogni virtù; perchè quando mancano le virtù, mancano le città, e non possono stare: e per questo, gli uomini litterati per non vi aver condizione, perirono le lettere;" ed. Frati, vol. III, p. 250). The most elaborate presentation of the theory of a parallelism between the political and literary development of Rome is found in Pietro Crinito's *De Poetis Latinis Libri V*, published at Florence in 1505—even though in this work from Poliziano's circle little has remained of the original republican roots of the theory. A similar parallelism between the politics and the visual arts of antiquity was proposed first, it seems, by Leon Battista Alberti in his *De Architectura*. In the 1480's this view found its most elaborate presentation in Antonio di Tuccio Manetti's *Vita di Brunelleschi*. This application to the history of art is well known from J. v. Schlosser's *Die Kunstliteratur* (Vienna, 1924), p. 131f., and *Präludien. Vorträge und Aufsätze* (Berlin, 1927), p. 276. See also W. Rehm, *Der Untergang Roms im Abendländischen Denken* (Leipzig, 1930), pp. 68, 150.

17. "Forma rei publicae gubernandae utimur ad libertatem paritatemque civium maxime omnium directa, quae, quia aequalissima in omnibus est, popularis nuncupatur." *Oratio in Funere Nannis Strozae*; in Baluzius' edn., p. 3.

18. ". . . libertas, sine qua nunquam hic populus vivendum sibi existimavit." *Laudatio*, *L* fol. 152v; ed. Klette, p. 98.

19. "Sed ne ipsi legum vindices in summa potestate constituti arbitrari possint non custodiam civium sed tyrannidem ad se esse delatam, et sic, dum alios cohercent, aliquid de summa libertate

', multis cautionibus provisum est. Principio enim supremus
tus, qui quandam vim regie potestatis habere videbatur,
la temperatus est ut non ad unum sed ad novem simul,
annum sed ad bimestre tempus, deferatur." *Laudatio, L*
152v; ed. Klette, p. 99.

20. *Laudatio, L* fol. 154v-155r; ed. Klette, p. 103.

21. "Aequa omnibus libertas . . . ; spes vero honoris adipiscendi ac se attollendi omnibus par, modo industria adsit, modo ingenium et vivendi ratio quaedam probata et gravis. Virtutem enim probitatemque in cive suo civitas nostra requirit. Cuicunque haec adsit, eum satis generosum putat ad rem publicam gubernandam. . . . Haec est vera libertas, haec aequitas civitatis: nullius vim, nullius iniuriam vereri, paritatem esse iuris inter se civibus, paritatem rei publicae adeundae. . . . Atque haec honorum adipiscendorum facultas potestasque libero populo haec assequendi proposita mirabile quantum valet ad ingenia civium excitanda. Ostensa enim honoris spe, erigunt sese homines atque attollunt; praeclusa vero, inertes desidunt; ut in civitate nostra cum sit ea spes facultasque proposita, minime sit admirandum et ingenia et industriam plurimum eminere." Ed. Baluzius, p. 3f.

22. Buonaccorso da Montemagno of Pistoia was a man about twenty years younger than Bruni and like him a newcomer from the Florentine territory to the intellectual middle-class of Florence. Again like Bruni he became a Florentine in spirit by his own choosing; he taught jurisprudence at the Florentine University and was employed in Florentine diplomatic missions abroad —activities which he preferred to the high offices in his native Pistoia to which he had been elected. His premature death in 1429 prevented him in the end from legally becoming a Florentine citizen. Since Buonaccorso was only 37 or 38 years old when he died, his *Disputatio* can hardly have been written very long before the 1420's; and since comparable Florentine literary documents that impugn mere privilege of birth, or insist upon the right of social ascent, do not fall before the late 1420's or early 1430's, it is most probable that the *Disputatio* was not written until shortly before Buonaccorso's death. That this work may be considered a product of the school of Bruni's civic Humanism is not only indicated by its tenor and line of thought, but also suggested by the somewhat embarrassing fact that in an unusual number of the manuscripts the work is ascribed to Bruni. The

widespread use of this ascription even in relatively old a[illegible] manuscripts, as well as the observation that the *Dispu*[illegible] reached us in two versions showing considerable stylistic[illegible] ences (see the discussion of some manuscripts in *Bruni, Sc*[illegible] pp. 180-184), arouse the suspicion that everything was not no[illegible] in the process of publication, and that Bruni may have had a ha[illegible] in it. After the present writer (in *Bruni, Schriften, loc. cit.*, and in "Studien über Leonardo Bruni Aretino," *Archiv für Kulturgeschichte*, XXII [1932], 356-359) had expressed his suspicions, R. Sabbadini (in *Carteggio di Giovanni Aurispa* ["Fonti per la Storia d'Italia," vol. 70; Rome, 1931], 174f.) also emphasized that "the uncertainties about the two orations [composing the *Disputatio*] are numerous and serious." The hasty rejection by L. Bertalot (*Archivum Romanicum*, XV [1931], 306-309) of any possible connection with Bruni fails to account for the undeniable discrepancies among the manuscripts. The most plausible assumption would seem to be that the work had not yet been formally released at the sudden death of its author, and that Bruni played some part in the final revision of the text, possibly by supplying the more polished version (beginning "*Aetate illa florentissima qua vastum Romae imperium adolevit*," instead of "*Claruit Romae quondam, cum florentissimum eius imperium adolevit*"). A close examination of the manuscripts is much needed. The text available in print is too corrupt to allow a conclusive answer to the critical questions. There also exists an early fifteenth-century translation of the "*Aetate illa florentissima*" version into the Volgare; their authorship, too, is variously ascribed. The second speech (the plea of the plebeian) has been edited in E. Garin's *Prosatori Latini del Quattrocento*, pp. 139-165 and 1128f., in both the Latin and the Volgare versions, based chiefly on Casotti's still indispensable edition of 1718, but substantially corrected according to a few good Florentine manuscripts.

23. As far as the writer knows, this dependence has never been mentioned by any student, but the similarities between Buonaccorso's plebeian and Sallust's picture of Marius are so unmistakable there can be no doubt that Sallust served Buonaccorso as a model.

24. "Sic itaque mortalium animus est: purus quidem ac liber ad suscipiendam nobilitatem ignobilitatemque dispositus. Nemo in hoc optimo et praestantissimo munere humanitatis naturae largi-

tionem accusare potest" (ed. Garin, p. 144). "Qui non sit clarus, se ipsum accuset; inique de fortuna queritur [preferable to Garin's reading "quaeritur"]" (ed. Garin, p. 162). "Etenim cum intelligerem praeclariora tum [so in numerous MSS; preferable to "tantum" in the printed editions] fore mortalium ingenia cum ad rempublicam accommodantur, totum me meae patriae concessi" (ed. Garin, p. 156).

25. The novelty of these ideas is further shown by the unusual success of Buonaccorso's disputation not only in Italy, but throughout Europe—a chapter in the history of the dissemination of Florentine early-Renaissance thought which is still to be written in detail, although today the major phases are known. The *Disputatio de Nobilitate* was one of the earliest works of the Quattrocento to be rapidly copied outside Italy and translated into the important vernaculars; its fortunes demonstrate the provocative impression made by the social notions of Florentine civic authors on northern readers.

We do not know the approval or disapproval with which the *Disputatio* was read at the court of Burgundy, focus of late medieval chivalrous culture. However, as early as 1449 a French translation, under the title of *Controversie de noblesse*, was made by Jean Mielot, secretary to Duke Philip the Good, was copied several times and eventually printed, not later than 1478, in Bruges by Collard Mansion, the collaborator of William Caxton. (See G. Gröber and S. Hofer, *Geschichte der mittelfranzösischen Literatur*, vol. II, Berlin & Leipzig, 1937 [in the series "Grundriss der Romanischen Philologie"], pp. 217, 282; Mitchell, *John Tiptoft*, to be quoted presently, p. 176f. and the table facing p. 216; F. S. Boas and A. W. Reed in their introduction to *Fulgens and Lucres*, to be quoted presently, p. xiv.) A translation into English was the work of one of the earliest English travelers to humanistic Italy, John Tiptoft, who during the years 1459-60 lived in Guarino's circle in Padua and Ferrara, and in the following year visited Florence (R. J. Mitchell, *John Tiptoft, 1427-1470* [London, 1938], pp. 50f., 66f.); most probably therefore, he became acquainted with the Latin text in Italy and, consequently, when translating, did not need to rely on Mielot's French version, as has long been assumed. (See Mitchell's convincing argument, *op. cit.*, pp. 176-178.) When in 1481 Tiptoft's English text was printed by Caxton under the title *The*

Declamacion of Noblesse (reedited by Mitchell, *op. cit.*, pp. 213-241), an epilogue was added from which we can observe that to the English printer the outcome of the altercation was not the implicit victory of a new cultural and social ideal over the prejudice and conduct of the patrician class, but rather the excitement of a delicate problem placed in the cross-light of opposing arguments. For in commenting on the concluding plea of the plebeian to his judges—"which character and conduct is the more noble, is now left to your decision (*utra earum nobilior sit, in vestra nunc sententia relinquitur*)"—Caxton remarks that the decision, then, had not been passed within the work itself, but had been left to the judgment of the reader. (See the quotation from Caxton's epilogue in Mitchell, *op. cit.*, p. 181 "As touchyng the sentence . . . I fynd none as yet pronounced. . . . Thenne I wold demaunde of theym that shall rede or here the book whiche of this tweyne was moost noble . . . and to him juge ye this noble and vertuous Lady Lucresse to be maryed.") That Caxton's understanding of the problem was the normal one in the countries north of the Alps, transpires from the prefatory remarks of the translator into German, Niclas von Wyle, who in 1470 included Buonaccorso's work among his *Translationen oder Teutschungen*, the earliest vernacular garner of Italian humanistic writings for the German reader. As Niclas von Wyle put it, the work of Buonaccorso represented "a plea and a counter-plea" on whose respective merits judgment was to be passed by the person to whom the translation was dedicated, "in order that this precious plea and counter-plea may not be found to lack a [final] verdict (*umb daz nit dise so costliche red und wider rede mer ăne urtail funden werd*)." This person was Count Eberhard of Württemberg who seemed to be an ideal judge of true nobility because he was so richly endowed with the three qualities producing "nobility" which Niclas von Wyle enumerated without discrimination: wealth, virtue, and high descent—a definition which in the German translator's hands obtained a strongly pre-humanistic flavor by the tracing of the Count's fabulous pedigree to Abraham, Aeneas, and Romulus. (See the edition of the *Translationen* by A. v. Keller in "Bibliothek des Litterarischen Vereins in Stuttgart," vol. LVII [Stuttgart, 1861], pp. 283-284.)

The difference between the social views held outside Italy and the civic standards of Florentine humanists was to have even stronger effects on the interpretation of the Italian work. We find the most striking illustration when the story of a contest between a Roman patrician and a Roman plebeian for the hand of a high-born lady was used, largely in a literal imitation, as plot for the earliest English secular drama, composed by Henry Medwall about 1497. (*Fulgens and Lucres. A Fifteenth-Century Secular Play*. Ed. by F. S. Boas and A. W. Reed, Oxford, 1926 [in "Tudor and Stuart Library"], on the basis of a unique copy of the long lost play, printed between 1516 and 1533 and rediscovered in 1919.) In the framework of a drama, of course, the verdict on each suitor's merits could not be left to the reader's good sense. The lady's decision had to be shown in the crowning scene; and given the inner structure of the contest, there was no doubt that the palm must be won by the plebeian's virtue. But while accepting this consequence, the English author did not conceal that such an ending was to himself and his audience an exciting exception from the rules of social life, by no means a new ideal realized. For when the lady, in his drama, has decided that "in this case" the plebeian was indeed "the more noble man" and that she must "condyscend" to him, she quickly deprecates any thought that her verdict might indicate a change in the social standards: "And for all that I wyll not dispise / The blode of cornelius, I pray you thinke not so: / God forbede that ye sholde note me that wyse, / For truely I shall honoure them wheresoeuer I go / And all other that be of lyke blode also, / But vnto the blode I wyll haue lytyl respect / where tho condycions be synfull and abiect. / I pray you all syrs as meny as be here / Take not my wordis by a sinistre way." Excited exclamations by the plebeian's servant emphasize still further the deviation from the normal course of life: "Yes by my trouth I shall witness bere, . . . / How suche a gentylwoman did opynly say / That by a chorles son she wolde set more / Than she wolde do by a gentylman bore" (ed. Boas and Reed, p. 81). Moreover in Medwall's presentation, the plebeian's victory does not impress the reader as a triumph of new values, because the author has cut the nerve of the humanist ideal by omitting the part in the hero's "nobility" played by his interest in studies and books and by his inner drive toward freedom of the mind and philosophic wisdom. In the English play, in short, an upstart distinguished by unusual ability and moral qualities has taken the place of the Florentine champion of a new civic virtue and education. (For the differences of Medwall's drama from Buonaccorso's *Disputatio*, see the excellent observations by Mitchell, *op. cit.*, pp. 182-185.)

26. Thucydides II, 37. Translation is that by B. Jowett.

27. See *Humanistic and Political Literature*, Chapter VIII, "An Epistolary Description by Bruni of the Florentine Constitution in 1413," where the letter is published.

28. "Leges igitur nostre omnes ad hoc unum tendunt ut paritas sit et equalitas inter se civibus; in quo est mera ac vera libertas."

29. "Nituntur enim leges nostre supereminentiam singulorum civium quantum fieri potest deprimere et ad paritatem mediocritatemque reducere."

30. "Est enim hoc mortalibus natura insitum, ut via ad amplitudinem honoresque exposita, facilius se attollant; praeclusa vero, inertes desideant. Tunc igitur imperio ad Romanos traducto, cum neque honores capessere neque maioribus in rebus versari liceret, Etrusca virtus omnino consenuit longe plus inerti otio quam hostili ferro depressa." *Historiae*, ed. Santini, p. 13.

31. Cf. note 21 above.

32. This origin from experience of Bruni's estimate of the role of liberty in the constitution of Florence deserves emphasis in view of the fact that the assertion of superiority in government and in the extent of liberty was in itself nothing original, but had been a typical topic of ancient city eulogies, especially in commendations of Athens. The Greek statements in praise of the Athenian constitution are listed by Th. C. Burgess in his *Epideictic Literature* (see note 5 to Chap. 9), p. 153.

33. The date of Uberto Decembrio's *De Re Publica* is 1420, or not much later, according to M. Borsa, "Un umanista vigevanasco," *Giornale Ligustico di archeologia, storia e letteratura*, XX (1893), 101f. Borsa, *ibid.*, gives the only available survey of the contents of the work, which seems to have been preserved merely in the manuscript Bibl. Ambrosiana B 123 sup. The following quotations from two sections dealing with the selection of "custodes" by the prince, fol. 90r and 94r-95r, are taken from extracts made many years ago; Prof. Paul O. Kristeller has been good enough to check most of these references against a microfilm he owns of Decembrio's work.

34. "Repugnare etenim nature nemo feliciter potest. Quinymo more Gigantum pugnare cum diis asseritur" (fol. 90r). "Agat

tamen unusquisque quod sibi proprium natura indulserit; . . . ut unusquisque proprium suum agat nec ad impropria se divertat, si forent etiam meliora. Grave est enim, ut sepe dixi, nature repugnare, et contra aquarum, ut aiunt, impetum enatare, cum secundo fluxu longe felicius vehi queat" (fol. 94r-94v). If the Prince, in his selection of the "custodes" of the state, allows himself to be guided by this knowledge, he will achieve "ut status sue rei p. utili stabilique regula gubernetur. Isto etenim ordine naturam suam singuli conservabunt" (fol. 95r).

35. "Nam si nobile electumque ingenium vili ministerio nutrietur, non in proficuum, sed in malignum et reprobum effectum potius commutabitur. Ut enim in electis generosisque seminibus accidit, si in alienum et difforme eisdem solum transferuntur, a priori natura degenerant, deterioraque nascuntur, sic talium ingenia preter naturam translata nonnumquam proditiones accutissimas, coniurationes pestiferas et alia exquisita scelera meditantur, ad que natura rudiores aspirare nequirent. Rude etenim ingenium, ut ad bonum tardum inspicitur, sic ad perniciem obtussum redditur et ignavum" (fol. 94v).

36. The Prince must take care, "ne parentum incuria, ut sepe fit, vel negligentia aut ineuntis etatis inexperientia talis nature proprietas . . . violetur," especially since every father wants his son to go into his own profession, as even Cicero did with his own son. "Propterea, ne id in nostra re p. possit accidere, eliget princeps ad omnia circumspectus aliquot graves expertosque viros, ad quos in electo aliquo urbis loco ab ineuntis etatis primordio pueruli a suis patribus deducantur, ut singulorum naturas queant diligenter inspicere, ad quas potissimum sunt proclives. Quo facto notent singulos et describant, quibus aptissimi videantur officiis, edicantque parentibus, ut illos ad ea ministeria exerceant, ad que fuerint designati, pena gravi transgressoribus imposita, nisi secus fortasse placuerit principanti. Hoc etenim ordine priscos Athenienses Laconasque suas res p. sentio stabilisse." Objection: "Sed si patres instruendorum filiorum expense forent fortassis inhabiles, nequirent agere quod intendis." Answer: "Ex publico, inquam, non obmittet princeps talium inhabilitati facere provideri." Objection: It will be difficult to make sons of noble families climb down the social ladder, and vice versa. Answer: There are no "nobiles" by birth. "Virtus est et vitium, que nobiles et degeneres efficit. Itaque princeps noster ex omni hominum sorte custodes

urbis aut philosophos aut medicos aut fabros eliget, nobiles vero et degeneres nulla alia ratione distinguet quam nature uniuscuiusque bonitate atque malicia" (fol. 94v).

37. *Περὶ τῆς πολιτείας τῶν Φλωρεντίνων*, listed in *Bruni, Schriften*, p. 179, among Bruni's undated works, must have originated (as G. Iorio pointed out in *Rivista Abbruzzese di scienze, lettere ed arti di Teramo*, x [1895]) during the time when the Greek scholar George of Trebizond, to whom it is dedicated, was in Florence at the occasion of the Council of union with the Greek Church. According to Sabbadini's brief biography in *Enciclopedia Italiana*, XVII (1933), p. 180, George of Trebizond was in Florence from 1438 to 1443. It is highly probable that Bruni's analysis of the Florentine constitution was composed in the early part of this span of time, as the following considerations (made on the basis of this writer's knowledge of the dates of Bruni's other works in those years) will show. Early in 1440, Bruni turned to the task of setting the record of his own life in order: he worked through his *epistolarium* to prepare it for the public, and he wrote his memoirs, the *Rerum Suo Tempore Gestarum Commentarius*. From the middle of 1441 to his death, he produced an adaptation of Procopius, and books X-XII of the *Historiae Florentini Populi* dealing with the recent events in Florentine history, some of which he had also touched upon in his memoirs. None of these works have any relation to a piece of writing whose main concern is with the diminution of the political rights of the masses of citizens following the disappearance of the citizen-army around the middle of the Trecento. In the ninth book of the *Historiae*, on the other hand, Bruni had given a lively discussion of the final abolition of military service in 1351, condemning it because of its evil long-term consequences for the citizenry. (See the passage in question in note 51 below.) This ninth book had been written in 1437-38. There is little doubt, then, that the pamphlet on the Florentine constitution, emphasizing the same turning point in Florentine history, was a by-product of Bruni's studies for *Historiae* lib. IX, that is, either within the year 1438 itself after the arrival of George of Trebizond, or during the next year before Bruni began to revise his *epistolarium*. For the Greek editions of Bruni's pamphlet on the Florentine constitution, see L. Bertalot in *Quellen und Forschungen aus italienischen Archiven*, XXVIII (1938), 278f.; a

Latin translation is found in Galletti's edition of Filippo Villani's *De Origine Civitatis Florentiae* (see note 33 to Chap. 3), pp. 94-96.

38. "Antiquitus siquidem populus cum armis in bellum exire . . . solebat. . . . Civitatis potentia maxime in multitudine erat, eamque ob causam populus primas obtinebat, adeo ut nobiles ferme omnes e Republica submoveret. Procedente vero tempore bellicae res conducto milite magis geri coeperunt. Tunc vero urbis potentia non in multitudine, sed in optimatibus et divitibus consistere visa est, quo pecuniam in Rempublicam conferrent et consilio magis quam armis uterentur. Hoc pacto attrita sensim populi potentia in hanc quam obtinet formam Respublica deducta est." Ed. Galletti, p. 96.

39. "Florentinorum igitur Respublica neque optimatium tota est neque popularis, sed ex utraque forma commixta. . . . Extrema declinans haec Civitas mediae sortis homines recipit. Attamen ad optimates potius, et ditiores, non tamen ultra modum potentes, inclinat." Ed. Galletti, p. 94. "Cum vero mixta Respublica sit, non a ratione abhorret, quaedam habere quae in popularem statum, quaedam vero quae in paucorum potentiam magis vergant. Popularia quidem illa. . . . Rursus ad optimatium statum tendunt multa. De omnibus quippe antea consulere, neque aliquid ad populum referre quod prius probatum non fuerit, et haec ipsa immutare populo non licere, sed opus esse probare simpliciter vel reiicere, maxime ad optimatium potentiam conferre mihi videtur." Ed. Galletti, p. 96.

40. "Conviene pertanto che, dove sono assai potestadi, vi surga assai valenti uomini; dove ne è poche, pochi." "Sendo adunque vero che, dove sia più imperii, surga più uomini valenti, seguita di necessità che, spegnendosi quelli, si spenga di mano in mano la virtù, venendo meno la cagione che fa gli uomini virtuosi." *Arte della Guerra*, historical excursus at the end of lib. II; in *Tutte Le Opere Storiche e Letterarie*, ed. Mazzoni e Casella (Florence, 1929), p. 301.

41. Giannotti, *Della Repubblica Fiorentina*, lib. III c. 5, lib. IV c. 7. "All active citizens," under the conditions of the Renaissance city-state, of course means those who possess "lo stato," i.e. the full citizen-rights—a group which excludes some of the lesser guilds and the laborers in the Florentine industries.

42. It is to be noted that the first six books of the *Historiae*

are not at all concerned with the Visconti; therefore, the fear of the Milanese must have been directed against Bruni's philosophy of history, and his reading of the Italian past, as they emerge from the *Historiae*.

43. "Neminem enim unum quasi dominum horremus, non paucorum potentiae inservimus," Bruni explains the Florentine attitude. Equality before the law and equal access to the civic rights, these foundations of liberty "nec in unius dominatu nec in paucorum possunt existere." "Ex quo fit ut monarchiae laus veluti ficta quaedam et umbratilis sit, non autem expressa et solida. Regibus, inquit historicus, boni quam mali suspiciores sunt, semperque his aliena virtus formid[ul]osa est. Nec multo secus accidit in dominatu paucorum. Ita popularis una relinquitur legitima reipublicae gubernandae forma, in qua libertas vera sit, in qua aequitas iuris cunctis pariter civibus, in qua virtutum studia vigere absque suspicione possint" (*Oratio in Funere*, ed. Baluzius, p. 3).

44. A history of these early Renaissance ideas and ideals of citizen-soldiership has never been attempted. Historians begin to pay attention to this aspect of Florentine thought only when they reach the time of Savonarola, or even not until they have to deal with the immediate background of Machiavelli. The consequence is that they fall into one of the customary misconceptions of the civic attitude in the early Quattrocento. The evidence discussed on the following pages (it could be enlarged by moving the focus of attention outside of Bruni's circle and the humanistic school) should be sufficient to prove that here again is a chapter that can and must be added to a history of Florentine thought during the period of the Viscontean menace.

45. "Noi, o superbo, le nostre mura defenderemo, e se fia bisogno, per la nostra libertà ruineremo nel ferro." Cino Rinuccini, *Risponsiva* (see above note 8 to Chap. 4), p. 216. For the relationship of this threat to the actual situation in 1397, cf. *Humanistic and Political Literature*, Chapter II, at the beginning of section 2, "The Date of Cino Rinuccini's *Risponsiva alla Invettiva di Messer Antonio Luscho*."

46. ". . . ipso populo Florentino exeunte atque armis fruente." *Laudatio*, *L* fol. 149v; ed. Klette, p. 97.

47. "Dispeream, nisi haec nostra ad illorum comparationem veluti puerilia quaedam ludicra existimare compellor, expertia ordinis, expertia disciplinae, expertia scientiae rei militaris, nun-

quam collatis signis dimicare ausa, sed levibus certaminibus fugisque et insectationibus instar puerorum contenta." *Bruni, Schriften*, p. 124. As to the date 1408, see note 24 to Chap. 17.

A middleman between Bruni and Machiavelli may have been Benedetto Accolti, who in his *De Praestantia Virorum Sui Aevi* talks at length about contemporary humanists (i.e. during the 1460's) who can find nothing good in the modern "*res militaris*" compared with that of antiquity, and accuse the *condottieri* and their mercenaries of lack of discipline and readiness to expose themselves to danger. For as these critics say, "raro ab eis aliquid egregium perpetratur facinus, et nedum urbes, sed nec etiam exigua oppida seu parva castella, nisi vix atque anxie, perraro expugnantur. Nullus in eorum castris ordo, nulla prorsus viget disciplina. . . . Unde accidit quod in magnis praeliis . . . vix decem ferro pereant [*rather* pereunt?], gravia etiam si quando imminent pericula ignavissime fugiunt. . . ." (ed. Galletti, pp. 107-108).

48. *Ethic. ad Nic.* III. 8. 1116b.

49. "Hic quantum inter externi militis ac civis amorem intersit, perfacile apparuit. Ceteri enim, nihil magis quam salutem propriam aestimantes, e vestigio cesserunt; hic [Strozzi] autem caritatem patriae saluti propriae anteferens obtulit sese statim pugnae, corporeque suo viam claudere hostibus perrexit, compellans commilitones atque adhortans, hostique manu et pectore resistens, impetum omnium aliquandiu sustinuit." *Oratio*, ed. Baluzius, p. 6.

50. *Bruni, Schriften*, p. 52f.

51. "Hoc profecto nil aliud fuit quam propriam domesticamque multitudinem imbellem efficere, ut alios suarum fortunarum inspiciat defensores, ipsa vero nec defendere sese, nec pugnare pro patria sciat." *Historiae*, ed. Santini, p. 186.

52. ". . . quali exerciti sieno migliori, o di soldati mercennarii et per prezo condotti, o veramente di proprii cittadini ragunati." *Della Vita Civile*, Ms. Florence Bibl. Naz. II, IV, 81, fol. 92r; ed. Battaglia, p. 156.

53. ". . . i quali sempre colle proprie arme principalmente combattevano, reputandosi quasi a vergogna, che delle vittorie romane fosse cagione altri che i propri cittadini." Porcari, *Orazione IV*, ascribed to Buonaccorso in *Prose del Giovane Buonaccorso da Montemagno*, ed. Giuliari ("Scelta di Curiosità Letterarie," fasz. 141; Bologna 1874), pp. 56-58; the quoted passage p. 57.

54. Not only did Porcari discuss in his orations many other themes that at that time were uniquely characteristic of Florentine civic literature (see H. Baron, "Lo Sfondo Storico del Rinascimento Fiorentino," *La Rinascita*, I [1938], 62-64, and "Franciscan Poverty and Civic Wealth," *Speculum*, XIII [1938], 22); he also stated in moving words how, in the decay of his native Rome, he had been dreaming of the still vigorous life of a Republic as had been the one which had once flourished in ancient Rome, and how through his experience in his office of Florentine *capitano del popolo* (during the same year of the war against Filippo Maria Visconti, 1427, in which Bruni became chancellor) all his former thoughts and sentiments had finally matured. See esp. his *Orazione VII, op. cit.*, pp. 70-72.

55. "L'effecto è che in tutti i passati secoli non si truova alcuna città essere divenuta degnissima, se non con la virtù et colle proprie mani de' suoi cittadini. I cittadini sono quegli che desiderono l'honore, la gloria, la riputatione et habondante imperio della città. I cittadini appetiscono la conservatione, la salute, lo stato et mantenimento d'ogni loro bene, et, quando che sia, cercano la pacie, tranquillità et riposo di loro, de' loro figluoli et di tutte loro cose. I soldati condotti contro l'honore proprio antepongono, et sopra ogni cosa il prezo amano et voglono; i terreni amici poco meglio stimano che de' nemici; fuggono i pericoli proprii, non curando della salute di chi gli paga; spesso habandonano quando truovono soldo migliore; se perdono l'amico, cercano d'un altro, et finalmente, perchè di guerre guadagnono et fannosi riputati et degni, sempre appetiscono et cercono guerra. Rade volti l'antiche potentie conducevano soldati, se non necessitati da gravi danni ricevuti et da timore di pericolo gravissimo; et colle proprie persone feciono aquisti grandissimi, come si vede de' Romani, Cartaginesi, Ateniesi et molti altri. Et similemente nella nostra città quasi tutto quello si possiede, fu colle proprie mani de' nostri antichi padri conquistato." *Della Vita Civile*, Bibl. Naz. II, IV, 81, fol. 92r-92v; ed. Battaglia, p. 156.

INDEX

INDEX

(Numbers in parentheses refer to note numbers in Volume Two)